the BOOK of the British Library

BRITISH
LIBRARY
BRITISH
LIBRARY
BRITISH
LIBRARY
BRITISH
LIBRARY
BRITISH
LIBRARY
BRITISH

the BOOK of the British Library

Michael Leapman

BRITISH LIBRARY

First published in 2012 by
The British Library
96 Euston Road
London NW1 2DB

British Library Cataloguing in Publication Data
A catalogue record for this publication is available from
The British Library

ISBN 978 0 7123 5837 8

Designed by Mercer Design, London
Colour reproduction by Dot Gradations Ltd, Essex
Printed in Italy by Printer Trento Srl

PAGE 2: The bronze gates at the entrance to the British Library.
PAGES 6–7: View out over the entrance hall, looking towards the King's Library.

Contents

Introduction

TODAY IT IS ONE OF THE world's great cultural institutions; yet the British Library was created not through the vision and determination of one person or group but through a series of sometimes random decisions, amalgamations and acquisitions over 250 years. Originating as the library of the British Museum, it was formally separated from its parent in 1973 and 25 years later moved into its own splendid home at St. Pancras. It has today amassed some 150 million items – not only books and manuscripts but paintings, photographs, sound recordings, maps, newspapers, stamps, historic documents and much else. Holdings increase by more than three million in an average year, largely because by law the Library receives copies of nearly everything published in Britain and Ireland. And it is all available to be consulted by members of the public, at no charge.

Such are the scope, variety and importance of the Library's collections that to write a coherent account of its history and holdings in a short book has been a challenging assignment. It amounts to just one page for every half a million objects: so in choosing what to describe in detail I have perforce been highly selective. And although I have taken much valued advice from the Library's specialists, the ultimate selection is my own.

Some items choose themselves. Among the acknowledged British treasures are two copies of *Magna Carta*, the seventh-century *St. Cuthbert Gospel*, William Caxton's early printed books, Shakespeare's First Folio and Lewis Carroll's original version of *Alice in Wonderland*. There is, too, a wealth of books and manuscripts from around the world that are notable both for their beauty and for their significance in tracing the history of language, art and religion – indeed of civilisation itself.

Alongside these I have highlighted less familiar items that caught my imagination. The Library has an especially rich collection of material relating to the British theatre, founded initially on the formidable collection of 1300 early English plays bequeathed by the eighteenth-century actor and theatrical impresario David Garrick. Today's collecting policy embraces not only the texts of plays but of personal letters, diaries and other items that offer insights into the theatrical world. Lurking amongst the modern manuscripts, for instance, is a carefully graded list by the playwright Terence Rattigan of the gifts to be given members of the cast after the first night of one of his works. While in no sense a seminal historical document, it provides a vivid snapshot of the social and cultural mores of mid twentieth-century England.

Among many other unexpected items in the Library's possession, the music collection boasts Beethoven's tuning fork, alongside priceless original manuscripts and recordings of his works. The voluminous scientific material includes a pamphlet by Benjamin Franklin on how to deal with smoky chimneys. There is a range of quirky nineteenth-century ephemera, including colourful advertisements for freak shows and patent medicines. To borrow an advertising slogan from a popular (now defunct) Sunday newspaper: all human life is there.

The Library's priority is to ensure that these extraordinarily diverse collections are preserved for future generations, and to this end a state-of-the-art Conservation Centre was constructed in 2007. Here highly-trained specialists combat the ravages of crumbling paper, insect infestation and the other ills that can befall its vulnerable holdings. As the years go by, more and more items are being digitised, so that they can be perused on screens, thus preventing wear and tear on the originals. And, keeping up with the rapid technological developments of recent years, the collections include increasing quantities of material that exists only in digital form.

My assignment would have been not merely challenging but impossible to fulfil without the generous guidance offered by scores of people in the Library, at all levels. In particular I am grateful to Colin Baker, Peter Barber, Nicolas Bell, John Falconer, Ed King, Scot McKendrick, Helen Peden, Ilana Tahan, Frances Wood and Christopher Wright for their invaluable assistance at various stages of the enterprise. The Library's head of publishing, David Way, and his colleagues Jenny Lawson and Sally Nicholls, have handled the complicated material with admirable care and professionalism. The Friends of the British Library have made a generous grant towards production costs, allowing a high standard of illustration and design in keeping with the values of the institution that the book celebrates.

MICHAEL LEAPMAN
JULY 2012

The ~~dew~~ ~~settling~~ through the ~~wreaths~~ in his

The air was sickly with an aftermath
of the day's heat - a clammy, lifeless, ~~~~
~~and atmosphere~~ ~~~~ air, as though it had been
breathed before, ~~thrice~~ exhaled & stale ~~second-hand~~.
Only his feet felt cold, as ~~~~ they
sank ankle deep in the dew. ~~~~
~~as though he trod in his own~~ ~~~~
~~sweat too through the meadows of~~
~~his sweat~~. It was as though he trod through
grass that was ~~heavy~~ ~~~~ with his own sweat
~~dripping~~

CHAPTER 1

The caretaker

> ❝ If only I could get down to Sidcup! I've been waiting for the weather to break. He's got my papers, this man I left them with, it's got it all down there, I could prove everything. ❞

∽ HAROLD PINTER, *THE CARETAKER* (1960)

IN 2007, SOME 18 MONTHS before his death, Harold Pinter, one of Britain's most celebrated playwrights, agreed to sell *his* accumulated papers, the archive of his lifetime's work, to the British Library. He was keen that they should stay in Britain, easily accessible to British researchers.

After he died his widow Antonia Fraser, herself a celebrated author of historical biographies, published a memoir of their marriage entitled *Must You Go?* In it she stated: 'It might surprise people who only knew of Harold's criticism of the government to learn that by his own standards Harold was extremely patriotic. … [He] felt strongly that his manuscripts should go to the British Library, whatever the lure of well-endowed American universities which some of his contemporaries had felt. Thus he began by letting his papers go on loan, and ended by selling them not long before his death for a handsome price with which he was more than content. As for me, just as I wanted to lie one day in the next-door grave to Harold, I decided that our papers should lie together too. So I joined him.'

The Pinter archive consists of more than 150 boxes of manuscripts, scrapbooks, letters, photographs, programmes and emails. Mementoes from the playwright's youth include a photograph of him playing Romeo in a school production.

❧ OPPOSITE

The prolific Mervyn Peake (1911–68) was known for his talents as both an artist and author, the two coming together memorably in the imaginative *Gormenghast* novels. On this page from one of his notebooks he has sketched an illustration for *Titus Groan*, the first novel in the series. It shows Lord Groan's manservant, Flay, stalking his arch-enemy, the chef Swelter, whom he believes to be trying to kill him.

❧ BELOW

Harold Pinter playing Romeo in a school production.

∂ BELOW

Thomas Hardy's manuscript of
Tess of the D'Urbervilles, first
published in 1891.

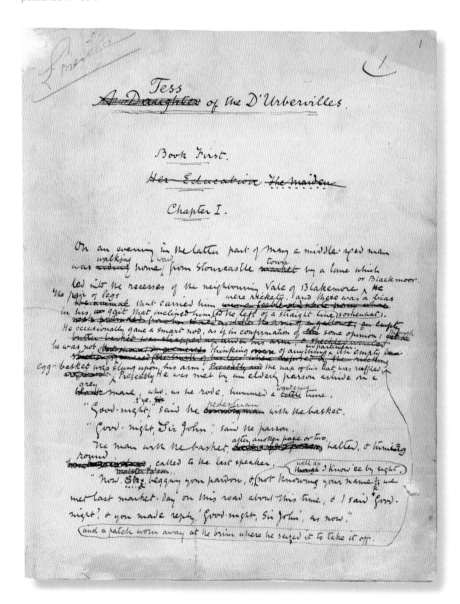

When the archive was catalogued and opened to researchers, the most popular single item was his book of early press cuttings, including the generally ferocious reviews of his first play, *The Birthday Party*. As well as the manuscripts and notes from nearly all his plays, poems, film scripts and other writings, there are thick files of personal and professional correspondence. Among the highlights are letters from Samuel Beckett and Philip Larkin, making frequent references to their common interest in cricket. 'May we meet again before the close of play,' wrote Beckett in 1977 – and they probably did, because the Irish playwright lived for another 12 years.

In its diversity, combined with a touch of quirkiness, the Pinter archive, the documents and keepsakes that mark out his creative life, is a microcosm of the British Library itself. Established in 1973, when it was severed from the British Museum, its holdings span over 3000 years, ranging from fragmentary manuscripts to football fanzines and deriving from nearly every country in the world. The Library is a storehouse of knowledge without equal. That is why Pinter and many other modern writers have chosen it to be the repository – the caretaker, if you like – of their legacy, rather than accepting higher offers from across the Atlantic.

Only after the Second World War did the manuscripts and working papers of living authors come to be recognised, at least in Britain, as a valuable resource for scholars and therefore a

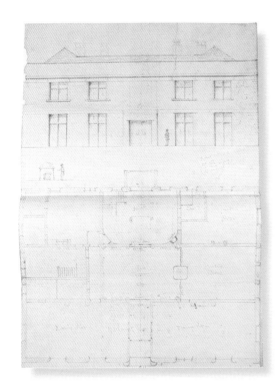

desirable addition to the libraries of educational institutions. Until then such bodies had customarily focussed on writers of the past, on the grounds that it was not possible to judge the true stature of authors until after their death. Thus when, in the 1920s, Thomas Hardy and John Galsworthy offered to donate their 'autograph' manuscripts (in the authors' own hands) of *Tess of the d'Urbervilles* and *The Forsyte Saga* to the British Museum library, the Trustees hesitated before agreeing. (They had less difficulty in accepting a bequest of £91,000 from

Hardy after his death in 1928. Other writers who were to remember the Museum in their wills with substantial legacies included G.K. Chesterton, J.M. Barrie and H.G. Wells.)

The Museum's attitude to modern manuscripts had changed in the decades after George Bernard Shaw's death in 1951. In his lifetime the querulous – but fundamentally generous – playwright had already given some material to the Museum, notably a sheaf of letters from the actress Ellen Terry, and the Trustees were glad to accept the bequest of his literary archive. In the will, Shaw said he wanted it to be placed 'where all the would-be biographers can find it and do their worst or their best'. The Museum also inherited a third of his residual royalties 'in acknowledgment of the incalculable value to me of my daily resort to the reading room of that institution at the beginning of my career'. The other joint legatees are the Royal Academy of Dramatic Art and the National Gallery of Ireland. Controversially the British Museum held on to its right to a third of the Shaw royalties after the Library separated from it in 1973, although in 2002 a settlement was reached. With the extension of copyright until 70 years after an author's death, the three beneficiaries will continue to enjoy their share of the royalties until 2021, mostly derived from frequent revivals both of the play *Pygmalion* and *My Fair Lady,* the musical based on it, first produced six years after Shaw's death.

Shaw acquired his reader's ticket soon after

Daily Mirror Studios
316 Oxford S.W.
Taken at the rehearsals of Pygmalion. H.M. Theatre 1913

arriving in London from Ireland in 1876 and, according to his biographer Michael Holroyd, could scarcely keep away from Great Russell Street. 'It became his club, his university, a refuge, and the centre of his life. He felt closer to strangers in this place than to his own family. He worked here daily for some eight years, applying for more than 300 books each year.' Shaw himself admitted that, 'My debt to that great institution … is inestimable', and he learned shorthand so that he could make notes more quickly. It was in the Reading Room that he met the eminent drama critic William Archer, who would prove a lasting friend. Archer wrote: 'There I used to sit day by day, beside a pallid young man with red hair and beard, dressed in Jaeger all-wool clothing which rather harmonised with his complexion.'

The extensive Shaw archive contains not only manuscripts of his plays and copious correspondence, but also a collection of works that he owned and the privately printed playscripts used for rehearsals. Many contain notes in his hand amending the dialogue or stage directions and, in the case of *Pygmalion*, providing instructions on how Eliza Doolittle's Cockney vowels should be pronounced, as well as detailed instructions on her initial appearance and clothing: 'Her ill-combed hair is dirty. Her shawl and skirt are old and ugly. Her boots are deplorable; her hat, an old black straw with a band of violets, indescribable.'

The impetus actively to solicit autograph

manuscripts from living writers had its origins in the United States. John Quinn, a manuscript collector and art patron based in New York, was a pioneer: in about 1912 he made an arrangement with the novelist Joseph Conrad to feed him the manuscripts of his works. Later Conrad supplied some material to T.J. Wise, a London-based collector (and, it later transpired, a forger and thief). Quinn successfully sought papers from other writers, including T.S. Eliot and W.B. Yeats, and his collection is now in the New York Public Library. In the 1930s Charles Abbott, Director of Libraries at the University of Buffalo, New York State, wrote to scores of leading British and American poets asking them to donate suitable material, then crossed the Atlantic to solicit in person. Among those who responded were Hilaire Belloc, Walter de la Mare, Stephen Spender, Alfred Noyes and Lord Alfred Douglas.

Abbott was not offering any payment for the manuscripts, but it soon became clear that other American universities – with the University of Texas taking the lead – were prepared to lay out useful sums for the archives of significant writers, and a market became established. Yet there were those who felt strongly that the records of British writers should stay in Britain. Notable among them was Philip Larkin. In 1958 he started a campaign both to persuade authors to take patriotism into account when deciding how to dispose of their papers and to convince British libraries that living writers, as well as the dead, should have a place in their collection strategies.

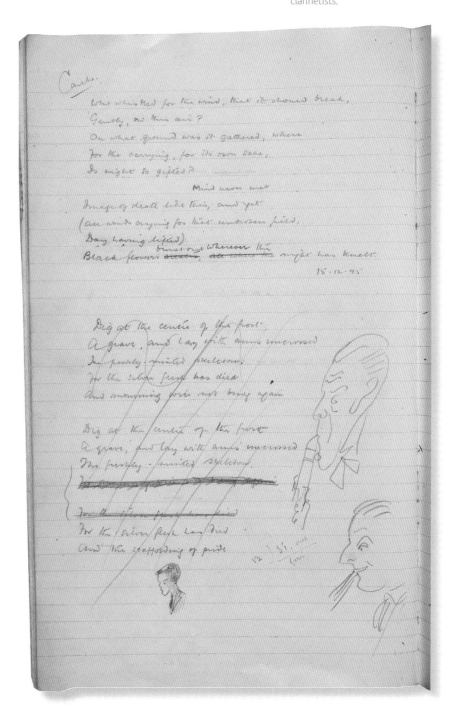

Social terms   Glossary of Christian and ~~Psych~~ Psychological terms

Social	Christian	Psychological	
Society, the ^{happy} ~~good~~	Heaven	The Unconscious	
Matter ~~The individual, the happy~~	Earth	The Conscious Mind	
Society the unhappy	Hell	The repressed unconscious	
The revolution	Purgatory	The consulting-room	

		(Body? / Mind)		
The collective	The Father	The Ego-instincts	The self ~~principle~~ ...
The individual	The Son	The Death-instincts	The Not-self for idea
History	The Holy Ghost	The Libido	The relation between ... of ...
~~Matter~~ Nature	~~Being~~ The Redeemer	Nature	
The C. Party	The four Archangels	The four great ganglia of the body	

Social	Christian	Psychological
The capitalist system ~~self...~~	Satan	The Censor
The ruling classes	The Devils	The repressed instincts
starvation, war, unemployment	Hell, Fire	Unhappiness and disease and mania

Social	Christian	Psychological
The appearance / class distinction	The Fall of Man	The advent of self-consciousness
The break up of the primitive food gathering communities	~~Sin~~ The Expulsion from Eden	The loss of the contentment of the so called Natural state / ... separation from the self & the kingdom
Anti-social acts	Sin	Substitute Pleasures
	Temptation	The deliberate stimulation of the

In a speech in 1979 Larkin said that his interest was aroused when he received requests for his own material, first from Abbott and then from others. 'It seemed dreadful to me that manuscript material was leaving the country just because American librarians could take the trouble to ask for it, and I wrote several letters to the papers grumbling.'

Larkin also elaborated on why he believed the material to be valuable. 'All literary manuscripts have two kinds of value: what might be called the magical value and the meaningful value. The magical value is the older and more universal: this is the paper he wrote on, these are the words as he wrote them, emerging for the first time in this particular miraculous combination. … The meaningful value is of much more recent origin, and is the degree to which a manuscript helps to enlarge our knowledge and understanding of a writer's life and work. A manuscript can show the cancellations, the substitutions, the shifting towards the ultimate form and the final meaning. A notebook, simply by being a fixed sequence of pages, can supply evidence of chronology. … His letters and diaries add to what we know of his life and the circumstances in which he wrote.'

Such a view signalled a shift in thinking about exactly what it was important to collect. Previously librarians, even if they had learned to value manuscripts of modern published work, did not, for the most part, seek what was still regarded as extraneous material. Only in the second half of the twentieth century did they begin to pursue whole archives, including the routine paraphernalia of everyday life that Larkin and others now believed to be of almost equal importance.

The bequest in 1958 of the papers of Marie Stopes, the birth control pioneer, proved a significant milestone in the Museum's collecting policy: the first such acquisition in the field of sociology, rather than politics or literature. Not only were people's lives being assessed holistically, but arbitrary barriers between disciplines were also starting to crumble.

Larkin was the prime mover in the establishment in 1963 of the National Manuscript Collection of Contemporary Poets. Under this scheme the Arts Council would buy papers from living poets (or from the estates of those recently deceased) and sell them on to the British Museum. The low value placed on such material at this time was reflected in the sum initially granted to the project when it was launched – a mere £2000, all donated by the Pilgrim Trust, founded in 1930 by the American philanthropist Edward Harkness to support British cultural and social projects. Yet the first two years saw the acquisition of valuable jottings from some of the leading poets of the era, including John Drinkwater, Dylan Thomas, Dom Moraes, Edmund Blunden, Kathleen Raine and George Macbeth.

In 1967 the Collection's remit was broadened beyond poetry to embrace writers of all kinds. The

LEFT
Dylan Thomas's handwritten
prologue to his *Collected Poems*,
1952.

success of that initiative is reflected in the growing number of authors who now donate or sell their papers to the British Library. Most significant British figures of twentieth-century literature are represented. Even where an author has sold his early archive to an overseas university, much important later material has come to St. Pancras. Tom Stoppard, for example, has donated original scripts of many of his plays, even though his archive is at the University of Texas.

The W.H. Auden collection includes his rare first book, privately printed by Stephen Spender in 1928. Among papers relating to Dylan Thomas are a manuscript of his early poems, a collection of 73 letters and a hand-written prologue to a volume of his *Collected Poems*, published in 1952. Students of George Orwell (Eric Blair) can even examine his pension and national health insurance cards. Lawrence Durrell's letters highlight his constant financial problems, while proofs of his 1946 collection of poems, *Cities, Plains and People*, are annotated both by Durrell and T.S. Eliot, who worked for his publisher, Faber and Faber. The study of writers' correspondence gives a sense of the communal aspects of literary life and the mutual dependence of its leading lights. Among items related to D.H. Lawrence, for example, is a copy of Bertrand Russell's *Philosophical Essays*, in which Lawrence has scribbled some highly critical comments about the philosopher. John Betjeman's papers include letters and postcards from Auden,

LEFT
Sketch of Dalston station and cartoons from John Betjeman's notebook, *c.* 1954.

Eliot and many other important writers of the first half of the twentieth century, including Louis MacNeice, Christopher Isherwood and Edith Sitwell. Ted Hughes corresponded at length with his contemporaries, most poignantly with his wife Sylvia Plath, who committed suicide in 1963 following their estrangement.

In his lifetime Hughes had sold material relating to his early work to Emory University in Atlanta, Georgia. However, when it came to the second, more substantive part of his archive, including a great deal of personal material, his widow Carol decided in 2008, ten years after his death, to accept an offer from the British Library. Coming soon after the purchase of the Pinter papers, the acquisition meant that in the space of six months the Library had greatly enhanced its collection of contemporary literary archives. Mrs. Hughes explained: 'Ted was a man of these islands – their landscapes, rivers and wild places – and it is fitting that papers covering such an important part of his creative life should be deposited with such a prestigious institution here in Britain.'

Some of the most important elements of the Hughes archive are the manuscript and documents relating to *Birthday Letters*, the award-winning collection of 88 poems regarded by many as his response to Sylvia Plath's suicide. They include drafts of poems not eventually included in the collection – which Hughes planned originally to call *The Sorrows of the Deer* – because he considered them too personal to be published. Another touching manuscript is that of *Capriccio*, about his mistress Assia Wevill, who in 1969 killed her daughter before committing suicide. Many of the poems are written in half-used exercise books that he bought from a local school.

Soon after acquiring the Hughes papers the Library came to an arrangement with Graham Swift, a writer who had been one of his close friends. Both men were keen fishermen, and Swift's archive contains letters and postcards from Hughes in which the poet offered tips for fishing the River Torridge in Devon, together with his sketches marking fish traps along the river. The 75 file boxes contain manuscripts, notes, revisions and proofs relating to all of Swift's novels, including *Waterland* and *Last Orders*, which won the Booker Prize in 1996. There is also correspondence with writers such as Andrew Motion, Kazuo Ishiguro and Pat Barker.

In 2010 the Library acquired the archive of the writer and artist Mervyn Peake, who died in 1968. As well as the notebooks for the *Gormenghast* novels, it features a complete set of his original drawings for Lewis Carroll's *Alice in Wonderland* and *Alice Through the Looking-Glass*, and correspondence with contemporaries including Graham Greene, Laurie Lee and C.S. Lewis.

Some of the papers of recently deceased writers come to the Library through the Acceptance in Lieu scheme, under which they are accepted by the nation as payment of the inheritance tax on the estate. Among these was the archive of the novelist J.G. Ballard who, before his death in 2009, told his daughters to ensure that his manuscripts and other significant documents should be offered to the Library. That same year saw the acquisition of the extensive papers of John Berger, the novelist and art critic. He offered to donate them to the Library on condition that a curator went to his home – a

The Eve of Pearl Harbor

= Chap 1 =

Wars came early to Shanghai,
overtaking each other like the tides
that raced up the Yangtze and
returned to this gaudy city all
the coffins cast adrift from the
funeral piers of the Chinese
Bund.

[Jim had begun to dream of
wars. At night the same silent
films seemed to flicker against the
wall of his bedroom in Amherst
Avenue, and transformed his sleeping

Manuscript of Virginia Woolf's
Mrs Dalloway, 1923.

farmhouse in an Alpine village in the Ardèche, close to France's border with Switzerland – to help him pack them up, then transport them to St. Pancras. Among unexpected gems was an account of a nineteenth-century postman in the Ardèche who collected stones on his rounds so that he could build an extraordinary castle, now a national monument.

The written archives are enhanced in many cases by recordings of the writers' voices held in the Sound Archive (see Chapter 10). And although the Library has no complete set of Virginia Woolf's papers, it does possess a copy of the sole remaining recording of her voice, in an extract from a BBC broadcast. The few Woolf manuscripts in the collection include her 1925 novel *Mrs Dalloway*, originally entitled *The Hours*.

Holdings in Pinter's own field, the theatre, have been strengthened enormously in recent years, again embracing both documents and sound recordings. The former include the papers of the playwrights Terence Rattigan, Ronald Harwood and Peter Nichols, as well as the agent Peggy Ramsay. The papers of the three giants of the twentieth-century stage – Laurence Olivier, Ralph Richardson and John Gielgud – all entered the Library in the first three years of the new millennium, along with those of the influential critic Kenneth Tynan, later literary advisor to the nascent National Theatre.

The acquisition of those significant archives in a few years, as well as the text of every play submitted for censorship to the Lord Chamberlain from

1824, encouraged the Library, in conjunction with the University of Sheffield, to launch the Theatre Archive Project. Between 2003 and 2008 it compiled a wealth of written and oral material on the history of British theatre between 1945 and 1968, the year in which the Lord Chamberlain's role as censor was abolished. Since 1968 there has been an obligation on producers to deposit in the library the scripts of all plays performed in licensed British theatres, although in the early years this was not systematically enforced.

An exhibition at the Library to mark the completion of the Theatre Archive Project highlighted the revolution in British theatre that occurred during those 23 years. It examined some of its key institutions, including the Old Vic, Theatre Workshop and the Royal Court, and documented the long, ultimately successful campaign for a National Theatre. Exhibits included a handwritten draft of *The Entertainer*, the script sent to Olivier by John Osborne in a fit of remorse after the successful young playwright had written an attack on Olivier in the London *Evening Standard*. Olivier, to the surprise of Osborne and everyone else, agreed to play Archie Rice, the seedy, clapped-out music hall comedian who was the entertainer of the title. The script was displayed alongside letters to Olivier from erstwhile admirers disgusted that this dignified Shakespearean actor should have agreed to play the lecherous old roué. The official censors in the Lord Chamberlain's office also disapproved of the play, decrying its 'sex, sexy references and … lavatorial dirt'.

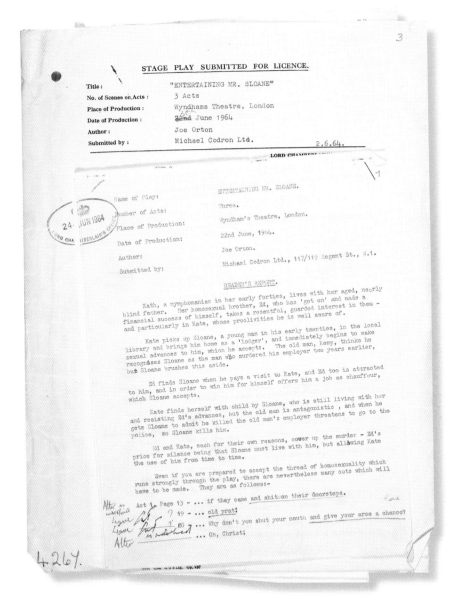

Terence Rattigan's list of gifts to the performers in *Joie de Vivre*, 1960.

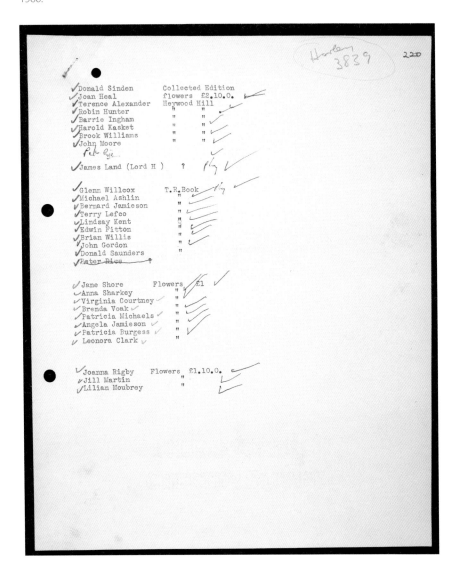

A case study of a particular West End production shows how rich these archives are in compelling detail. In 1960 Terence Rattigan, the most celebrated playwright of the old school challenged by Osborne and fellow 'angry young men', wrote *Joie de Vivre*, a musical version of his early successful play, *French Without Tears*. The musical was panned by nearly all the critics and closed after four performances. The archive begins with letters and documents showing how the project originated and early discussions about casting and finance. Rattigan, unaware of the looming débâcle, drew up an invitation list for the after-show party on the first night, along with a list of gifts to be presented to the performers: for the dancers, bouquets costing £1; for actresses, bigger bouquets at £1 10s. (£1.50); and for the leading lady, Joan Heal, one worth £2 10s. The men received copies of Rattigan's works, but only the leading man, Donald Sinden, was given the full collected edition. The last items in the file are letters from Rattigan's friends and some of the actors, offering him their commiserations and lambasting the critics, then the final accounts showing a loss of nearly £35,000.

The most vicious review, by Kenneth Tynan, was published in *The Observer* the day after the show closed. Rattigan was angry enough to write him a scathing letter, criticising his writing, his attitude and his mores – and adding that the show's director, Billy Chappell, was threatening to sue Tynan for appearing to compare him to a French prostitute. (Tynan replied that the offending phrase, *en cocotte*, actually referred to a method of cooking eggs with cream.)

Prior to this exchange another word in the show, the French expletive *merde*, had upset the Lord Chamberlain, who demanded its removal. Before the West End opening Rattigan wrote to him saying that in ten weeks of touring they had obeyed his instruction and 'we have tried every alternative, including a silent grimace, but nothing, I'm afraid, has worked at all'. He feared the whole scene might have to be cut. Perhaps because of that threat, the Lord Chamberlain gave way. On the day of the opening Rattigan received a letter from St. James's Palace which read: 'The Lord Chamberlain will agree to *merde* in this instance.' However, the concession was not enough to save the show.

Rattigan had other brushes with the official censor during his career. In 1954 he had been forced to change a plot line in his play *Separate Tables*. As he originally wrote it, a male character was accused of importuning other men: he was persuaded to change it to a man accused of 'nudging' women in a cinema. The portrayal of homosexual characters was a subject that worried the Lord Chamberlain. Under pressure to re-think his resistance to it, he sent a number of letters canvassing the opinions of 'wise and responsible men and women' – including Olivier, who was subsequently alleged to have been bi-sexual. In his letter the Lord Chamberlain fretted that any hint of homosexuality would be 'very distasteful and embarrassing in mixed company' and 'might start an unfortunate train of thought in the previously innocent'.

As in the literary archive, there are many cross-references among the memorabilia of the theatrical aristocracy. Thus, taken together, the papers of Richardson, Olivier and Gielgud, all of whom cut their teeth at the Old Vic, the home of Shakespearean productions in the 1930s, contain both sides of the many exchanges between them – although there are fewer in the case of the last two, who fell out early in their careers and were never close friends. Being in a profession where courtesy and mutual support are legendary, they nonetheless maintained contact; and Gielgud kept one letter from Olivier containing a thinly veiled insult. Written in 1959, it purported to congratulate him on a television performance of *The Browning Version*: 'Bravo dearest Johnnie, it's just fascinating and most inspiring – you seem still to find room for improvement all the time.'

The Gielgud archive is rich in theatrical mementoes from as early as the nineteenth century. He had a distinguished pedigree: his great-aunt was Ellen Terry, who frequently played the leading lady on the London and New York stage opposite Sir Henry Irving. His mother, Kate Terry Gielgud, kept numerous notes about plays she had seen and meticulously recorded the appearances of her son until her death in 1956. There is also a set of letters that he wrote to her, some containing indiscreet comments about fellow actors, and scores of scripts from the films and plays in which he appeared, with his own observations and *aides mémoires* written around the typewritten text. Thousands of press cuttings record Gielgud's stage career: there is even a set of reviews in Danish of his production of *Hamlet* at Elsinore in 1939. From later years come records of funeral and memorial services for his generation of actors, beginning with Vivien Leigh in 1967, where he gave the eulogy. And there is one non-documentary item in the archive: a silk-embroidered bag in which he, and before him his mother, stored important letters.

Ralph Richardson's papers include what appear to be some notes for a tribute to mark Gielgud's 80th birthday in 1984, never completed as Richardson died in 1983. He was a popular public speaker and a prolific writer, and much of this output is preserved, including a letter to young people, written in 1950,

RIGHT

A scene from the 1938 production of *Three Sisters* at the Queen's Theatre, directed by Michel Saint-Denis and starring John Gielgud, Michael Redgrave, Gwen Ffrangcon-Davies and Peggy Ashcroft. From the Gielgud archive.

laying down rules of behaviour in the theatre. An early letter in the archive is from Shaw, advising Richardson how to play Bluntschli in *Arms and the Man* in 1931.

Another significant archive is that of the French director Michel Saint-Denis, who exercised a profound influence on the British theatre of the twentieth century. He settled in London in 1934 and directed all the up-and-coming actors of the period. A memorable production of Chekhov's *Three Sisters* in 1938, featuring Gielgud, Michael Redgrave, Alec Guinness and Peggy Ashcroft, is well documented in the collection with scripts, casting notes, correspondence and production photographs.

After the Second World War Saint-Denis ran the Old Vic Theatre Centre with Glen Byam Shaw and George Devine, later the influential founder of the English Stage Company at the Royal Court Theatre. The Saint-Denis archive includes hundreds of letters between the two men, as well as plans and other documents relating to the renovation of the Old Vic, which had been damaged by wartime bombing. After leaving Britain temporarily, he returned in 1961 to work with Peter Hall at the Royal Shakespeare Company as artistic adviser and co-director.

If the British Library did not exist many such archives, vital for the comprehension of our cultural history, would surely be lost or dispersed. Many whose lives do not bring them into contact with the Library have an image of it – assuming they think of it at all – as a fusty place where ancient manuscripts and historic books are made available to scholars. That is certainly one of its most important functions, and always has been. Yet its role as caretaker of the national heritage is a lot wider than that. It is a constantly growing organism that has renewed itself through the ages to collect and store artifacts that will give future generations the means to interpret contemporary life and learning in all its aspects. It is a colossal undertaking, made possible by the vision of a determined group of men nearly 260 years ago.

✠ ihs xps · Matheus homo

incipit euangelii

genelogia mathei

ongunned   godspeller

boc

cynn
necce
nirxe

cnou
nixe

haelen
de
cnixxex

dauid
xunu

abnaham
ex xunu

LIBER

generati

onisihu

XpifiliidauidfiliIabRAHAM

CHAPTER 2

Foundations

'The scope of this petition is to preserve divers old books concerning matter of history of this realm, original charters and monuments into a library to be erected in some convenient place.'

~ SIR ROBERT COTTON'S PETITION TO ELIZABETH I (1602)

QUEEN ELIZABETH I, in the final year of her life, did not respond to this first serious attempt to establish what is now the British Library. Sir Robert Cotton, as well as being a dedicated book collector, was an influential, ambitious courtier and Member of Parliament; but Elizabeth appears to have been unmoved. Possibly she was discouraged by the proposal that the national library should incorporate, alongside Cotton's own holdings, the most significant items from the royal collection of books and manuscripts, much of it amassed by her father Henry VIII as loot following the dissolution of the monasteries.

Cotton, born in 1571 into a wealthy landed family in Huntingdonshire, was well educated (at Westminster School and Jesus College, Cambridge). He developed an early interest in history and historic artifacts, becoming a member of the College of Antiquaries shortly after its foundation in 1586. He was an assiduous collector of old manuscripts, initially for the purpose of compiling a history of his native county, although he soon began to broaden his interests.

⊱ OPPOSITE

The *Lindisfarne Gospels* were created by Eadfrith, Bishop of Lindisfarne between 698 and 721, at his priory on Holy Island. The book – 258 pages on vellum, produced from calf skins – was in the collection of Sir Robert Cotton, the early seventeenth-century bibliophile. It is written in Latin, but at some point in the tenth century a scribe added an Anglo-Saxon translation in red ink beneath the original words. This page (folio 27) is the beginning of St Matthew's Gospel, illustrated with patterns reminiscent of Anglo-Saxon jewellery and enamel work.

⊱ LEFT

Sir Robert Cotton, painting attributed to Cornelius Johnson.

Given the Queen's indifference to his proposal, Cotton donated some of his treasures to Sir Thomas Bodley, then in the process of establishing the Bodleian Library in Oxford. Cotton was generous in giving researchers access to his 800 volumes of manuscripts 'of the choicest sort', according to a contemporary, John Selden, who used to borrow from it frequently. The collection embraced Anglo-Saxon manuscripts, biblical works and state papers, some purchased from the library of Henry, Prince of Wales, James I's eldest son, after his death in 1612 at the age of 18.

Of the many priceless items in the Cotton collection, the best-known today include the *Lindisfarne Gospels*, created in the eighth century – the earliest copy of the four Gospels known to have been produced in England – and the only surviving manuscript of the fourteenth-century romance *Sir Gawain and the Green Knight*. Some of the works were politically or theologically sensitive, causing Cotton to fall foul of James I and, subsequently, Charles I, who perceived that the Library's materials were being used by scholars and Parliamentarians to challenge their cherished concept of the divine right of kings. Cotton was briefly arrested in 1629 and his library sealed on Charles's orders. It was still closed when Cotton died in 1631, and was not handed back to his descendants until 1650, during the interregnum. In 1700 Cotton's grandson established a trust that allowed the collection to become the property of the nation. Accommodation was eventually found for it at Ashburnham House in Westminster. Unfortunately a fire there in 1731 destroyed or seriously damaged several of its treasures, including the Cotton Genesis – the first book of the Old Testament, wonderfully illustrated in the fifth or sixth century.

In the 1620s Cotton had befriended Simonds D'Ewes, a young lawyer, and passed on to him his passion for ancient manuscripts. According to the

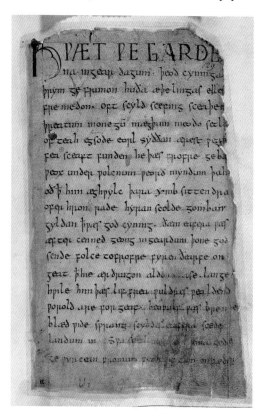

▶ RIGHT
The opening page of *Beowulf*, early eleventh century.

nineteenth-century historian John Bruce, D'Ewes believed that 'records, and other exotic monuments of antiquity, were the most ravishing and satisfying part of human knowledge'. He collected documents with a view to writing a definitive history of Britain, but he never completed it. In 1704 the bulk of his collection was bought by the politician Sir Robert Harley and formed the basis of his own library. This would eventually be as important as Cotton's, and likewise become one of the British Library's core collections.

Harley, born in 1661, came to prominence as a supporter of William of Orange in the 1688 revolution. He was elected to Parliament the following year and appointed Speaker in 1701. When Queen Anne came to the throne he was one

of her most influential advisers until forced from office in 1708, only to return as Chancellor of the Exchequer two years later. Harley was made the first Earl of Oxford in 1711.

In 1708 Harley appointed a curator for his library. He chose Humfrey Wanley, a scholar with a reputation in Oxford as a cataloguer of historic manuscripts. Wanley had done some work on the collection of Sir Hans Sloane – destined, like Harley's, to form part of the Library's foundation holdings. Together with Harley's son Edward, born in 1689, Wanley set out on an extravagant buying spree which would eventually cause Edward severe financial difficulties. Their most famous acquisition is the *Golden Gospels*, written entirely in gold lettering and dating from the ninth century. Wanley bought the manuscript from a Dutch collector in 1720.

When Robert Harley died in 1724, Edward inherited both his title and the library. By the time of his own death in 1741 the latter comprised nearly half a million items, including 50,000 printed books and 7618 manuscripts as well as many pamphlets, charters and antiquities. He bequeathed the collection to his widow, Henrietta, who was forced to sell most of it, including all the printed books, on the open market to settle the family's debts. Harley's collection would have made a superb foundation for a national library, but at that time no such institution existed and the prevailing government was in no mind to create one. Only the manuscripts remained in the family's hands and in 1753, when the need for a national library was at last being accepted, Henrietta sold them to the nation in for £10,000.

The event that proved to be the ultimate spur for the Museum's creation was the death in January of that year of Hans Sloane, at the age of 93. A prominent physician, naturalist and collector of curiosities, antiquities, manuscripts and books, Sloane was born in Ireland, but he moved to London as a youth and trained as an apothecary.

hic est elaphantus

Est animal quod dicitur elephans in quo non est con
cupiscentia cotus. Elephantem greci a magnitudine
corporis uocatuoy puttant. quod formā montis pferat. Grece
enim mons elephio dicit. Apud indos autē a uoce barro uo
catur. Unde .ē. & uox eius barrit, & dentes ebur. Rostrū
autē p muscida dicit qm illo pabula ori admouet, &
est angui similis. uallo munitur eburneo. Nullum

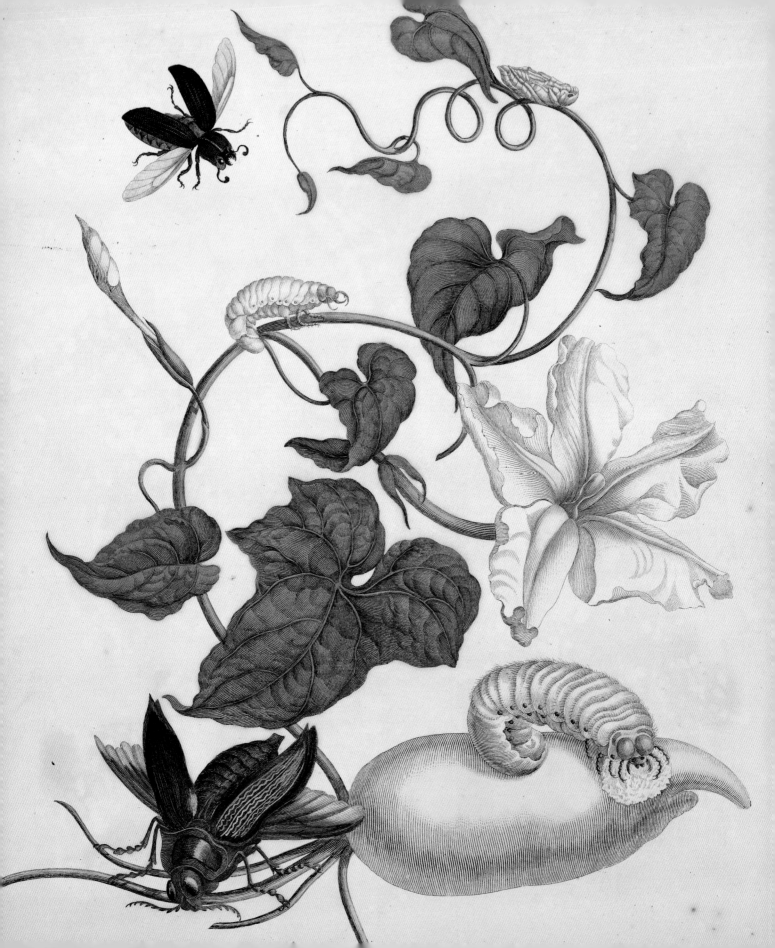

There he developed an interest in herbal remedies that broadened into a fascination with the entire plant world. In his early twenties Sloane travelled to continental Europe and gained a qualification in medicine. In 1687 he embarked on a longer journey, on his appointment as physician to the Duke of Albemarle, Governor of Jamaica. But the Duke died after two years, and Sloane returned to London.

During his travels he assiduously collected specimens of plants and manuscripts relating to botany, which he formed into a museum for the benefit of his friends and associates. (One of his lasting introductions to the national diet was the cocoa bean, leading to the production of chocolate, first as a drink and later as confectionery.) Sloane was elected to the Royal Society, a group of men linked by their intense curiosity about the natural world and fascination with the developing discipline of science, and he soon became one of the Society's most prominent members. The papers he contributed to its *Philosophical Transactions* included such intriguing subjects as the feathers of a condor and people who ate stones. In an era when nobody could be quite sure of the importance of various natural phenomena, or certain of how they related to one another, almost any such topic was of potential significance.

Sloane's medical practice flourished and in 1712, by then a wealthy man, he bought the Manor of Chelsea, where several thoroughfares still bear his

OPPOSITE

Sir Hans Sloane, whose collections formed the basis of the original British Museum library, sought out books about natural history and owned several works by the Swiss artist Maria Sibylla Merian (1647–1717), the leading botanical illustrator of her day. This plate from her closely observed *Insects of Surinam*, published in 1705, depicts a horned passalus beetle in various stages of development, against the background of a morning glory.

LEFT

Bust of Sir Hans Sloane by Michael Rysbrack.

BELOW

A medieval herbal from Sloane's collection.

name. Appointed physician to Queen Anne, he was made a baronet in 1716 in recognition of his services to her and her successor, George I. In 1727, on the death of Sir Isaac Newton, the Royal Society chose Sloane to succeed him as its President. His collection grew, as did its reputation among antiquaries and scientists. Among the many important scientific papers it contained were handwritten notes by William Harvey on his discovery of the circulation of blood. In 1743 the Rev. William Stukeley described a visit made to Sloane: 'His great house at Chelsea is full throughout; every closet and chimney with books, rarities, etc.' Five years later the 'great house' was visited by Frederick, Prince of Wales (who was to die in 1751 while his father, George II, was still on the throne).

At the time of Sloane's death in 1753 his collection consisted of nearly 100,000 items, half of them books and manuscripts. In his will he expressed the wish that it should be acquired by the state and made accessible to all, at a price of £20,000, payable to his two daughters. George II was as resistant to the idea of a national museum and library as Elizabeth had been 150 years earlier – but this time Parliament stepped in and agreed that the Sloane material should be combined with the Cotton and Harley collections in what would become the British Museum. The cost of purchasing the three collections, and finding a suitable place where they could be held, was estimated at £50,000. As the Treasury would not stump up that amount,

it was agreed that the money should be raised by a public lottery which, although conducted in a notoriously corrupt manner, raised £75,000, duly handed over to the newly appointed Museum trustees. To house the collections they bought Montagu House in Bloomsbury for £10,500, on the site where the present British Museum stands.

In 1757, three years before his death, George II agreed that his Royal Library (not to be confused with the King's Library, given to the Museum 66 years later) should be incorporated into the new institution. Known for many years as the Old Royal Library, this was and remains an eclectic assemblage of books and manuscripts, with the oldest material in it dating from the eighth century. The collection had been built up in piecemeal fashion by the King's predecessors – whose interest in the written word ebbed and flowed, partly in response to the political circumstances in which they found themselves. Some of the finest medieval manuscripts from the Old Royal Library, still in near-pristine condition, were displayed in an exhibition at the British Library in 2011.

Edward IV can lay claim to be the progenitor of the Royal Library. Although his 22-year reign was dominated by the Wars of the Roses, he found the time and inclination to acquire a quantity of manuscripts and printed books. It is probable that

A binding from the Old Royal Library incorporating Henry VIII's arms, *c.*1540.

Jean de Wavrin presents his *Chronique d'Angleterre* to Edward IV, depicted in the manuscript itself, *c.*1475.

Edward acquired his taste for rich illumination during his exile in Flanders in 1470–71, when he was briefly supplanted by his predecessor, Henry VI. In 1475, restored to the throne, Edward commissioned a chronicle of England from Jean de Wavrin in Bruges, and the work incorporates a picture of the author presenting the book to the King.

After Henry Tudor became King in 1485 he appointed a Burgundian, Quentin Poulet, as the first dedicated royal librarian. Henry VII seems to have been interested in books less for their content, more as status symbols and evidence of his wealth: his principal enthusiasm was for brightly coloured French copies of illuminated manuscripts. The King's partiality for bold display was confirmed by the rich bindings that cloak his books, a tradition continued by his successors. Some of the British Library's most spectacular bindings are to be found on the books that were in the Old Royal Library.

⋙ BELOW
The *Queen Mary Psalter*, early
fourteenth century.

Henry's son, Henry VIII, had an additional and
more practical use for books. Seeking the annulment
of his marriage to Catherine of Aragon, he hunted
for texts to support his case. His dissolution of the
monasteries between 1536 and 1539 released a huge
number of theological books and manuscripts, and
he took his pick. He made notes in the margins
when he found passages with which he strongly
agreed or disagreed.

Under his successor, Edward VI, more
theological works were acquired, as well as some
books that might be found in a schoolroom, such
as language primers and mathematical text books.
Edward was, after all, not yet 16 when he died. Mary I
garnered books that confirmed her Catholic faith:
the fourteenth-century psalter presented to her
in 1553 and which is now known as the *Queen
Mary Psalter* is one of the outstanding items in the
Old Royal Library. Many other volumes that have
been identified as Mary's personal copies show
signs of wear, suggesting that she frequently carried
them with her rather than leaving them unread on
library shelves.

James I acquired a number of treatises on the
turbulence in the Holy Roman Empire, culminating
in the defeat of his son-in-law at the Battle of White
Mountain in Bohemia in 1620. James also collected
pamphlets for and against his abortive plan to
have his son Charles marry the Spanish Infanta.
Naturally enough, James also kept manuscripts of
his own books in the Royal Library, most of them

✺ BELOW

From Ben Jonson's manuscript of
The Masque of Queens, 1609.

on political themes concerned with the role of
the monarch. In 1612 he gained possession of the
extensive and valuable library of Lord Lumley, a
renowned Elizabethan bibliophile. Lumley died
in 1609, whereupon his library was acquired by
Prince Henry, James's eldest son; it then passed
to the King on Henry's death. Several volumes on
hunting testify to an enthusiasm shared by James
and Henry. The collection also included volumes
formerly in the possession of Thomas Cranmer,
Henry VIII's Archbishop of Canterbury, among
them a ninth-century manuscript of the Gospels
from St. Augustine's, Canterbury.

James's second son Charles, who became Prince
of Wales after his elder brother died, took after his
father in his penchant for acquiring pamphlets on
politics and religion. He does not appear to have
been as enthusiastic about books as some of his
predecessors: his collecting was devoted principally
to the visual arts, painting and sculpture. Yet Charles
did acquire several volumes relating to heraldry,
in particular the Order of the Garter, as well as
books of music and scripts of plays. This reflected
his fondness for the pageantry and spectacle of
the annual court masques, mostly written by Ben
Jonson and designed by Inigo Jones, in which he
would occasionally perform, even after inheriting
the throne.

After the execution of Charles I in 1649
Parliament proposed that the Royal Library should be
available for public use. Had that happened, it would

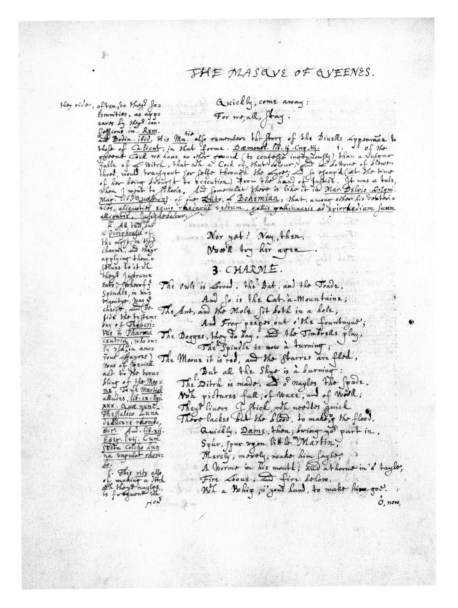

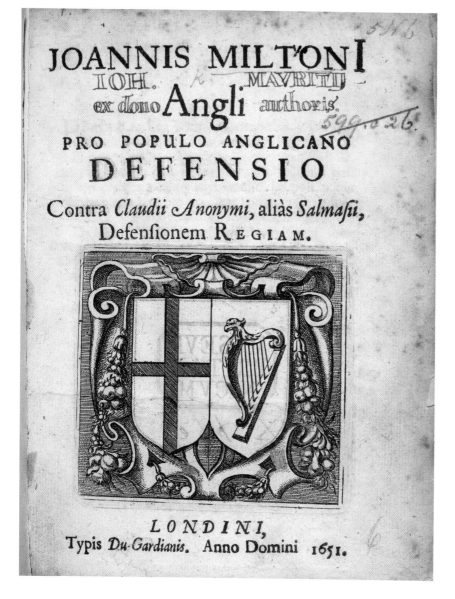

have advanced the creation of a national library by more than a hundred years. Instead, the books and manuscripts remained in the palaces of Whitehall and St. James's. All but a few escaped the fate of the bulk of the royal collection of art and antiquities, sold by auction to raise revenue for Oliver Cromwell's Commonwealth Government. Thus they reverted to Charles II on his Restoration in 1660, eventually coming to rest in the British Library's collections.

Charles II's library was the first to benefit from legal deposit legislation. The Licensing Act of 1662, reinforced in later years, stipulated that publishers must donate a copy of every new book to the Royal Library. Although not rigorously enforced for nearly two centuries, this did ensure a steady trickle of printed books into the collection. It had been already strengthened within just a few months of the Restoration when Charles and his librarian Thomas Ross, no doubt in a fit of jubilation at the King's return to his rightful kingdom, purchased the library of John Morris, a prosperous and well-connected scholar who died in 1658. Morris's wealth had derived from his ownership of the watermills by London Bridge, built by his father and providing much of the capital's water supply until they were destroyed in the Great Fire of London in 1666. His books clearly took precedence over his business: in his will Morris described his library as 'the chief pleasure and employment of my life'.

Although Morris's collection of around 1500 volumes covered a variety of disciplines it was especially strong in the fields of botany and natural history. He had been a keen gardener and a friend of the two John Tradescants, father and son, pioneer plant hunters and gardeners to the royal family. It also included some books formerly owned by Ben Jonson, who had died in 1637, and a copy of a political pamphlet by the poet John Milton, inscribed to Morris by the author.

The other significant acquisition during Charles II's reign came towards the end of it, in 1678, when he bought 300 items from the library of John Theyer, who had died five years earlier. Theyer, a lawyer and antiquary, was a devout Christian, and the most important part of his collection consisted of religious manuscripts inherited from a relative who had been a prior until the dissolution of the monasteries. That was to prove the last of the major additions to the Old Royal Library. It was moved to join the Cotton Library in 1707, but happily escaped the worst effects of the Ashburnham House fire in 1731. From there the two collections were moved to an unoccupied dormitory at Westminster School, until they found their permanent home in the new British Museum.

The British Museum and its library opened to the public at Montagu House in January 1759. From the start, it sought to embrace the concept of universal access that still guides the Library's admission policy today. Its regulations stated: 'Though chiefly designed for the use of learned and studious men, both natives and foreigners, into their researches into the several parts of knowledge, yet being a national establishment … it may be judged reasonable that the advantage accruing from it should be rendered as general as possible.'

Despite this bold statement of intent, the number of visitors to the first Reading Room – a narrow, damp and ill-lit space in the basement of Montagu House, with stuffed birds lining the walls – seldom reached double figures at any one time. (Any much greater number would indeed have been an embarrassment, since there were only 20 chairs.) Nonetheless, the early readers included some notable *literati*. The poet Thomas Gray was a regular attender from a few months after it opened, and Dr. Samuel Johnson, the lexicographer, visited the following year.

Not until 1774 were readers moved to larger and more salubrious accommodation on the ground floor. For the most part, in the early days, it was an all-male coterie. Two women are recorded as being admitted in 1762 and another in 1763, but these were apparently the only representatives of their sex to use the Reading Room in its first ten years. (According to G.F. Barwick, the historian of the Reading Room, it was not considered proper for women to study alone, where they could be prey to advances from lascivious scholars. They were thus admitted only if they could find another woman to accompany and chaperone them.)

The North Prospect of MOUNTAGUE HOUSE.

As soon as the British Museum and its library were established, they began to attract valuable donations of material. In 1759 Solomon da Costa, a Jewish broker from Amsterdam, gave a selection of early Hebrew printed books, some dating from the fifteenth century. Then in 1762 the young George III presented the Thomason Tracts, a collection of over 22,000 news sheets and pamphlets from the Civil War and Commonwealth periods, which over the years have proved an invaluable source for historians. The King had obtained them for £300 on the advice of the Earl of Bute, a trusted adviser who did much to inspire his interest in books and manuscripts, to the Library's eventual great benefit.

Other gifts followed. In 1766 Thomas Birch, one of the Museum's original elected trustees, died at the age of 61 after falling from his horse on Hampstead Heath. He bequeathed his books and manuscripts to the Museum's library, including correspondence from Sir Isaac Newton, and stipulated that the income from the rest of his estate should go to increasing the wages of the three under-librarians. Another valuable donation came soon afterwards from Earl Stanhope: the original Articles of the Barons, accepted by King John at Runnymede in 1215 and in effect the first draft of *Magna Carta*. The actor and theatrical impresario David Garrick, who died in 1779, bequeathed to the Museum his formidable collection of 1300 early English plays. This is one of the reasons why theatrical history is today one of the Library's strongest areas.

When George III succeeded his grandfather in 1760 there was no Royal Library as such, as it had been given to the nation three years earlier. The young King, though, already had his own collection of books, many of them inherited from his father, Frederick Prince of Wales, and he had appointed his first full-time librarian in 1755, at the age of 17. After George came to the throne the pace of his acquisitions increased: in 1762 he paid £10,000 for the important library and art collection of Joseph Smith, who had served as the British consul in Venice for 16 years. Smith's library was especially strong in Italian literature and early printed books from Britain and elsewhere, and included several rare manuscripts. The art collection featured many works by Canaletto (Smith was his agent), but these remain in the ownership of the royal family.

Once Smith's superb library had been absorbed into the King's and accommodated in the Queen's House – later to be known as Buckingham Palace – George was anxious to strengthen it further. In 1768 he deputed Frederick Augusta Barnard, a studious former page boy, to travel in Europe and buy significant books, allowing him a budget of £2000 a year for three years. Before Barnard left he received a long letter of advice on his assignment from no less an authority than Dr. Johnson, who frequently made use of the King's Library as well as of that in the British Museum. The King was so pleased with the results of Barnard's foray that in 1774 he appointed him Royal Librarian.

George III was also spending freely on acquisitions in Britain, and some scholars presented him with gifts of books. By the time of his death in 1820 the catalogue of his library contained nearly 50,000 titles in 65,250 volumes, as well as 17,500 pamphlets. The scale of the collection can be gauged by noting that it included 23 editions of Shakespeare's works, plus 38 texts of single plays, as well as the works of nearly every significant British writer up to the late eighteenth century. Virtually no branch of scholarship was ignored.

❧ BELOW
The King's Library in the Queen's
House (now Buckingham
Palace).

George IV did not share his father's passion for books. Moreover, he was planning a radical rebuilding of Buckingham Palace, aimed at turning it into the principal royal residence in London, and was irked by the space that of necessity had to be devoted to this extensive collection in addition to the cost of maintaining it – estimated at some £2000 a year. There were rumours that he was planning to sell it to the Tsar of Russia, but eventually, in 1823, George offered it to the nation. The British Museum was the obvious repository and the Trustees agreed to keep the collection intact, rather than dispersing its contents among the library's existing holdings.

The gift came at an apposite time, just as the Trustees had asked the architect Robert Smirke, who had been working for the Museum for some years, to enlarge and in effect rebuild Montagu House to accommodate the Museum's growing collections. Space allotted to the library had already been expanded twice because of the accelerating demand for readers' tickets, due in large measure to the energy and vision of Joseph Planta, Principal Librarian from 1799 until 1827. By the time Planta stepped down, to be succeeded by Henry Ellis, the number of users exceeded 20,000 a year.

For the King's Library, Smirke designed a much admired room of its own, which was ready to receive the books by 1827. There they remained for nearly 170 years, until they were moved out to occupy a vertical, glass-enclosed pillar that forms the dramatic centrepiece of the new British Library building: the background to thousands of holiday photographs taken by awestruck tourists. And 1857 saw the completion of the splendid Round Reading Room at the heart of the new Museum, which would become an object of such affection with those who used it that there was an outcry when it was eventually vacated 140 years on.

Incipit liber Bresith, quem nos Gene
A principio creauit deus celu sui vñ?.
et terram. Terra autem erat inanis et
vacua: z tenebre erant sup facie abissi:
et spiritus dñi ferebatur super aquas.
Dixitq; deus. Fiat lux. Et facta e lux.
Et vidit deus lucem cp esset bona: et
diuisit lucem a tenebris. appellauitq;
lucem diem et tenebras nocte. Factu
cp est vespere z mane dies vnus. Dixit
quoq; deus. Fiat firmamentu in me
dio aquaru: et diuidat aquas ab a
quis. Et fecit deus firmamentu: diui
sitq; aquas que erant sub firmamen
to ab hijs que erant super firmamen
tum: z factum est ita. Vocauitq; deus
firmamentu celu: z factum est vespere
et mane dies secundus. Dixit vero de
us. Congregentur aque que sub celo
sunt in locum vnu et appareat arida.
Et factum est ita. Et vocauit deus ari
dam terram: cõgregationesq; aquaz
appellauit maria. Et vidit deus cp es
set bonu. et ait. Germinet terra herba
virentem et facientem semen: et lignu
pomiferu faciens fructum iuxta genus
suu: cuius semen in semetipo sit super
terram. Et factum est ita. Et protulit
terra herbam virentem et facientem se
men iuxta genus suu: lignuq; faciens
fructu et habés vnuqdq; sementem scdm
specie sua. Et vidit deus cp esset bonu:
et factu e vespere et mane dies tercius.
Dixitq; aut deus. Fiant luminaria
in firmameto celi. z diuidat diem ac
nocte: z sint in signa z tepora z dies z
annos: ut luceat in firmameto celi et
illuminet terra. Et factu est ita. Fecitq;
deus duo luminaria magna: lumiare
maius ut pesset diei et lumiare min9
ut pesset nocti: z stellas. z posuit eas in
firmameto celi ut lucerent sup terra: et

pessent diei ac nocti: z diuideret lucem
ac tenebras. Et vidit de9 cp esset bonu:
et factu e vespere et mane dies quart9.
Dixit etiam deus. Producant aque
reptile anime viuentis et volatile sup
terram: sub firmameto celi. Creauitq;
deus cete grandia. et omne anima vi
uentem atq; motabilem qua produxe
rant aque in species suas: z omne vo
latile secundu genus suu. Et vidit de
us cp esset bonu: benedixitq; ei dicens.
Crescite et multiplicamini. et replete a
quas maris: auesq; multiplicentur
super terram. Et factu e vespere z mane
dies quitus. Dixit quoq; deus. Pro
ducat terra anima viuentem in gene
re suo: iumenta z reptilia. z bestias ter
re secundu species suas. Factu e ita. Et
fecit deus bestias terre iuxta species su
as: iumenta z omne reptile terre in ge
nere suo. Et vidit deus cp esset bonu:
et ait. Faciam9 homine ad ymagine z
similitudine nostra. z psit piscib9 maris.
z volatilib9 celi. z bestijs vniuseq; terre:
oiq; reptili qd mouet i terra. Et creau
it deus homine ad ymagine et simi
litudine suam: ad ymaginem dei crea
uit illu: masculu et femina creauit eos.
Benedixitq; illis deus. et ait. Crescite
et multiplicamini z replete terram. et
subicite eam: z dominamini piscibus
maris. z volatilibus celi: z vniuersis
animãtibus que mouentur sup terra.
Dixitq; deus. Ecce dedi vobis omne
herbam afferentem semen sup terram.
et vniusa ligna que habet i semetipis
semete generis sui: ut sint vobis i esca.
z cuctis aiantibus terre. oiiq; volucri
celi z vniuersis q mouetur in terra. et i
quibus e anima viues: ut habeat ad
vescendu. Et factu est ita. Viditq; deus
cuncta que fecerat: et erat valde bona.

CHAPTER 3

Growing pains

❝The expense requisite for … giving the necessary means of information on all branches of human learning from all countries, in all languages, properly arranged, substantially and well bound, minutely and fully catalogued, easily accessible and yet fully preserved, capable, for some years to come, of keeping pace with the increase in human knowledge – will no doubt be great; but so is the nation which is to bear it.❞

~ ANTONIO PANIZZI, KEEPER OF PRINTED BOOKS (1845)

PANIZZI, THE MOST INFLUENTIAL librarian in the history of the British Museum, was born in the Duchy of Modena, Italy, in 1797. He trained as a lawyer, but was forced to flee the country at the age of 25 because he had been active in secret societies opposing the ducal regime. Some of his fellow dissidents were less fortunate: they were arrested and charged with treason, and a copy of Panizzi's book attacking their trial is in the British Library. He came to England in 1823, the same year that he was sentenced to death in Modena in his absence.

When Panizzi arrived he spoke no English: although he soon became fluent, he would never lose his pronounced Italian accent. He settled for a while in Liverpool, where he taught Italian, but in 1828 moved to the capital on his appointment as Professor of Italian at the newly established London

University. He attracted few students, however, and, since his pay was determined by the size of his classes, it was with some relief that in 1831 he accepted the post of an assistant librarian at the British Museum on the recommendation of two Trustees, the lawyer Henry Brougham and Thomas Grenville, the statesman and diplomat. Throughout his career Panizzi would prove adept at forming connections with influential people: today we would call it networking.

He was assigned to the Department of Printed Books whose holdings, not taking the King's Library into account, amounted to 240,000 titles – fewer than in some of the principal libraries of Europe. Although the King's Library was by now comfortably accommodated in the splendid space that Smirke had designed for it, the rest of the collections remained in the old Montagu House. They still awaited transfer to the replacement building that would be constructed in stages over the next 25 years. At that time the number of users of the Reading Room was around 200 a day and rising rapidly, although only about half that number could be accommodated at any one time. Even when a new Reading Room was opened in 1838, it could seat only 161.

A year after his appointment, Panizzi became a British subject. Two years after that he was involved in the first of the passionate and often poisonous disputes that characterised his career. This one was about the Museum's library catalogue – whether it should be in manuscript form or printed, with the consequent possibility of error. The Trustees wanted it printed but Panizzi was strongly opposed to the idea: he advocated a written master catalogue that would be simple to correct and update. This apparently technical issue became a point of principle that rankled for many years, with some Trustees bristling at what they saw as an upstart foreigner challenging their authority.

Panizzi's most sustained enmity was with Frederic Madden, his junior by four years, who was Assistant Keeper of Manuscripts when Panizzi arrived at Montagu House, and whose reputation for thorough, painstaking work would later be enhanced through his careful restoration of some of the Cotton manuscripts damaged in the fire at Ashburnham House. The two men were of roughly equal status and never became friends. Their rivalry deepened in 1837 when Panizzi was confirmed as Keeper of Printed Books three days before Madden's appointment as Keeper of Manuscripts, meaning that Panizzi, although he had fewer years of service, technically held the senior ranking. Madden tried to get the Trustees to ante-date his own appointment so that he would displace his rival in the pecking order. His request was refused; yet he bested Panizzi in their first major power tussle, when he was allowed to take over the house in the Museum grounds previously occupied by Panizzi's predecessor, Henry Baber.

There followed repeated bitter arguments about whether Panizzi was authorised to poach staff from Madden's Manuscripts Department to help out during busy times in the Reading Room. Their next serious clash came in 1840 when Madden, claiming that he had Panizzi's permission, removed manuscripts from the King's Library, arguing that they should properly have been assigned to his department in the first place. Panizzi was furious, pointing out that this violated a condition attached to the acquisition of the King's Library, that it should be kept together as a unit. The Trustees again took Madden's side, but these early victories were misleading. Panizzi was destined to triumph in the end, and on balance it was the library's good fortune that he did.

One of Panizzi's first reforms as Keeper was to introduce some order into the formerly casual method of issuing materials. Instead of writing down the titles of the books required on scrap paper, and letting the hard-pressed attendants hunt them down, readers now had to use printed forms, one for each book they wanted. On these forms they had to note the shelfmark, having first looked it up in the catalogue. The forms also set out the conditions for the supply of books, including the requirement that they be returned to the desk before the reader left the premises, rather than simply abandoned on the tables. This procedure, only slightly modified, still remains in place, even with the computerisation of the catalogues in the late twentieth century.

The aim of making the Museum library run more efficiently was greatly advanced in 1827 when first the Reading Room and then the first of the book storage areas were moved out of Montagu House into the new building. They were put into rooms specifically designed by Smirke for those purposes. Ten years later Panizzi began broadening the collections by increasing the number of maps, newspapers, music, pamphlets and official publications, ensuring that it would in time become the unparalleled resource for researchers that it is today.

Panizzi's talent for cultivating the great and the good earned a rich dividend in 1845 when the 90-year-old Thomas Grenville – one of the Trustees who had championed his engagement – told him he was going to bequeath his library of more than 20,000 volumes to the Museum. After he retired from politics nearly 30 years earlier, Grenville had been appointed to a sinecure through which he received an annual stipend of more than £2000 from the public purse. Having no official duties, he could devote much of his time to collecting books, an interest he had pursued since he was a young man. From the outset he had been generous in allowing access to his library, rich in rarities of early printing – notably a Gutenberg Bible on vellum and the first illustrated edition of *The Canterbury Tales* printed by Caxton. He collected material in several languages, and it was through his interest in Italian books that he had first made Panizzi's acquaintance.

As he grew older, Grenville worried about what would happen to the collection after his death. His first plan was to bequeath it to his great-nephew, the Duke of Buckingham and Chandos, who, when told of the impending legacy, set about

∽ ABOVE
Thomas Grenville by Charles Turner after John Hoppner.

Of dubbyl worstede was hys semy cope
That rownd was as a belle out of presse
Somwhat he lispyd for hys wantownesse
To make hys englyssche swete vpon hys tonge
And in hys harpyng whan he hadde i sunge
Hys eyen twynklyd in hys hed a ryght
As don the sterris in the frosty nyght
Thys worthy frere was callyd hub berd

A Marchaunt ther was wyth a forkyd berd
In motley on hygh on hys hors he sat
Vp on his hed a flaundres bever hat
Hys bootis claspyd feyr and fetously
Hys resons he spack ful solempnely
Shewynge alway the encresse of hys wynnynge
He wold the see were kept for ony thynge
Betwyx Myddelburgh and orewelle
Welle coude he in hys eschaunges selle

Thys worthy man hys wytte ful wel besette
Ther wyst no wyght that he was in dette
So estatly he was of gouernaunce
Wyth hys bargayns and wyth hys cheuesaunce
Forsothe he was a worthy man wyth alle
But soth to say I not how men hym calle

Clerk ther was of Oxenford also
That vnto logik hadde longe I go
As lene was hys hors as a rake
And he was not ryght fat I vndertake
But loked holw and therto sobyrly
Ful threedbare was hys ouerest courtby
For he hadde gote hym yet no benefyce
Ne was not worldly to haue an offyce
For hym was leuyr to haue at hys beddys heed
Twenty bokys I clad in whyt and reed
Of Aristotle and of hys phylosophye

Triumphs of Charles V, one of
12 miniatures by Giulio Clovio,
c.1556–75.

enlarging the library at his ancestral home of Stowe, Buckinghamshire, to make room for it. Just a year before his death, though, Grenville wrote to the Duke to say that he had changed his mind. Noting that without his annual stipend from the Exchequer he would have been unable to buy so many valuable books, his conscience now dictated that he bequeath them to the nation. The Duke was furious (he went bankrupt a few years later), but Grenville stood firm. When he told his old friend Panizzi about his decision, the librarian, in his own words, was 'strongly moved, almost to tears'.

Grenville died in December 1846 and Panizzi lost no time in having the books transferred the following month from the collector's home in Piccadilly to the Museum – an operation that involved 21 journeys over five days by specially adapted horse-drawn vans. The acquisition was a personal triumph for Panizzi; but, almost inevitably, it fuelled yet another row with Madden. The collection included 59 manuscripts, among them 12 images of the Triumphs of Charles V ascribed to Giulio Clovio, the highly regarded Renaissance illuminator. In a replay of the row over the King's

Library manuscripts, Madden immediately laid claim to the Clovio images, despite the stipulation in Grenville's will that the collection should be kept together as a unit. This time the Trustees ruled in Panizzi's favour – although in 1890, after both combatants were dead, the Grenville manuscripts were indeed transferred to Madden's former department.

Madden was by no means the only man with whom Panizzi had difficulties. According to his biographer, Edward Miller, he could be quite charming to his circle of friends but 'to those whom he disliked or scarcely knew, he could appear morose, proud and distant, hiding his essential shyness and simplicity under a grim and forbidding exterior'. Writing of a particular feud with an errant employee, Edward Edwards, Miller implies that this was due to his Italian heritage: 'He pursued his victim with all the energy and determination of one to whom a vendetta was second nature.'

One eminent reader with whom Panizzi fell out was the historian Thomas Carlyle. In 1848 a Royal Commission was appointed to look into the running of the Museum and its library and, in his evidence to it, Carlyle was intensely critical of the Reading Room (too noisy and too crowded) and of the man who ran it. He was an interested party, because seven years earlier he had been instrumental in founding the London Library, a private lending library that might have regarded the Museum, in some respects, as a competitor. In any event his protests, along with

those of other critics of the conduct of the Library, carried little weight with the Commissioners. Their report, published in 1850, paid tribute to Panizzi, remarking that he had achieved much, despite unjustified and often misguided interference by the Museum Trustees.

Carlyle, though, did not agree with the report, and continued to needle Panizzi. In 1853 the historian wrote in his journal about a request he made to Panizzi 'whom I do not love and who returns the feeling' to be given a private room where he could study Library materials in isolation from *hoi polloi*. Panizzi penned a haughty reply: 'All readers should be … treated alike. … I do not see how I can of my own account make any exception in favour of any reader, however high his literary claims.'

When he was not dealing with disgruntled *literati,* Panizzi was conducting a campaign that would eventually alter the character of the library. Under the Copyright Act of 1709, an extension of the Licensing Act of 1662, a copy of everything printed in England had to be donated to the King's Library. The Copyright Act of 1814 had transferred this right to the British Museum, and further legislation in 1842 laid down that it was the responsibility of the publisher to deliver the books to Great Russell Street. The Museum Secretary was supposed to enforce these laws, but it was low on his list of priorities and he allowed more than half of eligible titles to slip through the net. This angered Panizzi, who refused

to authorise the purchase of books that should by law have been presented free.

In 1850 the Trustees put Panizzi in charge of enforcing the Act and authorised him to prosecute publishers who refused to comply. In some cases the threat of legal action was enough to prise the books from reluctant publishers, but those who still refused were taken to court, where they were convicted and fined. One particularly acrimonious dispute, with the publisher Henry Bohn, was played out in the correspondence columns of *The Times*. Eventually, though, publishers bowed to the inevitable, and new books and pamphlets now arrived at the Museum in their thousands. By 1858 nearly 20,000 new items a year were being received – more than double the number that had come in just five years earlier.

The resolution of one problem gave rise to another: the Museum's library was again running out of space, both for storing the books and consulting them. There were increasing complaints about overcrowding in the Reading Room, with some readers claiming that it was infested with fleas. In 1852 Panizzi made his best-known contribution to the history of the library when he drew a rough sketch showing how the central courtyard at Great Russell Street, then merely an open space in the centre of the new building, could be converted into a large circular Reading Room.

The Trustees approved and Sydney Smirke, who had taken over the architectural brief from his elder brother, designed the magnificent domed room,

similar to the Pantheon in Rome, much as Panizzi had envisaged. There were 25 miles of shelves in the surrounding book stacks, as well as modern heating and ventilation to ensure the comfort of readers. There was, though, no artificial lighting. Use of the room was restricted to the daylight hours until electric lights were installed in 1879.

The great public interest in the Reading Room project was symbolised by the visit paid by Queen Victoria and Prince Albert in June 1855 to inspect the work in progress. Here Panizzi gave full rein to his networking ability, to the chagrin of Madden, who wrote in his diary that 'with his usual licence "as a foreigner" [he] rudely shouldered everybody out of place. … Alas! For a poor, modest Englishman who knows his place and keeps it!' The Queen, however, was impressed, recording in her diary that 'Mr. Panizzi, a very amusing Italian librarian, met us there'.

When it opened in 1857 the Round Reading Room was widely admired. The French writer Prosper Merimée called it 'the new marvel of London', and

many agreed. It soon became such an established part of the landscape of literary London that in 1891 George Gissing used it as the principal setting of his novel, *New Grub Street*. Describing it as 'the valley of the shadow of books', he gave a wry insight into the difficulties in those days of obtaining a reader's ticket: 'It was necessary to obtain the signature of some respectable householder, and Reardon was acquainted with no such person. His landlady was a decent woman enough, and a payer of rates and taxes, but it would look odd, to say the least of it, to present oneself in Great Russell Street armed with this person's recommendation.' Instead, he wrote to a prominent novelist who, after a meeting, agreed to give him a reference. In 1965 David Lodge wrote *The British Museum Is Falling Down*, another novel set mostly in the Reading Room.

In 1929 Alfred Hitchcock used the Room and its dome in the climax of *Blackmail*, his first sound film. Ten years later Louis MacNeice wrote a poem, *The British Museum Reading Room*, that began:

Under the hive-like dome the stooping haunted
    readers
Go up and down the alleys, tap the cells of
    knowledge –
Honey and wax, the accumulation of years –
    Some on commission, some for the love
    of learning,
Some because they have nothing better to do
Or because they hope these walls of books will
    deaden
The drumming of the demon in their ears.

He described the readers as:
    Cranks, hacks, poverty-stricken scholars,
    In pince-nez, period hats or romantic beards…

The room served that motley clientele for more than 140 years. Some had their favourite seats and would arrive before opening time to be sure that they secured them. Regular readers fought long and hard, but in vain, to keep it as the library's main Reading Room even as the St. Pancras building was being constructed.

By the time the Round Reading Room was opened, Panizzi had reached the summit of his career. On the retirement of Sir Henry Ellis in 1856 he was appointed Principal Librarian, despite

ABOVE
Climax to Hitchcock's *Blackmail* filmed on the roof of the Round Reading Room.

OPPOSITE
The completed Round Reading Room.

opposition in the press and elsewhere based principally on his foreign origin (although one of his most notable predecessors, Joseph Planta, had himself been Swiss). The post involved taking responsibility for the whole Museum, not just the books. Madden, who had proposed himself as a candidate, gave vent to his rage and disappointment in his diary: 'The devil choke him with it, say I. ... It is hard to think that if this cursed fellow had never come to England with a rope round his neck, and entered the Museum as a subordinate in 1831, I should now have had the fairest chance of a good house and £1000 per annum. And what has he done for the Museum and the public that I have not done, ay and ten times more? My bitter ban on him!'

He refused to engage in direct contact with Panizzi for several months after the appointment. Although he relented after the intervention of the Archbishop of Canterbury, the Museum's senior Trustee, Madden never became reconciled to what he saw as a snub and an intolerable defeat. More trivial clashes ensued over his pets. Panizzi tried to prevent him from keeping his Blenheim spaniel Fido in his Museum apartment. This time Madden prevailed – but then he blamed Panizzi when his cat Mouton was locked in a basement for two days.

Nor, predictably, was Madden impressed with the new Reading Room, and he declined his invitation to attend the opening ceremony. He denounced the Room in his diary as 'perfectly unsuited to its purpose and an example of reckless extravagance occasioned through the undue influence of a foreigner', adding: 'Had Mr. P. been an Englishman, the Treasury would not have granted £20,000 for such a purpose. ... I rejoice much I had nothing to do with it.' Madden did, it is true, have genuine concerns about the looser supervision envisaged for readers of the manuscripts in his care, but it was clear that his disapproval was chiefly personal. 'I wish the Trustees and Mr. P. in a hot place 50 times a day,' he wrote.

There are two ways of looking at the ferocious rivalry and hostility that existed not just between Panizzi and Madden, but also between other colleagues, officials and politicians involved in running this ever-fractious public body. You could argue that in fighting their corner so stubbornly on every conceivable issue, these men were demonstrating their passionate regard for the library and the culture it symbolised. Or you could say that they were inordinately jealous and implacably resentful of rivals. In a climate in which promotion to senior posts usually depended more on patronage than on ability, the few positions that required expertise were especially fiercely contested.

Now that he was responsible for the entire Museum, Panizzi assumed the role of adjudicator, or sometimes helpless spectator, rather than being a participant in the turf wars. The persistent problem was lack of space, with the curators of each collection – ethnography, science, natural history, prints and drawings – all laying claim to already overcrowded rooms occupied by others. The difficulties eased when in 1860 the Trustees agreed to move the natural history collection to a new building in South Kensington, opened in 1881.

In 1866 Panizzi stepped down on health grounds, having been plagued with gout and other complaints for several years. Madden, who was again passed over for the succession, resigned on the same day, but he thought his pension provision inadequate and his grievances lived on. As late as 1872, just a year before his death, he confided in his diary: 'Daily, hourly I curse him!' Madden's biographers, Robert and Gretchen Ackerman, summed up his blighted career thus: 'All historians of the British Museum emphasize that [his] acerb disposition, his insistence on his prerogatives, and his arrogance towards those he considered his social or intellectual inferiors impaired his effectiveness as an administrative officer.'

Panizzi received a knighthood in 1870 and lived to the age of 81, dying in April 1879. Many agree with Edward Miller that 'Panizzi was in every respect a librarian of librarians, perhaps the greatest we have yet seen'.

❁   ❁   ❁

From Dr. Johnson onwards, a list of the eminent men and women who have made use of the Library and its collections since its inception would in effect be a *Who's Who* of the intellectual life of Britain –

indeed of much of the world – in the last two and a half centuries. While the natural history collections were still held on the site, biologists and scientists were frequent visitors. Charles Darwin was first admitted in 1837 and was a constant presence until he moved to Down, Kent, in 1842. Thomas Huxley was allowed a reader's ticket in 1840 when he was only 14, even though the regulations stipulated that nobody under 18 should be admitted.

Charles Dickens was an early reader at Great Russell Street, while political theorists and activists also flocked there to absorb the writings of thinkers who would add weight to their conceptions of how the world should be changed. Giuseppe Mazzini, one of the architects of modern Italy, made for the Library only days after he arrived in London in 1837; he paid repeated visits during his many stays in the capital, until his death in 1872. Karl Marx moved to London in May 1849 and remained for the rest of his life, working long hours in the various Reading Rooms on his books, notably *Das Kapital*, that would have such a profound effect on world history.

❧ ABOVE
The entry for Karl Marx in the 1873 reader register.

Marx's most influential disciple, Vladimir Ilyich Lenin, came to London for the first time in April 1902. He applied for a reader's ticket almost immediately, signing his letter Jacob Richter, the name he had assumed to cover his tracks from the Russian authorities. After a bureaucratic delay due to a mix-up over the address of the trade union official who had given him the required reference, Lenin's ticket was issued on 29 April. It was initially valid for only three months, but was twice extended until he left London a year later.

He returned in 1905 and spent time in the Reading Room transcribing extracts from the works of Marx and Engels. He returned in 1907 and 1908, when he applied for his ticket under his real name, Vladimir Ulyanov, to work on his book *Materialism and Empiriocriticism,* published that year. After another delay over his references, he was again given a three-month reader's ticket. During this visit he donated four books to the Museum, three of them his own works. His last recorded use of the Reading Room was during a short visit in 1911, when he donated a further book.

※   ※   ※

The two World Wars of the first half of the twentieth century inevitably affected the operations of the Museum library, although it never closed. The danger of bombs was a principal concern, even in the First World War: a bomb fell in Russell Square, quite close to the Museum, in September 1915. As a precaution, the most valuable of the books and manuscripts were moved to the building's deep basements, and early in 1918 some were sent to the National Library of Wales at Aberystwyth for safe keeping. Germans were not admitted to the London Reading Room for the duration of the hostilities.

Among other inconveniences were attempts by the Government to requisition Museum accommodation for national purposes. Space was found for the Medical Research Committee and the Registry of Friendly Societies, while another room housed the personal effects of interned German nationals captured from their former dependent territories in Africa. However, the Museum did manage to fend off a request in 1917 that its entire building be given over to the Air Board.

The Second World War affected the Museum and the Library far more seriously than the First. Plans had been made some years earlier to send the most valuable items out of London for safekeeping, and in August 1939, a few weeks before the official declaration of war, they were put into effect. Once again the National Library of Wales took most of the rarest books and manuscripts, around 30,000 of them – although later that was also thought to be vulnerable, and many items were moved to a disused quarry in Wiltshire.

The Museum suffered substantial bomb damage in the early stages of the Blitz, from September 1940. In one raid the King's Library was hit and several hundred books were destroyed or damaged beyond repair. The worst raid occurred in May 1941, when incendiary bombs scored direct hits on the Museum. About 240,000 books were damaged or destroyed, both by fire and by the water used to control the flames. There was also a hit on the outstation at Colindale, north London, where most of the newspaper collection had been housed since the early years of the century. Some 6000 volumes of

∾ ABOVE
Bomb damage to the Newspaper Library at Colindale in 1940.

English and Irish provincial newspapers were lost. All this prompted the transfer of further Library material to Aberystwyth and the Wiltshire quarry, while some items were dispersed among stately homes. Part of the contents of the King's Library went to the Bodleian Library in Oxford.

The immediate post-war years were occupied with restoring the damage to the building and reclaiming the scattered treasures from their secure locations. Once that was accomplished, the perennial issue of accommodation had to be addressed once more. The shelves were again full to bursting. Temporary relief was achieved by leasing space in the Royal Arsenal at Woolwich in the early 1960s, and later a northern outpost was established at Boston Spa in Yorkshire, initially to house the National Lending Library for Science. But by then a more radical and more durable solution was being canvassed.

CHAPTER 4

The new Library

❝A great library is like a coral reef whose exquisite structure as it grows proliferates a living network of connections; and its ramification is all of a piece like knowledge itself that bridges the endless curiosity of the human mind from the first pictogram to the latest microchip. It is of its essence that it grows.❞

∾ COLIN ST. JOHN WILSON, *THE DESIGN AND CONSTRUCTION OF THE BRITISH LIBRARY.* THE BRITISH LIBRARY, 1998

IN 1951, THE YEAR in which the Festival of Britain celebrated the nation's gradual emergence from the deprivations of the Second World War, the London County Council formulated the County of London Development Plan, to revive the city so devastated by enemy bombs. Since the beginning of the century the British Museum had been in ever-increasing need of extra space to house its expanding collections – and the library was in the greatest need of any of its departments.

It was therefore proposed to construct a new building immediately to the south of the existing one to house the library, as well as the Museum's collection of prints and drawings. The plan would have involved the destruction of many of Bloomsbury's atmospheric Georgian streets, but the pleas of conservationists initially went unheeded. Partly because of the planning issues that had to be resolved, it was eleven years before Colin St. John Wilson (customarily known as 'Sandy' Wilson) and Sir Leslie Martin were appointed as architects, to give substance to the proposal. The two men had worked together for the London County Council, for which Martin's best-known work was as the leader of the team that designed the Royal Festival Hall, opened in 1951. In 1955 Martin was appointed the first professor of architecture at Cambridge University; he took Wilson with him as an assistant lecturer.

While teaching at Cambridge the pair jointly designed several buildings. Wilson believed that it was their work on a group of three libraries in Oxford that won them the contract for the British Museum expansion. In 1964 they produced the first blueprint for the new building. It was approved by the then Conservative Government, shortly before a General Election that returned Labour to power.

The new Government proved more responsive to the conservationists' cause and reduced the area of the proposed Library site so as to preserve the west side of Bloomsbury Square. To add to the difficulties, the Science Reference and Patents Office libraries, which had been part of the British Museum library since 1966, were now also to be incorporated into the new, independent British Library that would sever its ties with the Museum – a place which a Government White Paper in 1971 had declared to be 'bursting at the seams'. Adding the Science and Patents libraries to the new British Library was a far-reaching decision. Now the old institution, firmly rooted in literature and its comfortable academic traditions, would have to accommodate the modern, restless needs of science and – even more alien – of business. This dichotomy would form the heart of some of the impassioned disputes about the Library's purpose and its future that were destined to drag on into the present century.

The new British Library was established by an Act of Parliament of 1972 and came into existence the following year. It was then still the intention to house it on the now-reduced Bloomsbury site. By this time Martin had, in Wilson's words, 'withdrawn from the fray', and Wilson was asked to produce a scaled-down plan. When it became apparent that there would simply be insufficient room in Bloomsbury a new site was sought, and duly found in an old rail goods yard in Somers Town, alongside St. Pancras Station. 'The fact that twelve years' work

and two whole projects in Bloomsbury came to nothing is a sorry tale,' Wilson wrote in his book, *The Design and Construction of the British Library*. He produced a design for this new site, with significant input from his second wife, Mary Jane (known as M.J.) Long, whom he had married in 1972.

The St. Pancras design was approved by the Government in 1978, despite the rearguard action by scholars who could not bear to quit the familiar Round Reading Room: they formed themselves into the Regular Readers Group and mounted a concerted campaign of sniper fire as the project stumbled on. Even when the new building was eventually completed the Group sought to have it converted into a simple book repository, with the Round Reading Room continuing to serve its traditional function as the main point of access to the collections. The Labour MP Gerald Kaufman wrote in *The Times* on 23 July 1994: 'That the Reading Room is beautiful, that it is aesthetically captivating, that it could be argued to have a soul, does not seem to enter into the British Library's pragmatic considerations.' He had earlier likened Wilson's building to 'a Babylonian ziggurat seen through a fun-fair distorting mirror'.

The critics were reinforced by traditionalists who instinctively opposed most modern architecture, and were convinced that Wilson's creation would clash with Sir George Gilbert Scott's neo-Gothic St. Pancras Station next door. Among them was the Prince of Wales, who described the proposed

2

The **Guardian**

This is the building we all love to hate

(But not ~~~ Fay.

A thirty years war. By Fiona MacCarthy. Photographs by John Reardon

3 The Observer Review 2 November 1997

No hair? No chance?

Left on the shelf
Suddenly everyone loves the new British Library. But no one loves the man who built it

Colin St John

2

The **Guardian**

COLIN St John Wilson started work on the British Library 30 years ago. The cost so far is £450 million and no one yet knows when it will open. The only thing that comforts him is that his library is better than the Mitterrand is building in Paris: 'Grim.'

MPs recount sorry saga of British Library

By SHEILA GUNN, POLITICAL CORRESPONDENT

PUBLIC ACCOUNTS

THE sorry saga behind the construction of the British Library's new £450 million building in London was disclosed in full to Parliament yesterday.

According to the Commons public accounts committee, the building, one of the largest civil projects of the century, has been blighted by delays, costs and poor management. To make matters worse, MPs disclose that when the St Pancras building is opened in 1996 it may soon run out of shelf space to fulfil the library's statutory duty to house a copy of every United Kingdom publication.

The Prince of Wales entered the controversy two years ago over the design by the architect Colin St John Wilson, former head of architecture at Cambridge University, by comparing the new building to a railway station; while the gothic-revival St Pancras station, he added, looked like a library.

The original plan, costed at £250 million, was for the new building to meet the library's storage needs up to the year 2030. The number of reader seats was also going to be trebled. The committee said that, as well as running out of storage space, the new building would increase the present number of 1,103 reader seats by less than 7 per cent. The Office of Arts and Libraries decided to press ahead with plans for a 260-seat auditorium, entrance hall, large restaurant despite the shortage of working space.

The committee said: "It seemed to us that the auditorium and the large entrance hall may have been built at the expense of the space for books, and the facility may be full and the provision of galleries which are due to open only moderately overcrowded. According to...

Labour hurries to meet foes

By PHILIP WEBSTER
CHIEF POLITICAL CORRESPONDENT

THE Labour leadership has decided on the earliest possible confrontation with its Militant Tendency foes in Liverpool.

Neil Kinnock, the Labour leader, and his senior colleagues decided yesterday to bring forward the Liverpool Walton by-election to July 4, a week earlier than had been planned only last weekend.

A writ signalling the start of what is likely to be a rough contest will be moved in the Commons today, as Labour moves to conclude a battle that will undoubtedly be exploited by...

building as 'a dim collection of sheds groping for some historic significance', resembling 'an academy for secret police'. (Lord Quinton, then chairman of the Library's Board, gave a spirited response: 'If a nation has a secret police, its assembly hall will inevitably be one of the most beautiful rooms in the country.')

There was also opposition from those who looked towards the future rather than the past. They foresaw that the world was at the brink of a digital revolution, where computers would radically change the working habits of scholars, researchers and everyone else engaged in the field of information. They argued that visits to a traditional library would prove unnecessary when not only the verbal content of books and manuscripts but also images of them would be available online. To them, the construction of an enormous building for the storage and viewing of such obsolete artifacts as books was therefore quite misconceived.

Resisting these conflicting objections, the Government made an initial grant of £74m to the project, with the aim of opening the new library by the late 1980s. However, scores of practical hurdles had to be to overcome before it would be a reality, many of them organisational. Governments came and went, with some new ministers proving less enthusiastic than others. Worse, responsibility for overseeing the construction was shared between the Library itself and the Office of Arts and Libraries (later subsumed into the Department of National

Heritage), each with a different set of priorities and neither with a tight grip on the building's progress. Extra funds were granted only grudgingly – ever more so as budgets were regularly exceeded and target dates for completion missed.

When Margaret Thatcher's Government came to power in 1979, building was yet to begin and the whole project was reconsidered. It was given a second green light and construction began in 1982, to be carried out in phases. By this time the target for completion of the first phase had already been moved back to 1990. When it became clear that this date would not be met it was moved again, to 1993, at which point the estimated cost of this first phase – the principal Reading Rooms, storage areas and Conference Centre – had ballooned to £450m. Progress was painfully slow and the timetable continued to slip, as serious defects were discovered in the work already carried out. Some cables had been damaged during installation and had to be replaced. The fire detection and sprinkler system proved inadequate. Tiles had to be re-fitted because they had not been installed according to the architect's specification.

The failure that attracted most publicity was the saga of the mechanical book stacks, designed to be installed in the building's four basements. These were on a larger scale than any previously installed, and in retrospect it is scarcely surprising that they should have suffered from teething troubles. In 1991 prototypes of the new shelves had been installed on the Bloomsbury site to allow staff to familiarise themselves with the high-tech system for retrieving books. They found that, as the shelves were moved, the books on them were displaced, tumbling backwards and forwards uncontrollably.

Modifications were made to the prototypes, and the production models began to be installed in the fourth basement of the new building, their designated permanent home. At this point their gear mechanism jammed, making them unusable. To resolve this some of the shelves had to be dismantled, revealing already alarming signs of rust. It transpired that inappropriate paint had been used, failing to give the shelves adequate protection. Such errors, analysed in detail in a report by the National Audit Office in 1996, seemed to symbolise the confusion and poor management that, according to the report, had dogged the project from the outset.

The views expressed by critics were so negative that the Library's chairman, Sir Anthony Kenny, felt obliged in 1994 to publish a booklet defending the whole concept and its creators. The criticisms, he wrote, were based on 'misunderstanding and misinformation', with some people blaming the Treasury for its parsimony and the others attacking the Library Board for incompetence. 'More damaging than either of these ideas is that the whole St. Pancras project is misconceived, and that even when completed the building will be a white elephant that will do nothing to further

the purposes which the British Library exists to serve.' He elaborated: 'Opposition takes two forms, traditionalist and futurist. Traditionalist opposition is motivated primarily by the desire to retain in its present function the Round Reading Room in Bloomsbury. Futurist opposition is inspired by a vision that the printed book is being superseded by the computerised database.'

Eventually the Library opened its doors to readers in November 1997, with the Queen performing the formal opening ceremony the following June. By then five of the eleven Reading Rooms were open, with the rest coming into service within months. To mark his achievement, Colin St. John Wilson was granted a knighthood.

BELOW

HM The Queen performs the opening ceremony of the new British Library, June 1998.

The King's Library in its vertical,
transparent gallery.

And, after all the earlier criticism and controversy, the reaction to the finished building was broadly favourable. Wilson had always been keen for the Library to blend with St. Pancras Station, its gigantic eastern neighbour. If the relationship could not exactly be seamless, at least it could be conducted graciously, playing proper court to the older structure. To this end he used bricks as the principal facing material, obtaining them from the same Leicestershire source that had provided them for the terminus more than a century earlier. The tiles for the large sloping roof, and the metal that covers the ground floor panels and columns, were again chosen to reflect the materials and colours used in the station.

Writing in *The Guardian* on 11 May 1995, the journalist Stephen Fay noted what he called 'one of those unfathomable shifts in public taste'. He described how 'suddenly, the clean twentieth-century Scandinavian lines of Wilson's building seem to complement rather than clash with Scott's pointed arches and decorative steeples'. While there was still a hard core of critics who objected to the exterior, most agreed that the interior was splendid, both beautiful and functional. The central hall pivots around the King's Library, displayed in a vertical, transparent gallery that pierces the building, visible from the restaurant and other public areas.

Sir Colin recounts in his book the stormy history of the project and reveals the principles that lay behind his creation. 'Most powerful of all, the bronze and glass tower housing the King's Library … soars up in all its splendour of leather and vellum bindings from the basement below to rise six floors high as the symbolic centre of the whole building; the suggestion of its origin in the deep book basements below is emphasised by the use of polished black marble around its base whose reflections convey by *trompe l'oeil* the impression of receding into limitless depth. By this means the architecture has been able to signal to the visitor in the main entrance hall the existence of the huge underworld of stored treasures.' More prosaically, he added: 'In the ratio of above-ground to below-ground accommodation the building has much in common with an iceberg.'

In his book's postscript, Sir Colin quoted Edmund Burke: 'Those who would carry on great public schemes must be proof against the most fatiguing delays, the most mortifying disappointments, the most shocking insults and worst of all the presumptuous judgment of the ignorant upon their designs.' For his own part he commented: 'From the time when the first project for this building was launched in 1962 to the time when the last of the reading rooms will be opened in 1999, thirty-seven years will have elapsed. There is no precedent for such a timescale in the genesis of a building until we reach back to the building of St. Paul's Cathedral: and even then the longevity of the realization was due more to

the nature of traditional building methods than in the irresolution of authority that has dogged the course of our project. Slow progress towards an agreed end is one thing: it is quite another to experience constant change (of site, of funding, of supervising authority, of scale of operation) without any assurance of continuity. For that, I believe, there is no precedent.'

❀ ❀ ❀

ABOVE
The basement book stacks.

❧ BELOW
Bronze gates by David Kindersley
and Lida Cardozo.

In designing the Library, Wilson adhered to the tenets of the English Free School of architecture. The School's defining principle was to break out from the confines of symmetry in favour of shapes and patterns that responded both to the building's function and to the environment in which it was set. In this respect Wilson was harking back to a Gothic tradition and moving away from the neoclassical designs that had dominated the country's public buildings (including the British Museum itself) at least until the early twentieth century. In his book he quoted the art critic John Ruskin: 'It is one of the virtues of the Gothic builders that they never suffered ideas of outside symmetries and consistencies to interfere with the real use and value of what they did.'

In their book, *The Architecture of the British Library at St. Pancras*, Roger Stonehouse and Gerhard Stromberg made the point that the design amounted to 'an intimate response to monumentality'. By its nature, a great public library has to aspire to the status of a monument, but at the same time the readers need an intimate place to perform the 'essentially introverted nature of their activities'. They added: 'This intimate experience of monumentality is not imposed, but closely orchestrated from the purpose of the building and its location. … The building is book-like, revealing its inner world only when entered.'

The brick wall on the north side of Euston Road is broken by David Kindersley and Lida Cardozo's bronze gates whose pattern, incorporating the words

BRITISH LIBRARY, informs visitors in the most direct possible way that they have arrived at the right place. Entering them, the first object to catch the eye is Sir Eduardo Paolozzi's massive bronze statue of a stooping Sir Isaac Newton, based on an image by William Blake. (Wilson and Paolozzi had been close friends for years.) The other major art work here is Anthony Gormley's *Planets,* a series of stone sculptures of human figures encircling boulders, placed around a sunken amphitheatre in front of the entrance.

There are plenty of places to sit on the piazza, the fashionable name that the Library bestowed on its forecourt. Built-in benches are complemented by a scattering of chairs and tables, where in fine weather people can enjoy refreshments from the little café or simply sit and pass the time of day. The relaxing atmosphere was created to counter the earnest, forbidding connotations once attached to the concept of a research library; but one of Wilson's ambitions for it was never fulfilled. He wanted the piazza to accommodate a row of second-hand bookstalls, but the Library's administrators did not approve – fearing, so it was said, that people might think they were selling off surplus volumes.

Internally, the entrance hall is the most important space, setting the tone for the building as a whole. Lit by natural daylight through glass roofs, the dominant material is pale and fine-grained travertine marble, enhancing the sense of lightness. Other materials – leather and brass for the handrails on the stairs, American oak for the door handles – were chosen for their tactile qualities, what Wilson described as 'their sensuous response to touch'. Busts of literary figures and of the Library's founding fathers underline its central ethos, as does Roubiliac's full-length statue of Shakespeare, bequeathed to the British Museum by David Garrick. Above the wide,

BELOW
Sir Eduardo Paolozzi's bronze statue of Sir Isaac Newton in the piazza.

gentle staircase leading to the Reading Rooms, the colossal tapestry designed by R.B. Kitaj (another friend of the architect) adds bright colour to what otherwise would be a sober space.

Wilson played an important role in commissioning and choosing the artworks. In an address in 2006 to a conference at the Pallant House art gallery in Chichester – his last major architectural project – Sir Colin spoke of the vital relationship between buildings and the works of art displayed in them, mentioning in particular the Paolozzi statue and the Kitaj tapestry. 'I think I can claim that I practised what I preached in believing that painting and sculpture and architecture really can make a difference when they are together, rather than when they are separate.'

Off the entrance hall are the galleries housing permanent and temporary exhibitions. The Sir John Ritblat Gallery is where some of the Library's principal treasures are shown in a display that changes frequently but nearly always includes such iconic items as *Magna Carta* (in a dedicated ante-room), the *Lindisfarne Gospels* and Shakespeare's First Folio. The gallery is in semi-darkness so as not to harm the exhibits. Wilson wrote that 'the intended ambience is of a low-lit cavern in which the treasures of the collection are displayed in showcases lit from within by small fibre-optic lenses'. Stonehouse and Stromberg regarded the exhibition spaces as among the most successful features of the building. 'For the first time', they wrote, 'the British Library can mount exhibitions which do justice

to its collection in excellent galleries.' Two major exhibitions every year, highlighting different aspects of the collections, are staged in the PACCAR gallery on the lower ground floor.

Wilson took immense care in designing the eleven Reading Rooms, giving each a distinct character depending on the function it was to serve. The Reading Rooms for humanities, manuscripts and rare books, occupying the western side of the building, are dominated by desks for readers, with a single range of open-access bookshelves lining the walls. The reason for this is that most readers will be working on material supplied to them over the counter, from the basement stacks or from off-premises storage, with comparatively few using the open access shelves.

❧ OPPOSITE
The tapestry by the wide staircase in the entrance hall is based on *If Not, Not*, a 1976 painting by R.B. Kitaj (1932–2007), the American-born artist who worked for most of his life in London. It portrays figures in stages of agony or emotion strewn across a multi-coloured landscape with the gatehouse at Auschwitz looming in the background: Kitaj was ever conscious of his Jewish heritage. The artist described the original painting – which hangs in the Scottish National Gallery of Modern Art – as having 'a certain allegiance to Eliot's *Waste Land* and its ... family of loose assemblage'.

❧ BELOW
One of the two Humanities reading rooms.

'Most of the readers in these rooms are committed to an extended period of research,' he wrote, 'so that the Reading Room becomes a long-term place of work. The prime consideration has therefore been to create a working ambience for sustained occupation and study. To this end the employment of daylight as the primary source of ambient light is given priority, and it is poured into the centre of the space by means of clerestory and lantern lights housed in pitched roofs.' This is achieved in the first-floor Reading Rooms by placing them at the lowest level of a stepped atrium, three stories high, letting the light in from the top. The Reading Rooms above, on the second and third floors, are in effect perched on balconies within that tall space.

When he came to design the Reading Rooms for the Science and Patents collections, in the eastern wing of the building, Wilson adjusted the relative positions of the book stacks and the desks. His reason was that a large quantity of the material consulted here – patent applications, official reports, learned journals and the like – is selected from open-access shelves. These therefore occupy the centre of the Rooms, with the reading desks on the perimeter.

The requirement to house the former India Office Library – previously in the custody of the Foreign and Commonwealth Office – was added to the architect's brief in 1982, late in the design process; it was decided to accommodate it in the science wing together with the existing Oriental collections. The result is that the Reading Room for what are now called Asian and African Studies (formerly the Oriental and India Office collections) is something of a hybrid of the humanities and science models, with a roughly equal balance between reading desks and open-access shelves. To exploit one of the most attractive resources of the India Office collection, Wilson incorporated wall space where the best of its portraits could be hung, high above the desks and bookshelves (see Chapter 9). He also inserted an alcove for a bust of Warren Hastings, governor-general of India from 1773 to 1785. Other busts are placed near the entrance, and outside the Reading Room is a small display case for one or two pieces of exquisite oriental furniture that once graced the London offices of the East India Company.

The Conference Centre abuts on to the southern end of the science Reading Rooms. Although joined to the main building, it forms a discrete unit with its own entrance. On the ground floor is a cloakroom and information desk, with stairs leading to the main entrance of the auditorium on the first floor, where comfortable, steeply raked seats can accommodate audiences of up to 255. In the first floor lobby is the bar area, connected to the upper entrance of the auditorium by a flight of broad, shallow stairs. A few nooks at the side of the stairs are furnished with padded benches where small groups can socialise in the intervals of conferences or performances, or while waiting for them to begin. Wilson dubbed the stairs the Spanish Steps, as he sought to duplicate the ambience of the much-admired eighteenth-century steps leading up from the Piazza di Spagna in Rome.

❧ BELOW LEFT
Conserving the *Diamond Sutra*,
2010.

❧ BELOW
Work benches in the
Conservation Centre.

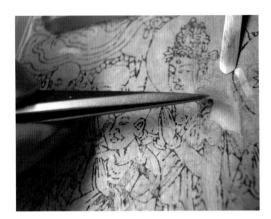

The only major addition to his building has been
the Conservation Centre, completed in 2007. It was
constructed to the north of the Library, on land that
was part of the Government's original purchase,
retained so that it could expand when necessary.
To get there, visitors have to pass through the main
building at first floor level and walk along the terrace
alongside the staff restaurant. The exterior of the
Conservation Centre is faced in the same red brick
as the rest of the Library, making a smooth transition
from the older structure to the more recent one.

At the Centre's entrance is a small exhibition
space explaining the vital work of the conservators
in maintaining the Library's priceless collection of
books and manuscripts. The great age of the most
precious items means that they have to be treated
with extreme delicacy and, although the Centre is
equipped with state-of-the-art machinery, many of
the most vital processes still have to be undertaken

by hand. It is a highly skilled trade, and one of the most important activities of the Centre is to train conservators – not just those destined to work in the Library itself, but also those who will take their skills to other institutions in Britain and abroad.

The lower floor of the Centre is occupied by the technical sections of the Sound Archive, formerly part of the British Institute of Recorded Sound, which merged with the Library in 1983. Until 1997 it was housed in its own building in Kensington, but the collection was then moved to St. Pancras. As well as recordings of historic speeches and performances, the Archive has a large collection of bird calls and other wildlife sounds (see Chapter 10). Many of the oldest recordings were made on devices that no longer exist, and in formats that deteriorate with age. Part of the Archive's work is to transfer these to modern digital formats that enhance the quality of the original and can more easily be preserved. When the Princess Royal performed the opening ceremony of the Conservation Centre, she listened to a recording of the voice of Florence Nightingale originally made on a wax cylinder.

❁   ❁   ❁

Those who criticised the St. Pancras project on the grounds that digitisation would rapidly make it redundant were correct in one aspect. Their prediction that, in the last two decades of the twentieth century, computers would radically alter the way we access information has certainly been fulfilled. Yet they were wrong to conclude from this that large libraries are no longer required. The actual books and manuscripts that constitute our national heritage are a priceless treasure that has to be preserved in perpetuity. The British Library has been designed to perform this function at the same time as it provides state-of-the-art electronic facilities both for researchers, able to call up much important information at the touch of a keyboard, and for interested visitors, who can view some of the most important and beautiful items in the collection on interactive screens.

The atmosphere is certainly very different from that in the old Round Reading Room, as the diehards feared it would be. All the Reading Rooms, and many of the public spaces outside them, are fitted with plugs to power laptop computers and other equipment. This has coincided with a relaxation of the rules governing the issue of readers' passes. Previously intending readers, unless they were published authors, would have to show that the material they wanted to consult was unavailable elsewhere, and were often required to produce supporting evidence from a senior academic. Now, in accordance with the Government's desire to increase access to this publicly funded resource, these restrictions have been eased. The result is that the Library is daily filled with hundreds of young students, and it is sometimes hard to find a vacant desk in the Reading Rooms. This has provoked complaints from some more traditional users; but the Library has stood

The once-familiar trolleys used in the Newspaper Library at Colindale.

firm against their pressure to reimpose the former conditions on issuing readers' passes.

The impact of the new technology also brought major changes to the newspaper collection, most of it housed in a 1930s building at Colindale, on the northerly reaches of the London Underground. In the 1970s work began on photographing the most popular newspapers and journals on microfilm, seeking to protect the original copies from excessive wear. Gradually, regular readers saw fewer and fewer of the familiar trolleys, once used to wheel the heavy bound volumes from the storage areas to its Reading Room. Instead, they picked up small rolls of microfilm from the issue desk and spooled them on to the ever-growing number of machines provided. Some 20 years

later, a programme was launched to digitise much of the collection, making it available and easily readable on remote computers. Within a few years the hard-copy newspapers will have moved to a purpose-built store at Boston Spa in Yorkshire, and very many will be accessible on-line from St. Pancras.

Boston Spa, the site of a munitions factory in the Second World War, has served as an off-site storage area for British Library materials for many years, as well as the headquarters of the much-used Document Supply Centre. Recently it has introduced a commercial service for digitising academic theses. A large, ultra-modern storage unit has just been completed there, from which requested materials are extracted by giant robotic machines.

❧ RIGHT
'Turning the Pages'.

❧ OPPOSITE
This state-of-the-art storage facility at Boston Spa is like a honeycomb, with hundreds of cells for storing containers filled with documents. No people work inside the climate-controlled storage area. Items are called up on a computer, which passes the message to a giant robotic retrieving mechanism that fetches the material to librarians outside.

As far as visitors to St. Pancras are concerned, the most appealing example of new technology has been the interactive 'Turning the Pages' device. Historic items in the collection can be viewed on touch screens in the entrance hall and other strategic sites. Readers simply pass a finger over the screen, mimicking the turning of a real page in a real book, and the next page is revealed to them. This device can now also be accessed through remote computers.

Although its birth was painful and excruciatingly slow, and the completed building at St. Pancras represents a significantly scaled-down version of the original plans, the British Library has, as Stephen Fay predicted, quickly established itself as a familiar and greatly valued feature of London's physical and intellectual landscape. Even those who retain nostalgic memories of the Round Reading Room accept that the new building is user-friendly and admirably fit for purpose, even if sometimes overcrowded. As Stonehouse and Stromberg declared: 'St. Pancras has undoubtedly brought the British Library's existence to the attention of a public far wider than that which would have otherwise known what it stands for. Many people who might in earlier years have only gazed at the entrance now have good reason to enter, not only to view the treasures in the exhibitions but to attend the lectures, concerts and celebrations which are part of the wide range of events in the buildings.'

One of those who used it with enthusiasm is the poet Theresa Shiban. Her 2007 poem, *From Piazza to Reading Room*, begins:

The first thing you notice is what you don't
it is not imposing
overwhelming
you are not made to feel insignificant

with monumental humility
it is the box the words come in

storey upon storey hidden below
not towering above
to impress or oppress

its exalted purpose democratised
grandeur and majesty achieved by an honest brick

A British institution
wrestled down to size
to a human scale.

CHAPTER 5

Let there be light

'You know also that forms of speech change
within a thousand years, and words, lo!
that had a value, now wondrous odd and strange
we think them: and yet they spoke them so.'

∾ GEOFFREY CHAUCER, *TROILUS AND CRESSIDA*,
IN A VERSION BY A.S. KLINE (2001)

THE FIRST KNOWN ATTEMPTS to communicate
language visually by converting it into identifiable
symbols were made around 4000 BC in the Middle
East, initially as a means of recording business
transactions. Early writing systems involved
carving characters into stone and clay tablets and
were largely dependent on pictorial depictions of
meaning, or hieroglyphics. The next stage was the
cuneiform script, whose more abstract symbols
represented syllables of words. The Romans often
used wooden tablets as a writing surface, but the
Egyptians developed something more portable
from the pith of the papyrus plant – hence the word
'paper' – and the Greeks introduced parchment,
made from animal skins.

The Chinese were by then making a paper-like
substance from linen, tree bark and other ingredients:
in 2006 a fragment discovered in the Yumen Pass,
through which the Silk Road ran, was dated to
8 BC. This was more than a century before the first
recorded invention of Chinese paper in AD 105, by
a courtier named Cai Lun. By the eighth century
crude machinery for papermaking had also been
developed in the Middle East. As a result words, and
the ideas they expressed, could more readily spread
from place to place, from community to community,
from leaders to the people they led. And it was not
long before it became customary to add freestanding
images to significant documents, to illustrate and
enhance the ideas contained in them and extend their
appeal to people who could not read the text.

BELOW

Chinese oracle bone from about
1600 BC.

The British Library's oldest artifacts are Chinese oracle bones, dating from as early as 1600 BC. They consist of pieces of mammal bone containing inscriptions of religious and historical texts, scratched with a bronze pin. They are followed chronologically by fragments of manuscripts from the third and fourth centuries BC, mostly written in Greek. In 1840 the Trustees of the British Museum decreed that all early Egyptian written material, whether on tablets or papyri, should be assigned to the Department of Antiquities, while the Greek and Coptic papyri should be held by the Department of Manuscripts. When the Museum and its library separated in 1973, the Egyptian antiquities remained with the Museum.

Among the oldest manuscripts, one that stands out is part of a document detailing the constitution of Athens, often attributed to Aristotle. Other early survivals include 29 scrolls bearing Buddhist texts from the first century AD; they originate from Gandhara, today part of Pakistan and Afghanistan and for years the centre of Buddhism, from where the religion spread to many Eastern countries. Written on birch bark in a script known as Kharosthi, these scrolls are believed to be the oldest surviving Buddhist texts. Religious and philosophical in content, they feature fragments of verse, including one known as *The Rhinoceros Horn Sutra* because it contains the following passage: 'Leaving behind son and wife, and father and mother, and wealth and grain, and relatives, and sensual pleasures to the full extent, one should wander solitary as a rhinoceros horn.' Sutras were originally short, concise texts on a variety of subjects, designed to be memorised. The format was used to record the teachings of Buddha, which were first passed on orally.

A later Buddhist treasure, dating from the ninth or tenth centuries, is a scroll listing the various

RIGHT
Scroll of Buddhist text from Gandhara, first century AD.

names by which Buddha was known in different communities. It formed part of the immense haul of some 40,000 priceless manuscripts and other objects discovered in 1900 (including the *Diamond Sutra,* described in Chapter 6). They were found in the 'Cave of the Thousand Buddhas' at Dunhuang, a city on the old Silk Road in Gansu province in northwest China. Tens of thousands more items were excavated from other Silk Road sites and many were purchased in 1907 by Sir Marc Aurel Stein, a Hungarian-born archaeologist and explorer. The British Library is today a key partner in the Dunhuang Project, through which the most significant of these items, scattered as they are in institutions across the world, are being digitised to facilitate electronic access by scholars everywhere.

The Library's manuscript collection provides a graphic panorama of the origins and practices of the world's major faiths, through texts and images that date from their very earliest manifestations. Its oldest Qur'an (the Islamic holy book, also spelt Koran) is the *Ma'il Qur'an* from the eighth century. The document is precious not only on account of its age, but because it is believed to originate from the Hejaz region of Saudi Arabia, embracing the holy places of Mecca and Medina where the prophet Muhammad lived. It is written on parchment in an early Arabic script known as ma'il – which means 'sloping'. The Library's next oldest Islamic treasure is a *Kufic Qur'an*, copied on vellum in about 850. It is also named after its distinctive Arabic script

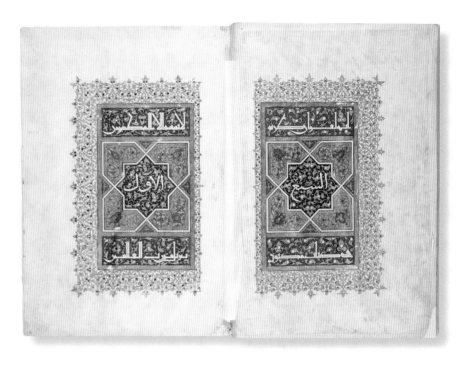

developed in Kufah, a town in Iraq that was one of the earliest centres of Islamic scholarship. The end of each verse is indicated by a golden symbol.

Qur'ans do not include images of humans or animals: their beauty lies in their calligraphy and illumination. The most splendid in the Library's collection is *Sultan Baybars' Qur'an,* made for Baybars in Cairo between 1304 and 1306, shortly before his brief reign as head of the Mamluks – the dynasty that ruled Egypt and Syria for 250 years from the middle of the thirteenth century. Each of its seven volumes has a frontispiece combining elaborate geometric patterns with ornamental lettering, known as 'carpet pages' because of their similarity to oriental carpets. The text is written in gold in the highly ornamental thuluth style, and some of it can be viewed on *Turning the Pages*. Made at roughly the same time, although

❧ ABOVE
Sultan Baybars' Qur'an, 1304–06.

slightly less ornate, is *Sultan Uljaytu's Qur'an.* Uljaytu, a descendant of Genghis Khan, ruled over Iraq, the Caucasus, parts of Asia Minor and Iran. Written with gold and black lettering, this large-format book is volume 25 of a 30-volume edition of the holy book: most of the other volumes have been lost.

Although images are not to be found in the Qur'an, Muhammad's ascent to heaven on Buraq, a winged white horse with a human face, is frequently depicted in other Islamic material, secular as well as religious, in Persian manuscripts in particular. Among the masterpieces at the Library is an illuminated manuscript of *Khamsa,* the five epic poems of the twelfth-century Persian poet Nizami Ganjavi, created in about 1540. As is traditional, the prophet's face is whitened out, but the features of the archangel Gabriel and the other escorting angels are finely portrayed.

A revealing and beautiful curiosity among the Islamic material is a fifteenth-century *Hajj certificate,* a scroll that commemorates the *hajj* – the pilgrimage to Mecca – undertaken by a woman named Maymunah between 1432 and 1433. It confirms that Maymunah duly visited Muhammad's tomb at Medina, depicted in an illustration along with many of the places she passed through *en route.* The images of the tombs and other landmarks are carefully labelled and the pages adorned with quotations from the Qur'an.

Hinduism has inspired many beautiful manuscripts, notably the colourfully illustrated

Devimahatmya, a Sanskrit hymn written on palm leaf in the mid-sixteenth century in Nepal, honouring the goddess Devi. The Library also owns a superb version of the celebrated Hindu epic *Ramayana,* created in Udaipur about 100 years later. It describes the heroism of Rama, Prince of Ayodhya, who wins the hand of Sita, Princess of Mithila, but is exiled to the forest for 14 years through the plotting of his stepmother. Sita is kidnapped, so Rama recruits an army of bears and monkeys to search for her. The quest is successful and Rama inherits his rightful crown. This manuscript was contained in seven large volumes (four of which are in the British Library) and profusely illuminated by artists in the court studio of the Ranas of Udaipur. The remaining parts are held by libraries in India. A project is underway to reunite the whole manuscript digitally, making it freely available on the internet.

A wealth of material also illustrates the remarkable history of Judaism, with two of the oldest Hebrew manuscripts dating from the ninth century. One is the *Gaster Bible,* named after Moses Gaster, Chief Rabbi of the Spanish and Portuguese synagogue in London, from whom the Museum

acquired it in 1925. This rare early Bible shows the influence of Islamic art in its decorative elements, especially in the Book of Psalms, adorned with gilded leaves and spirals. The second ninth-century work is a *Torah* (the first five books of the Old Testament) that includes instructions from early scholars on how to spell and pronounce the sacred text to ensure that its message is communicated correctly, even including rules about intonation.

The collections include thousands of fragments of old Hebrew manuscripts believed to be derived from the Genizah – a store room in the Ben Ezra Synagogue in Old Cairo. Acquired by the British Museum at various times during the nineteenth and twentieth centuries, they include documents, letters and religious and literary texts that provide insights into Jewish life in the Mediterranean region during the Middle Ages. Among these are two autograph manuscripts of Moses Maimonides, the greatest medieval Jewish scholar, philosopher and physician.

The *Lisbon Bible*, bought by the Museum in 1882, is the foremost example of the Portuguese school of medieval Hebrew illumination. Poignantly, it was produced in 1482 – just 15 years before Jews were expelled from Portugal or forcibly converted. It is the joint work of a scribe, with a penchant for ornate lettering and flourishes, and a team of artists who created the images and adornments in styles derived from a variety of Renaissance influences. A second scribe wrote notes and comments on the text in the margins.

The most surprising Jewish manuscript is the *Kaifeng Torah*, a scroll ostensibly made for the small and isolated community of Jews at Kaifeng in central China, on the banks of the Yellow River. They maintained their religious identity for about a thousand years until their last rabbi died in 1810. The Library's scroll, made in the mid-seventeenth century, was presented in 1851 to Christian missionaries, who gave it to the British Museum the following year.

The Library has a number of *ketubah*s, Jewish marriage contracts, from many eras and many parts of the world, some with intricate decoration.

ᘒ OPPOSITE
A *haggadah* contains the order of service to be conducted in Jewish households on the eve of Passover. This *Golden Haggadah* – so called because of the gold-tooled background to the illustrations – was created in Barcelona in about 1320, incorporating many miniatures that illustrate scenes from the Old Testament. These four panels depict Moses, in a blue cloak, summoning three of the ten plagues of Egypt inflicted on the Pharaoh because he would not liberate the Israelites: the plague of boils, the plague of frogs and the plague of diseased livestock.

ᘒ LEFT
The *Lisbon Bible*, 1482.

The *Ashem Vohu*, ninth or tenth century.

Other historic faiths are also represented in the collections. Two rare manuscripts highlight the doctrines and traditions of Zoroastrianism, a religion that originated in Iran several hundred years before the birth of Christ. Widely followed until challenged by Islam in the seventh century AD, it still has followers in Iran, India and other Eastern countries. The oldest known Zoroastrian text is the *Ashem Vohu,* a prayer transcribed in the ninth or tenth century in the language of the Sogdians, who lived around Samarkand and were active traders all along the Silk Road. The manuscript was one of those found at Dunhuang.

Another Zoroastrian treasure, from about 300 years later, is the *Videvdad,* a book that sets out rules for dealing with pollution and crime. (The Zoroastrians do not bury their dead in open ground through fear of polluting the earth.) It was copied in 1323 in Gujarat, India, where Zoroastrian refugees from Iran had settled in the tenth century, becoming known as Parsis. Each

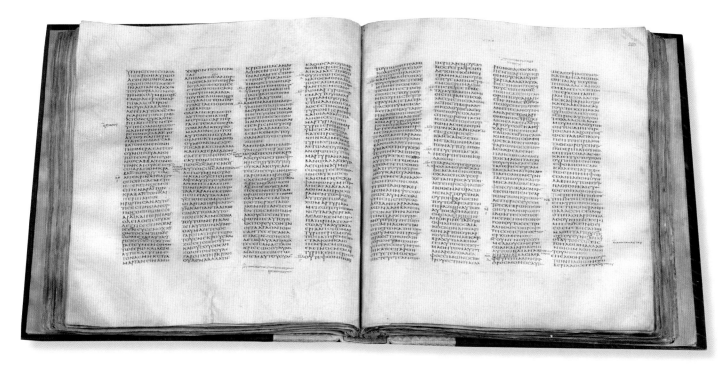

sentence is written first in the original Avestan (Old Iranian) language, then in Pahlavi (Middle Persian). The manuscript was one of hundreds acquired by Samuel Guise, surgeon in the Bombay Army from 1775 to 1796, while he was head surgeon at the General Hospital in Surat, Gujarat. They were auctioned in London after his death in 1812.

The most important Sikh manuscript in the collection is the *Guru Granth Sahib*, which contains verses by Guru Nanak, the founder of Sikhism, and by other gurus and saints. It was compiled in 1604 and this copy was made about 60 years later, making it one of the 20 oldest in existence. The work was bought by the Museum in 1884 from the principal of a missionary school in Amritsar.

Of the Library's many Christian treasures, the greater part of the fourth-century *Codex Sinaiticus*

stands out. A codex is a manuscript in the form of a book rather than a scroll, and this is one of the two earliest known Christian Bibles, the other being the *Codex Vaticanus* in Rome. The 694 pages of the *Codex Sinaiticus* held by the British Library were discovered by Constantin von Tischendorf, a German biblical scholar, at St. Catherine's Monastery, near the foot of Mount Sinai in Egypt, in 1859. Von Tischendorf presented them to the Tsar of Russia, and in 1933 the Soviet Government put them up for sale. The British Museum bought the pages for £100,000, provided by the Government and through public subscription. A smaller set of leaves from the codex remains in Russia, while others are at Leipzig in Germany and in St. Catherine's Monastery itself. All have now been reunited digitally and can be consulted in the Library and on the internet.

❧ ABOVE
The *Codex Sinaiticus*, fourth century.

The *Codex Sinaiticus*, handwritten in Greek on parchment, employs magnificent calligraphy but no illustrations: the practice of illustrating Christian books did not begin until much later. Originally it comprised more than 1,460 large pages, of which just over half have survived, containing the entire Old and New Testaments, together with two first-century Christian texts, the *Shepherd of Hermas* and the *Epistle of Barnabas*. Earlier versions of the Gospels and the Old Testament were contained in much slimmer volumes, with smaller pages, covering only a handful of texts.

Production of the *Codex Sinaiticus* is roughly contemporary with the reign of Constantine the Great, the first Christian emperor of Rome. One of the *Codex*'s intriguing aspects is the number of times it has been corrected by different hands – initially by the original scribes and their colleagues, then, over the next 800 years, by men of the Church seeking to correct or clarify the meaning of key passages. Such alterations are not unusual on ancient manuscripts, but here they occur on every page, providing rich material for theologians and historians seeking to trace the vagaries of belief through the ages – a kind of textual archaeology.

The spread of Christianity during the first millennium is reflected in the variety of languages represented in the Library's collections. The *Syriac Bible*, a translation of the first five books of the Old Testament dated 463–64, is about a century younger than the *Codex Sinaiticus* and is signed by its scribe, a deacon called John. Syriac is a dialect of Aramaic, the language of Jesus; it was spoken at the time in an area covering what is now northern Syria and Iraq and southern Turkey. This particular Bible was produced at Amid, now Diyarbakir in eastern Turkey.

From the late fourth century onwards, for more than a thousand years, the standard version of the Bible was St. Jerome's Vulgate, commissioned by Pope Damasus in 382 and written in what was then the everyday form of Latin. The Library holds one of the earliest known manuscripts of this work, the *Vulgate Gospels*. The work contains the four Gospels authorised by the Council of Nicaea in 325 to be included in the Christian Bible, as well as a set of 'canon tables' comparing the four Gospellers' accounts of key events in the life of Christ.

In 2012 the Library purchased the *St. Cuthbert Gospel*, the earliest surviving intact European book. Created in the seventh century and formerly known as the *Stonyhurst Gospel*, it is a copy of the Gospel of St. John, produced in the north of England and buried alongside St Cuthbert on Lindisfarne Island in Northumbria, apparently in 698. It was found in the saint's coffin at Durham Cathedral in 1104. The Gospel had been on long-term loan to the Library since 1979, and is regularly on view in the Treasures Gallery.

Another highlight of the large collection of early British manuscripts is the *Lindisfarne Gospels*, produced on Lindisfarne in the early eighth century. It is believed to be the work of a monk named Eadfrith, who succeeded Cuthbert as Bishop of Lindisfarne in 698 and died in 721. Written in Latin, in the 'insular' script, the elaborate illumination contains strong elements of the Roman and eastern styles then associated with Christian documents, but with modifications based on Celtic and Anglo-Saxon traditions. The Gospels were originally encased in a leather binding covered with jewels, but this was removed by the Vikings in one of their frequent raids on the island. The manuscript remained in Durham until the sixteenth century.

Like many other early English manuscripts, the *Lindisfarne Gospels* came to the nation from the Cotton Library in the eighteenth century. Also from that source is the early eleventh-century *Old English Hexateuch* – the first known attempt to translate into Anglo-Saxon the initial six books of the Old Testament, pared down and in some cases paraphrased. The chief translator was Aelfric, Abbot of Eynsham, a Benedictine monk who died in 1020. He was a notable and persuasive preacher whose core belief was that the Day of Judgement was close at hand and that people could not properly prepare themselves for it if they had no direct access to key works of scripture in their own language. In his preface to the work Aelfric declared that the Bible is not to be regarded as literal truth, but that its meaning is essentially spiritual. As well as the words, the manuscript contains more than 400 vivid illustrations – unusual in such a work at that time.

⟋ **OPPOSITE**

The *St. Cuthbert Gospel* was bought by the Library from the Society of Jesus in 2012 for £9 million, with the aid of a large grant from the Heritage Lottery Fund, topped up through a public appeal. A small, handwritten copy of the Gospel of St. John, it was produced in northern England shortly before being buried in Lindisfarne in 698 alongside the body of Cuthbert, a venerated leader of the early English Church. A unique feature of the book is that it retains its original red goatskin binding. *(Reproduced actual size)*

The story of Noah's Ark from
the *Old English Hexateuch*, early
eleventh century.

Another treasure from the Cotton Library is a copy of the Venerable Bede's most important work, the *Ecclesiastical History of the English People,* made in the south of England in the ninth century. Beginning with Julius Caesar's invasion in 55 BC, this unique document, again written in Latin, records early English history and the spread of Christianity. A key feature is Bede's detailed account of the pivotal Synod of Whitby in 664, where clerics opted to observe the Roman rather than the Celtic version of Christianity. Bede also wrote at length here about how to calculate the correct date for Easter, a subject of heated argument between the two Christian traditions. There is also an eleventh-century manual of services, some sections of which date from before 1066 and were probably written at Sherborne Abbey in Dorset. The work is in Latin, but prayers in English were added later.

Among the oldest illuminated manuscripts is the *Benedictional of St Aethelwold*, Bishop of Winchester from 963 to 984. This is a rare and outstanding example of Anglo-Saxon book decoration, with 28 illustrations in the sumptuous style of the so-called Winchester School of painting that flourished in the tenth and eleventh centuries, before being overlain with influences from continental Europe. The book contains an inscription explaining how it originated:

'A bishop, the great Aethelwold, whom the Lord had made patron of Winchester, ordered a certain monk subject to him to write the present book. … He commanded also to be made in this book many frames well adorned and filled with various figures decorated with many beautiful colours and with gold. … Let all who look upon this book pray always that after the term of the flesh I may abide in heaven – Godeman the scribe, as a suppliant, earnestly asks this.'

In 1831 the Museum strengthened its holdings of early manuscripts when it acquired from the Royal Society the collection amassed in the early seventeenth century by Thomas Howard, fourteenth Earl of Arundel. It contains two fine Anglo-Saxon Psalters, one from the early and one from the late eleventh century. The earlier is the *Arundel Psalter,* created in Canterbury about 1020 by the scribe Eadui Basan. Illustrations include ink drawings of the evangelists, of animals and of Biblical scenes, among them the slaying of Goliath by David. The second Psalter, made about 50 years later in Winchester, contains a fine drawing of the Crucifixion. Its unique feature is that, although most of it is in Latin, it has a few additions in Old English. The Arundel collection also includes an early thirteenth-century copy of Henry of Huntingdon's *History of the English* – essentially an updating of Bede's work with little evidence of original research, although it was copied frequently in the Middle Ages. A reference to Arundel Castle, ancestral home of the Earls, was highlighted by an early reader, possibly a member of the family.

EA
ta
di
TVS
per
UIR
re pene
QVI NON
fgide
ABIIT

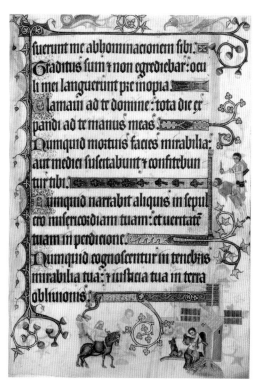

Some of the most spectacular illuminations are to be found in the *Luttrell Psalter* and the *Bedford Hours*. For years these had belonged to the Weld family, who lived (as their descendants do still) in Lulworth Castle in Dorset, a mock medieval fortress built in the seventeenth century. When the manuscripts were put up for sale at Sotheby's auction rooms in 1929, a legal dispute occurred over who in the family actually owned them. The courts decided in favour of Mary, wife of the poet Andrew Noyes: she had formerly been married to a Weld heir, killed in action in the First World War. The Museum bought the two manuscripts from her for £64,000, aided by a loan from the American financier John Pierpont Morgan.

The *Psalter*, which had been on loan to the Museum since the early years of the century, was produced around 1340 for Sir Geoffrey Luttrell, a wealthy landowner. Believed to be the work of more than one artist, the illuminations do not represent purely religious subjects. Charming scenes of rural life in the fourteenth century feature, with depictions of farmers, musicians, cooks, animals and much more.

Books of hours were collections of Christian prayers, written in Latin, to be recited in the home at specific times, based on the regular, more elaborate periods of prayer observed in monasteries. The *Bedford Book of Hours* is thought to have been made in Paris, a leading centre of illumination, for the wedding of John, Duke of Bedford, to Anne of Burgundy on 13 May 1423. Following Henry V's victory at Agincourt in 1415, the Duke became Regent of France after the death of his brother the King in 1422. (In this role, John's best-remembered act was to order in 1431 that Joan of Arc, following capture by his troops, should be burnt at the stake.)

Another gem of the period, the *Sherborne Missal*, came to the Library in 1998 from the Duke of Northumberland, whose family had owned it for nearly 200 years. Made for St. Mary's Abbey in Sherborne around 1400, it is the largest and most colourful book of church services to have survived the Reformation: its 697 parchment pages weigh more than 20 kilos. Famed for the quality and variety of its illustrations, it has been called the unrivalled masterpiece of English book production in the fifteenth century. Apart from the Latin texts of services, with musical notations, it is remarkable for its representations of many of the birds to be seen in England at that period, with the English names by which they were then known.

One of the most appealing English manuscripts is the fourteenth-century *Holkham Bible*, so called because until 1951 it was owned by the Earls of Leicester and kept at Holkham Hall in Norfolk. It tells a somewhat free version of the Bible story in Norman French, backed up by revealing illustrations of everyday English life at the time of its production. At the start of the book the friar who commissioned it is portrayed instructing the artist: 'Now do it well and thoroughly, for it will be shown to important people.' This indication of the target audience is confirmed by the language in which the book is written: Norman French was the tongue of the nobility at this time. The pictures amount to a catalogue of tools, weapons, skilled trades, buildings and styles of dress in fourteenth-century England. The high-spirited tone is well caught by an image of the infant Jesus sliding down a sunbeam.

The first known English translation of the Bible was the *Wycliffe Bible*, initiated in the fourteenth century by the religious reformer John Wycliffe – twice acquitted on charges of heresy. The translation appears to have been undertaken by Wycliffe himself, along with some of his followers, known as Lollards. Several copies were made of it although it was not officially recognised by the Catholic Church, which banned any English version of the scriptures. The Library's copy, dating from about 1408, is decorated with pictures cut from other Bible manuscripts. There is also an attractively decorated copy of a commentary on the Gospels by the Lollards, produced in about 1400.

ꝶ ꝑ pꝛe
lus. e
ꝛeꝛ ꝺe
roit.

ꝰ coment iꝉc mountoit
ꝺu foleꝉꝉ. � les auтres quiꝺoꝛecᴛ iꝉi
moter � tꝛebucheꝛecᴛ ateꝛe � baiſeꝛecᴛ
loꝛgauꝛles
e iꝉc leꝛgaꝛit

la raſe

ꝰ comɇt iꝉc ala qꝛeꝺ
leuꝛe ala fontaꝑnee
baiſeꝛt les poꝛ a les coꝑ
moꝛns · � puꝑs les feſoꝑ
eтere enтers ·

❧ LEFT

The infant Jesus on a sunbeam,
from the *Holkham Bible,*
fourteenth century.

The Book of Margery Kempe,
early fifteenth century.

With most of the early manuscripts having a religious connotation, one that does not is of particular literary interest. The eleventh-century copy of *Beowulf* is the longest known epic poem in Old English, the language of Anglo-Saxon England before the Norman Conquest, reflecting strong influences of Old Norse. In more than 3000 lines it recounts the story of the valiant Scandinavian prince as he overcomes the monster Grendel and his revenge-seeking mother, only to be fatally wounded 50 years later as he slays a rampaging dragon. Slightly damaged in the Ashburnham House fire, making it perilously fragile, the manuscript has since suffered from excessive handling. It is a precious survival, providing a rare insight into the language of Anglo-Saxon England (see page 30).

Making notes in the margins of early manuscripts was quite common, and the Library's copy of William Langland's *Piers Plowman,* from the late fourteenth century, is rich in such addenda. The poem is a powerful allegory that denounces the immorality and sinful excesses of contemporary society, aimed at provoking spontaneous indignation in readers. In a passage describing the evils of drink, referring to the story in Genesis of Lot's intoxication and subsequent incest, an early owner of the book has written, 'Through drunkenness all mischief is wrought'.

The Book of Margery Kempe, from the early fifteenth century, is notable for two reasons: it is the earliest surviving autobiography in the

English language and it was discovered in 1934
by a retired colonel clearing out a cupboard in his
ancestral home to make room to store table tennis
equipment. Kempe, who lived in Norfolk, gave birth
to 14 children before she had a vision of Christ
and decided to eschew worldly pleasures, instead
devoting her life to God. Unable to read or write,
she dictated the book to a scribe. Written in the
third person, it records her redemption and her
subsequent pilgrimages to holy places such as Rome,
Jerusalem and Santiago de Compostela.

(The year 1934 was a remarkable one for the
discovery of long-lost manuscripts. It was then that
a rare copy of Malory's *Morte d'Arthur,* believed
to be the source of Caxton's printed version of
1485, was found in a safe at Winchester College:
it was sold to the Library by the College in 1976.
And 1934 was also the year when Samuel Taylor
Coleridge's manuscript of his poem *Kubla Khan*
came to light, eventually acquired by the British
Museum in 1961.)

Splendid examples of illumination originating
from all over the medieval world have come to
rest in the British Library. The *Gospels of Tsar
Ivan Alexander* were commissioned by the ruler
of Bulgaria in 1355, during the nation's last years
of independence before becoming part of the
Ottoman Empire. As well as commissioning this
lavish edition of the Gospels, Ivan Alexander was
a generous patron who had several large churches
built during his reign. The Gospels, written in

The *Macclesfield Alphabet Book* is a rare 'pattern book' dating from around 1500, and thought to have been used by scribes in medieval Britain to produce luxury manuscripts. It contains 14 ranges of singular lettering styles including alphabets of initials with faces, animals, leaves and flowers and alphabets in Gothic script. There are in addition two sets of borders, some illuminated in colours and gold. It had been in the Earl of Macclesfield's library from around 1750 to 2009, when it was bought by the British Library for £600,000.
(Reproduced actual size)

Cyrillic script, are magnificently adorned with 367 miniature illustrations in gold and other rich colours. The scribe, a monk named Simeon, wrote that the book's binding was originally encrusted with precious stones. He stressed, though, that its beauty was only a secondary concern: the main purpose was 'to express the inner Divine Word, the revelation and the sacred vision'. The work was bequeathed to the Museum in 1917.

The *Sforza Hours*, a spectacular piece of Renaissance illumination, comprises delicate work by both the Italian miniaturist Giovan Pietro Birago and the Flemish illuminator Gerard Horenbout. Birago began the assignment around 1490 for Bona Sforza of Savoy, widow of the Duke of Milan. He had delivered the bulk of the book to her when the

Silos Apocalypse, depicting the end of the world, twelfth century.

rest of his work in progress was stolen from him. It therefore remained incomplete until 1517 when Bona's heir, Margaret of Austria, commissioned Horenbout to execute 16 miniatures to complete the project. She then presented the volume to her nephew, Emperor Charles V. The book was donated to the Museum in the 1890s.

The *Ethiopic Gospel*s, created in the late seventeenth century, were copied from an early fifteenth-century illuminated manuscript. As well as the four Gospels, the dazzling manuscript includes the first eight books of the Old Testament and other religious texts, all colourfully illustrated with depictions of Biblical characters and events. The language is Classical Ethiopic, the language of the Ethiopian Church, unusual among Semitic languages in that it is written from left to right. It was commissioned by Emperor Iyasu I Yohannes, a devotee of Christian art and scholarship, for a new church, Dabra Birham Selasse, in the royal city of Gondar.

The Library holds a twelfth-century copy of *Silos Apocalypse* – a graphic account of the end of the world as forecast in the Book of Revelation, written in about 776 by Beatus of Liébana, a Spanish monk. Its 106 startling illustrations, representing death, chaos and damnation, are in vivid colours, set off by gold and silver leaf. The British Museum bought the manuscript in 1840 from Napoleon's elder brother Joseph Bonaparte, formerly King of Naples and Sicily and then King of Spain, where he

probably acquired it. The two scribes who produced the manuscript, named as Munnio and Dominico, added a touching description of the back-breaking nature of the enterprise and an appeal to readers to treat the results of their toil with respect. 'The work of writing makes one lose his sight, it hunches his back, it breaks ribs and bothers the stomach, it pains the kidneys and causes aches throughout the body. Therefore, you the reader, turn the pages carefully and keep your fingers from the letters, because just as hail destroys the fields, the useless reader erases the text and destroys the book.'

Relief for such put-upon scribes would not come to the Western world for a further 300 years, until the invention of the printing press – the key development in information technology that changed the nature and scale of the dissemination of ideas.

Adorem9 dñm qui fecit nos, Ps venite aũ Seruite·

Eatus vir qui
non abijt in
consilio impiorū et in
via pcōrꝫ nō stetit: ⁊ in
cathedra pestilēcie nō se=
dit, Sed ī lege dñi vo
lūtas ei9: et in lege eius meditabit die ac
nocte, Et erit tanꝗ lignū qd plātatū iste
secus decursus aqē: qd fructū suū dabit in
tpe suo Et foliū ei9 nō defluet: ⁊ oīa ꝗcūꝗ
faciet plperabūt, Nō sic impij nō sic sed
tanꝗ puluis quē piicit ventus a facie terre,
Ideo non resurgi t impij in iudicio: neꝗ
pcōres in cōsilio iustorꝫ Q̄ nouit dñs
via iustorꝫ: ⁊ iter impiorꝫ pribit, Tha P

CHAPTER 6

Spreading the words

' Books are not absolutely dead things, but do contain
a potency of life in them to be as active as that soul was
whose progeny they are; nay they do preserve as in a vial
the purest efficacy and extraction of that living intellect
that bred them. '

~ JOHN MILTON, *AREOPAGITICA* (1644)

ALTHOUGH PRINTING WITH movable metal
type was not introduced to the Western world until
the fifteenth century, the Chinese had experimented
with a similar system, initially using porcelain
characters, at least 400 years earlier. It is thought
that the first metal typefaces were produced in
Korea in the thirteenth century; but the intricacies
of the Chinese alphabet (used in Korea at the time)
were a barrier to its wide adoption. Block printing,
by which letters and images are reproduced from
carvings on wooden blocks, had long existed in the
East. It featured on textiles for decoration as well as
on documents for information – particularly for the
propagation of Buddhism, which relied heavily on
the circulation of printed texts.

The world's earliest surviving dated block-printed
document is a Buddhist scroll, the *Diamond Sutra*. It
was discovered in 1900 at the 'Cave of the Thousand
Buddhas' at Dunhuang (see Chapter 5) and is today
one of the Library's most prized possessions. The

scroll is written in Chinese, and a note at the end
records the precise date of its production – 11 May
868, by the Western calendar. It consists of seven
sheets of paper printed from individual blocks and
pasted together in a scroll more than five metres

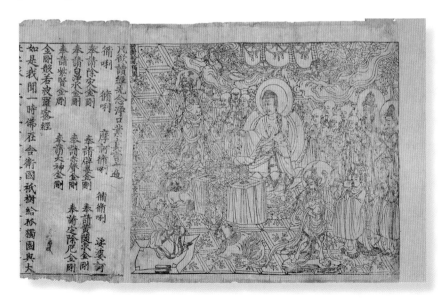

RIGHT

Isaac Ibn Sahula's *Meshal ha-Kadmoni* (Ancient Fables), 1491

ועתה הבה לכו עצה ' דבר מקובל (נרצה ' ונשמור דברי פיך ומוצא' שפתיך לא

יפול דבר ארצה ' ויאמר שמעו נא קציני ' האזינו קולי כבוני ' לכו ונעלה אל

הרים ונבוחה עד עיר היונה ' מקנטרת מגר ולבונה ' הר המור גבעת הלבונה

' נפש תמצאו מרגוע ' ואכלתם אכול ושבוע ' ותבכלו מצרה ומקטוב ' שמעו

אלי ואכלו טוב ' ויאמר הגד לכו טוב הארץ העליה ' השמינה היא אם רזה '

ומה מעלת יושביה וגריה ' זקיכ'ה וכעריה '

צודת הארי שואל הצבי מעלת הארץ וערכה '   והצבי משיבו בענין וכהלכה '

ויאמר קבלה היא בידינו

מאבותינו ' וכך

אמרו רבותינו ' הדר בארץ

ישר'א דומה כמי ש לו שא

בחבלו ' והדר בחוצה לארץ

דומה כמי שאין לו ' וכל 'מ

משביל מעיד על מאמר זה

ומסביס ' אוריא דארץ ישרא

מחכיס ' ואמרין לגולס ידור

אדס בארץ ישראל אפילו

מריב גויס בעריס ' ואל

ידור בחוצה לארץ ואפילו

בעיר מרובה ישרא דריס '

ואמר להתהלל בקדושתה ו

ולהשתבח ' כל הקבור בארץ ישר'א כאילו קבור תחת המזבח ' ונשאלו אל החכמיס

הקדמונים ' גוי צדיק שומר אמוניס ' היתמחייב לילך בחוצה לארץ למצות יבוס '

ועל דרך התמימה הטיבום ' ואמרו אחיו של זה נשא גויה ' ברוך המקוס אמר הרנג

בצדייה ' ואמר כל המהלך ד'אמות בא" מובטח לו ' שהוא בן עולס הבא'יחיה

ויזכה כלי שמן ודבה ' ועל זה תקנו רבותינו ' לומר ביום מנוחתינו 'מעניץ כוכת

לככנו ומאנויינו ' רמס על ביון כי היא ' בית חיינו ' ואמרו דבר ברור להודיע'

מציץ מכלל יופי ה'הופיע ' ואמרו דבר אחר לכל משכיל לא נעלס 'א' יושבת ב

באמצעיתה של עולס ' וירושליס באמצע א" והיא הנקראת ההד'ל ' ובית המקדס

באמצע ירושליס ' במהלת היתחניס ' ההוכל באמצע בית המקדס ' והארון

long. The lettering was painted on paper that was placed face down on wood, allowing the carver to trace the letters in reverse. An illustration portrays the Buddha delivering the sutra to a disciple and telling him that it should be known as 'the diamond of transcendent wisdom' because its message will cut through worldly illusion like a diamond. The sutra can be viewed in detail on the *Turning the Pages* terminals in the Library, or online.

In about 1440 Johannes Gutenberg, a goldsmith and publisher from Mainz, devised the system for large-scale printing of books and documents that has formed the basis of publishing for more than 500 years. As well as introducing metal typefaces that could be mass produced, he invented a wooden printing press, based on the screw press widely used in agriculture, and mixed an oil-based ink suitable for the process. The most important work that he printed by this method was the *Gutenberg Bible,* in the then standard Latin Vulgate version (see page 46).

The significance of Gutenberg's invention was quickly recognised, especially for widening the circulation of the Bible. A few months before the *Gutenberg Bible* became available Enea Silvio, the future Pope Pius II, reported at the Diet of Frankfurt that he had met a man who claimed he was about to produce a Bible that might be read without spectacles in 180 identical copies. He marvelled at the prospect, no doubt foreseeing the wide changes in religious observance that the development would initiate.

Books printed with movable type before the end of the fifteenth century are known as incunabula, and the Library has about 12,500, representing 10,390 editions. A high proportion of early printed books were Bibles, produced in mainland Europe in the accepted Latin version. One of the best known is that printed by Johann Amerbach in Basel in 1479. It contains this touching introduction: 'I am a Bible thoroughly corrected from Greek and Hebrew sources, and I am also beautiful. I call upon the gods and the stars as my witnesses: there is no printed Bible like me in the whole world. There are concordances to every passage and the lettering is neatly printed.' Many early Bibles have been 'glossed' by commentaries on the text written between the lines or in the margins.

The Library's fine collection of 100 Hebrew incunabula were mostly printed on the very early Hebrew presses in Italy and the Iberian peninsula. One of the rarest is a Pentateuch printed in Faro in 1487 – the only known copy of the first book printed in Portugal. Another remarkable item is Isaac Ibn Sahula's *Meshal ha-Kadmoni* (Ancient Fables) published in Brescia in 1491, possibly the very first illustrated Hebrew printed book.

In 1476 William Caxton, a merchant and book dealer, established the first English printing press at Westminster. He had become familiar with the new technique in the Low Countries and Germany, where he spent much of his early working life. In Bruges in 1473 Caxton had produced the first known book printed in English, *Recuyell of the Historyes of Troye* – his own translation of Raoul Le Fèvre's stories of the Trojan Wars. At the end of it he wrote: 'I have practised and earned at my great charge and dispense to ordain this said book in print after the manner and form as you may here see, and is not written with pen and ink as other books have been, to the end that every man may have them at once, for all the books of this story … thus imprinted as you see here, were begun in one day and also finished in one day.' (Several incunabula carry similar self-congratulatory messages. The *Catholicon* of Joannes Balbus, printed in Mainz in 1460, announces that it has been 'printed and accomplished without the help of reed, stylus or pen, but by the wondrous agreement, proportion and harmony of punches and types'.)

Caxton, before his death in 1492, printed and published some 18,000 copies of about 100 books, most in English but some in French or Latin. They included two editions of Chaucer's *Canterbury Tales,* the first in 1476 and the second in 1483, the latter illustrated with woodblock prints and including some textual corrections and alterations. The Library has a good copy of each edition, the earlier one part of the King's Library and the later from Thomas Grenville's collection (see page 50). Like the *Gutenberg Bible,* both have now been digitised for consultation electronically. There are also copies of Caxton's translation of *Aesop's Fables,* printed first by him and later by Richard Pynson,

the Frenchman who succeeded him as court printer to the Tudor kings.

Several of the books and pamphlets printed and published by Caxton give clues to the tastes and mores of his time. One, entitled *Ghostly Matters,* contains sections on 'seven points of true love' and 'the twelve profits of tribulation'; others include *The Book of Good Manners* and *Fayts of Arms and Chivalry.* After Caxton's death his business was taken over by a former assistant, Wynkyn de Worde, who moved the press from Westminster to Fleet Street, on the western edge of the City of London. The Library's holdings of de Worde's publications include several written by John Lydgate, the prolific Suffolk-born poet and monk who died in 1451 and whose works were among the sources of some of Shakespeare's plays.

In 1994 the Library paid over £1 million, partly raised in a public appeal, for what was then the only known surviving complete edition of William Tyndale's English translation of the New Testament, printed in Worms, Germany, in 1526. Tyndale was a priest attracted to the Protestant reformers, especially Martin Luther. He took his translation, partly derived from the 140-year-old Wycliffe Bible, to be printed in Germany because the Catholic Church disapproved of the project and no English printer would dare to be associated with it. When copies were brought into England they were denounced by bishops and burned outside St. Paul's Cathedral and elsewhere.

BELOW
The Gospel of St. John from the only known complete edition of Tyndale's translation. *(Reproduced actual size).*

Tyndale himself stayed abroad for his safety. Yet his Bible was clearly in demand, since by 1534, the year in which the Act of Supremacy established Henry VIII as head of the Church of England, it had been reprinted four times in Antwerp. In that year Tyndale produced a slightly revised translation: the Library has a copy that was owned by Anne Boleyn and is inscribed with her name. The following year he was arrested in Antwerp as a heretic, and in 1536, after 16 months in prison, he was executed by strangulation and his body publicly burned.

Tyndale's translation made a lasting impact on English literature. More than 80 per cent of the New Testament in the King James Bible of 1611 – the Authorised Version most used in the Anglican Church – was based on his work, including the most memorable phrases and figures of speech that have passed into the language: 'fight the good fight', 'the powers that be', 'the last shall be first' are just three of very many examples.

The year before Tyndale's death the first complete Bible in English, the *Coverdale Bible,* embracing both the Old and New Testaments, was printed in Cologne. In 1539 Henry gave his approval to this version, which became known as the 'Great Bible', and ruled that it should be made available in every church in England. Twenty-one years after that came the *Geneva Bible,* translated by followers of Calvin, sometimes called the 'Breeches Bible' because the word was

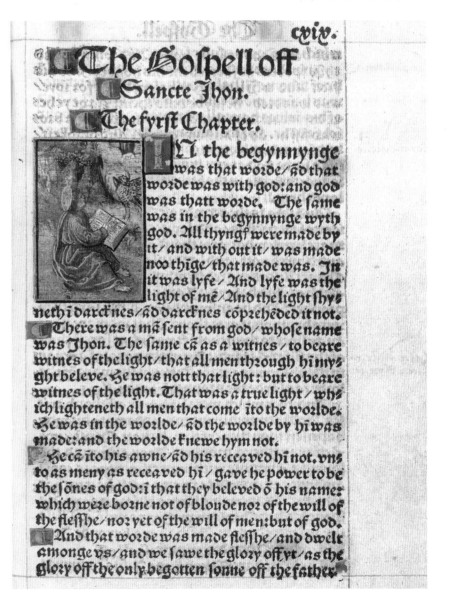

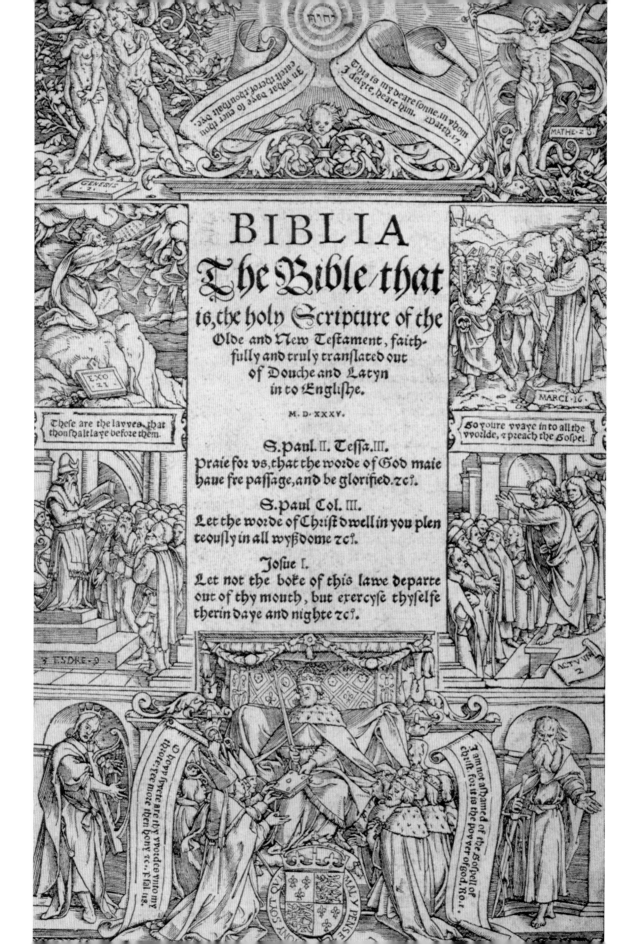

This is my deare sonne, in whom I delyte, heare him. Math. 17.

MATHE 3

These are the lavves, that thou shalt laye before them.

3 ESDRE 9

BIBLIA
The Bible, that
is, the holy Scripture of the
Olde and New Testament, faith-
fully and truly translated out
of Douche and Latyn
in to Englishe.

M. D. XXXV.

S. Paul. II. Tessa. III.
Praie for vs, that the worde of God maie
haue fre passage, and be glorified. zcʔ.

S. Paul Col. III.
Let the worde of Christ dwell in you plen
teously in all wyssdome zcʔ.

Josue I.
Let not the boke of this lawe departe
out of thy mouth, but exercyse thyselfe
therin daye and nighte zcʔ.

MARCI 16.

Go youre vvaye in to all the vvorlde, ⁊ preach the Gospel.

ACTVM 2

I am not ashamed of the Gospel of Christ, for it is the povver of god. Ro. 1.

used in Genesis Chapter 3. This proved a popular translation, printed in England after 1576 and reprinted many times, with explanatory diagrams, charts and marginal notes. The Library has 106 copies, representing 80 editions.

The King's approval of the 'Great Bible' was necessary, because in 1538 he had introduced state control of printing, ruling that all new books must be approved by the Privy Council so as to stamp out potentially seditious publications. In 1557 Mary I transferred that responsibility to the Company of Stationers. In the 1580s the Court of Star Chamber imposed an upper limit on the number of printing presses. Despite these restrictions, by the end of the sixteenth century a wide variety of works were being printed and published. They included poems, romances, books of history, philosophy and travel and pamphlets that expressed opinions on topics of the day. Among the books that have endured, one of the most remarkable is Sir Thomas More's *Utopia*, printed in Antwerp in 1516 – one of the first works in which authors have fleshed out their vision of a perfect but unattainable world order. More than a century later Francis Bacon wrote his treatise *New Atlantis*, and in 1651 Thomas Hobbes's *Leviathan* argued the case for an all-powerful protector (such as Oliver Cromwell) to shield the populace from its anarchic instincts.

Among the most popular items published in the sixteenth and seventeenth centuries were almanacs, consisting principally of astrological information and predictions. The first almanacs printed in England were translations from European languages, but home-grown examples began to appear; by 1567 at least 19 titles were on sale, although the number declined when the Government granted a monopoly in their production to two London stationers. The survivor is *Old Moore's Almanack*, first published in 1697, by which time annual sales of almanacs amounted to 400,000. The Library's holdings were strengthened in 2004 with the purchase of 14 early examples from the collection of Col. W.A. Potter.

There were plays, too, their publication stimulated by the growing popularity of the theatre in Elizabethan England. From the 1590s there appeared a succession of texts written by the leading playwright of his or of any time, William Shakespeare. The plays first appeared in individual quarto editions and were not collected together until the publication of the First Folio in 1623. The Library has no original copy of the first Shakespeare play to be printed – *Titus Andronicus*, in 1594 – but it does have copies of *Henry VI Part II*, printed later that year, and, from a year earlier, of his poem *Venus and Adonis*. From 1597 Shakespeare's plays were published more and more frequently, with *Romeo and Juliet*, *Richard II* and *Richard III* among the first to appear, though with no attribution to the author. In 1598, *Love's Labour's Lost* was the first to be published under Shakespeare's name, subsequently attached to all the plays.

The quarto editions varied significantly in quality and accuracy. Most notorious was the 'bad' first quarto of *Hamlet,* published in 1603, only about half as long as later versions and with heavily mangled verse. The first lines of Hamlet's famous soliloquy, for example, are rendered thus:

> To be or not to be, I there's the point,
> To die, to sleep, is that all? I all:
> No, to sleep, to dream, I mary there it goes…

A second quarto, much closer to the version we know today, was printed the following year. In all, five quarto versions of *Hamlet* were published, all based on the second or 'good' quarto. The Library has copies of all of them, some deriving from the rich collection of theatre-related texts bequeathed to the British Museum by the actor/manager David Garrick in 1779.

Only 19 of Shakespeare's plays were published in his lifetime. Seven years after his death the First Folio, containing 36 plays (the entire canon except *Pericles*), was compiled by two of his actor friends, John Heminge and Henry Condell. On the title page is Martin Droeshout's portrait of Shakespeare, and on the facing page this comment on it by the poet and playwright Ben Jonson:

> O, could he but have drawn his wit
> As well in brass, as he hath hit
> His face; the print would then surpass
> All, that was ever writ in brass.
> But, since he cannot, reader, look
> Not on his picture, but his book.

A second folio edition of the plays was published in 1632. No further editions appeared during Oliver Cromwell's Commonwealth, when theatres were closed. Not until after the Restoration of the monarchy did the third folio appear, in 1663, including not only *Pericles* but six plays that were not Shakespeare's work. (One of the Library's copies of this was originally owned by Charles II.) A fourth folio followed in 1685, since when countless editions of Shakespeare's plays and sonnets have been produced on printing presses throughout the world.

The poet most associated with the Commonwealth is John Milton, and the Library has many editions of his masterpiece *Paradise Lost*. Equally significant is its copy of Milton's *Areopagitica* of 1644, the pamphlet quoted at the beginning of this chapter. It is an early plea for freedom of expression, a reaction to the punishment of John Lilburne, who had been arrested in 1638 for importing seditious books. Lilburne was fined £500, flogged and sent to prison. In the pamphlet, Milton urged members of Parliament: 'You cannot make us now less capable, less knowing, less eagerly pursuing of the truth, unless you first make yourselves, that made us so, less the lovers, less the founders of our true liberty.'

Despite that impassioned plea, restrictions on publications remained in place until 1695. Yet an increasing number of books were still produced, treasured by their owners and bound as richly as they could afford. Many of the Library's most valuable examples of printed books, apart from

Mr. WILLIAM
SHAKESPEARES

COMEDIES,
HISTORIES, &
TRAGEDIES.

Published according to the True Originall Copies.

Martin Droeshout sculpsit London.

LONDON
Printed by Isaac Iaggard, and Ed. Blount. 1623.

those that came with the King's and the Grenville Libraries, derive from two major collections – one of them bequeathed in 1799 by former Trustee of the Museum Rev. Clayton Cracherode. In 1977 part of the Broxbourne Collection, amassed by Albert Ehrman in the twentieth century, was bequeathed to the Library and further items from it were bought on the open market.

✿   ✿   ✿

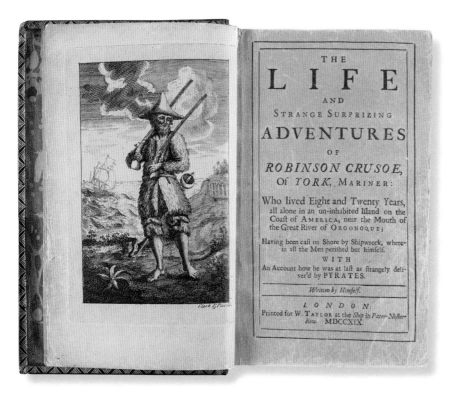

Towards the end of the seventeenth century the novel began its progress from an occasional literary form to the prominent position it occupies on bookshelves today. One of its exponents was the playwright, poet and part-time spy Aphra Behn, among the first of a long line of distinguished women writers of fiction. Her first major work in the field (running to three volumes and totalling more than a thousand pages) was *Love-Letters Between a Nobleman and his Sister*. This long novel featured real people and events connected with the 1685 Monmouth Rebellion that challenged the rule of James II. Better known today is *Oroonoko*, a story that arose from a brief period in Behn's early twenties when she and her family lived in Surinam, then a British colony. *Oroonoko* addresses the issue of race, and in particular of slavery, although scholars have never decided conclusively whether she approved of the practice or not.

The eighteenth century saw exponential growth in publications of every kind, but especially novels, most of them imbued with powerful elements of morality and philosophy. In 1719 Daniel Defoe gave a fresh slant to the concept of Utopia in *Robinson Crusoe*. Like *Oroonoko*, the novel was set in an island off the coast of the Americas, reflecting the great interest in that part of the world inspired by the first European settlements. The influence of Aphra Behn is suggested by Defoe's naming the island's great river Oroonoque, both names presumably deriving from the South American river Orinoco.

Seven years after *Robinson Crusoe*, the poet, clergyman and wit Jonathan Swift published *Gulliver's Travels*, a satire on eighteenth-century society and its foibles, again set on fictional islands. Such leaps of the imagination formed the basis of the genres of fantasy and science fiction explored in the twentieth century by writers such as H.G. Wells and George Orwell, and more recently by J.G. Ballard and Terry Pratchett. An exhibition on science fiction, mounted in the Library in 2011, traced the genre back even further, to the second century AD, when Lucian wrote his *True History*, an account of a journey to the moon. (The Library's earliest copy of this was printed in 1647, in Dutch.) The first known work of science fiction in English is *The Man in the Moone*, by Francis Godwin, which appeared in 1638.

Samuel Richardson's *Pamela, or Virtue Rewarded*, published in 1740, is generally considered the first romantic novel. It tells the story of a nobleman and his maid who fall in love, and it ends happily. Richardson, a printer and publisher by trade, was 51 when *Pamela* was published. He followed it eight years later with *Clarissa, or the History of a Young Lady*, a very different and immensely long novel (nearly a million words), featuring rape, prostitution and the eventual death of the heroine. Although both novels sought to point a moral, they were principally enjoyed for being packed with erotic incident. The same was true of the works of Henry Fielding, who became a novelist chiefly because he resented Richardson's success. Just a year after *Pamela* appeared, Fielding wrote an

LEFT

Flying to the moon via a flock of trained birds, from the first edition of *The Man in the Moone* by Francis Godwin, 1638.

anonymous parody of the work entitled *Shamela*. Then he created *Joseph Andrews*, in which the main character was depicted as the brother of Richardson's heroine Pamela. Fielding's best-known novel is *Tom*

OA′RY. *adj.* [from *oar.*] Having the form or use of oars.

His hair transforms to down, his fingers meet
In skinny films, and shape his *oary* feet. *Addison.*

The swan with arched neck,
Between her white wings mantling, proudly rows
Her state with *oary* feet. *Milton.*

OAST. *n. s.* A kiln. Not in use.

Empty the binn into a hog-bag, and carry them immediately to the *oast* or kiln, to be dried. *Mortimer.*

OATCAKE. *n. s.* [*oat* and *cake.*] Cake made of the meal of oats.

Take a blue stone they make haver or *oatcakes* upon, and lay it upon the cross bars of iron. *Peacham.*

OA′TEN. *adj.* [from *oat.*] Made of oats; bearing oats.

When shepherds pipe on *oaten* straws,
And merry larks are ploughmens clocks. *Shakespeare.*

OATH. *n. s.* [aith, Gothick; að, Saxon. The distance between the noun *oath*, and the verb *swear*, is very observable, as it may shew that our oldest dialect is formed from different languages.] An affirmation, negation, or promise, corroborated by the attestation of the Divine Being.

Read over Julia's heart, thy first best love,
For whose dear sake thou then did'st rend thy faith
Into a thousand *oaths*; and all those *oaths*
Descended into perjury to love me. *Shakespeare.*

He that strikes the first stroke, I'll run him up to the hilts as I am a soldier.
—An *oath* of mickle might; and fury shall abate. *Shakespeare.*

We have consultations, which inventions shall be published, which not: and take an *oath* of secrecy for the concealing of those which we think fit to keep secret. *Bacon.*

Those called to any office of trust, are bound by an *oath* to the faithful discharge of it: but an *oath* is an appeal to God, and therefore can have no influence, except upon those who believe that he is. *Swift.*

OA′THABLE. *adj.* [from *oath*. A word not used.] Capable of having an oath administered.

You're not *oathable*,
Altho' I know you'll swear
Into strong shudders th' immortal gods. *Shakespeare.*

OATHBREA′KING. *n. s.* [*oath* and *break.*] Perjury; the violation of an oath.

His *oathbreaking* he mended thus,
By now forswearing that he is forsworn. *Shakesp.*

OA′TMALT. *n. s.* [*oat* and *malt.*] Malt made of oats.

In Kent they brew with one half *oatmalt*, and the other half barleymalt. *Mortimer.*

OA′TMEAL. *n. s.* [*oat* and *meal.*] Flower made by grinding oats.

Oatmeal and butter, outwardly applied, dry the scab on the head. *Arbuthnot.*

Our neighbours tell me oft, in joking talk,
Of ashes, leather, *oatmeal*, bran, and chalk. *Gay.*

OA′TMEAL. *n. s.* An herb. *Ainsworth.*

OATS. *n. s.* [aten, Saxon.] A grain, which in England is generally given to horses, but in Scotland supports the people.

It is of the grass leaved tribe; the flowers have no petals, and are disposed in a loose panicle: the grain is eatable. The meal makes tolerable good bread. *Miller.*

The *oats* have eaten the horses. *Shakespeare.*

It is bare mechanism, no otherwise produced than the turning of a wild *oat* beard, by the insinuation of the particles

---

If when you make your pray'rs,
God should be so *obdurate* as yourselves,
How would it fare with your departed souls? *Shakesp.*

Women are soft, mild, pitiful, and flexible;
Thou stern, *obdurate*, flinty, rough, remorseless. *Shakesp.*

To convince the proud what signs avail,
Or wonders move th' *obdurate* to relent;
They harden'd more, by what might more reclaim. *Milt.*

Obdurate as you are, oh! hear at least
My dying prayers, and grant my last request. *Dryden.*

2. Hardned; firm; stubborn.

Sometimes the very custom of evil makes the heart *obdurate* against whatsoever instructions to the contrary. *Hooker.*

A pleasing sorcery could charm
Pain for a while, or anguish, and excite
Fallacious hope, or arm th' *obdurate* breast
With stubborn patience, as with triple steel. *Milton.*

No such thought ever strikes his marble, *obdurate* heart, but it presently flies off and rebounds from it. It is impossible for a man to be thorough-paced in ingratitude, till he has shook off all fetters of pity and compassion. *South.*

3. Harsh; rugged.

They joined the most *obdurate* consonants without one intervening vowel. *Swift.*

OBDU′RATELY. *adv.* [from *obdurate.*] Stubbornly; inflexibly; impenitently.

OBDU′RATENESS. *n. s.* [from *obdurate.*] Stubbornness; inflexibility; impenitence.

OBDURA′TION. *n. s.* [from *obdurate.*] Hardness of heart; stubbornness.

What occasion it had given them to think, to their greater *obduration* in evil, that through a froward and wanton desire of innovation, we did constrainedly those things, for which conscience was pretended? *Hooker.*

OBDU′RED. *adj.* [*obduratus*, Latin.] Hardned; inflexible; impenitent.

This saw his hapless foes, but stood *obdur'd*,
And to rebellious fight rallied their pow'rs
Insensate. *Milton.*

OBE′DIENCE. *n. s.* [obedience, Fr. obedientia, Latin.] Obsequiousness; submission to authority; compliance with command or prohibition.

If you violently proceed against him, it would shake in pieces the heart of his *obedience*. *Shakespeare.*

Thy husband
Craves no other tribute at thy hands,
But love, fair looks, and true *obedience*. *Shakesp.*

His servants ye are, to whom ye obey, whether of sin unto death, or of *obedience* unto righteousness. *Rom.*

It was both a strange commission, and a strange *obedience* to a commission, for men so furiously assailed, to hold their hands. *Bacon.*

Nor can this be,
But by fulfilling that which thou didst want,
Obedience to the law of God, impos'd
On penalty of death. *Milton.*

OBE′DIENT. *adj.* [obediens, Latin.] Submissive to authority; compliant with command or prohibition; obsequious.

To this end did I write, that I might know the proof of you, whether ye be *obedient* in all things. *2 Cor.*

To this her mother's plot
She, seemingly *obedient*, likewise hath
Made promise.

Jones, a raunchy tale of a foundling who struck it rich, since dramatised many times on stage and screen.

The most significant book to appear in the eighteenth century, in terms of the development of the English language, was Samuel Johnson's *Dictionary,* published in 1755. Dr. Johnson, one of the British Museum library's earliest readers, laboriously compiled the work, together with a team of helpers, over more than eight years. More than 40,000 words were listed and defined, with more than 110,000 quotations employed to illustrate their usage. The Library has many copies, including first editions that belonged to George III (in the King's Library) and to the statesman Edmund Burke.

Johnson understood that a dictionary can never be definitive but amounts to a snapshot of a language in constant evolution. He wrote: 'When we see men grow old and die at a certain time one after another . . . we laugh at the elixir that promises to prolong life to a thousand years; and with equal justice may the lexicographer be derided, who being able to produce no example of a nation that has preserved their words and phrases from mutability, shall imagine that his dictionary can embalm his language, and secure it from corruption and decay.'

⚜   ⚜   ⚜

It was around this time that books specifically for children achieved significant popularity and distribution. A few had appeared in the previous century. The Library has the only known copy of the earliest English illustrated alphabet, *The Childes First Tutor* by Festus Corin, published in 1664; and John Bunyan wrote *A Book for Boys and Girls, or Country Rhimes for Children,* in 1686.

The eighteenth century saw the rise of chapbooks. Small, slender and printed on poor paper, these were sold cheaply by chapmen, or street traders, hence their name. Many contained fairy tales, mostly translated from the French, with woodcut illustrations. The Library has bound some of them together in volumes. The stories of Charles Perrault, the father of the fairy tale, first published in France in 1697, appeared in an English translation by Robert Samber in 1729; but the earliest English edition in the Library's collections is a bilingual version dating from 1764, *Tales of passed times by Mother Goose with morals, Englished by R. S.*

The London publisher and bookseller Thomas Boreman established himself as a specialist publisher of children's books, many relating to the natural world. His first, published in 1730, was *A Description of Three Hundred Animals,* followed by *A Description of a Great Variety of Animals and Vegetables.* A few years later John Newbery entered the market in a much bigger way, publishing nearly 400 titles by the end of the eighteenth century. Although his books were written and designed for children, he did not shy away from tackling difficult subjects. One of the earliest, appearing in 1761, was *The Newtonian System of Philosophy.*

The Library has examples of about 170 of Newbery's books, including the only known copy

of the 1765 first edition of *The History of Little Goody Two-shoes*, one of his best loved works – although it has been questioned whether he was the original author. An indication that he might have been comes in the death of the heroine's father, who was 'seized with a fever in a place where Dr. James's powder was not to be had'. Much of Newbery's wealth came from the sale of a medicine called Dr. James's Fever Powder – an early example of what we now call product placement.

Newbery died in 1767, but his children's publishing business was continued first by his son Francis, then by his nephew, also Francis, and in turn by the nephew's widow Elizabeth. John Harris at first managed the business for Elizabeth before branching out on his own, notably publishing *The*

FRONTISPIECE.

Comic Adventures of Old Mother Hubbard and Her Dog in 1805. The Library has a copy of the second edition of 1806.

One of the most enduring authors of the nineteenth century also wrote for children, and his work is represented in two of the Library's treasures. Lewis Carroll (whose real name was Charles Dodgson) wrote *Alice's Adventures Under Ground* as a tale to tell the three daughters of his friend Henry Liddell, Dean of Christ Church, Oxford. The Library holds the original 90-page manuscript, meticulously penned and illustrated by the author in 1864, inscribed to Alice Liddell

"The Queen of Hearts she made some tarts
  All on a summer day:
The Knave of Hearts he stole those tarts,
  And took them quite away!"

"Now for the evidence," said the King, "and then the sentence."

"No!" said the Queen, "first the sentence, and then the evidence!"

"Nonsense!" cried Alice, so loudly that everybody jumped, "the idea of having the sentence first!

"Hold your tongue!" said the Queen.

"I won't!" said Alice, "you're nothing but a pack of cards! Who cares for you?"

At this the whole pack rose up into the air, and came flying down upon her: she gave a little scream of fright, and tried to beat them off, and found herself lying on the bank, with her head in the lap of her sister, who was

with the words: 'A Christmas gift to a dear child, in memory of a summer day'. It also has the first edition of the longer book that was developed from it, *Alice's Adventures in Wonderland,* published in 1865, inscribed by Carroll to Alice Fannie Thomas. The illustrations by John Tenniel, some based on Carroll's drawings, are held in as much popular affection as the story itself.

The nineteenth century saw the continuing development of the novel as the dominant form of literature and the emergence of formidable female authors such as Jane Austen, Charlotte Brontë and George Eliot, the pen name of Mary Ann Evans. They are well represented in the library both by manuscripts (see Chapter 7) and printed editions of their books, as are their distinguished male

contemporaries such as Charles Dickens, Anthony Trollope and, later, Thomas Hardy.

A major introduction in nineteenth-century fiction was the detective novel. The American writer Edgar Allan Poe is credited with writing the first of them in the English language; *The Murders in the Rue Morgue* was published in 1841. Dickens's *Bleak House,* written 12 years later, included a murder and a detective to solve it. Later in the century Wilkie Collins perfected the form with *The Woman in White* and *The Moonstone,* while Sir Arthur Conan Doyle created, in Sherlock Holmes, the most famous detective in English literature. In 2004 the Library acquired a significant group of Conan Doyle's manuscripts and correspondence.

These authors paved the way for the mystery writers who became household names in the twentieth century – Edgar Wallace, Agatha Christie, Dorothy L. Sayers, Ruth Rendell, Dick Francis, Raymond Chandler and countless others. That was also the period when espionage became a fruitful theme for novelists, beginning with Erskine Childers's *Riddle of the Sands* in 1903, then on to John Buchan and his character Richard Hannay in *The Thirty-Nine Steps* and other adventures. The form remained popular after the Second World War, developed by such as John le Carré, Len Deighton and Ian Fleming, creator of the suave James Bond.

PSYCHE BORNE OFF BY ZEPHYRUS, DRAWN BY EDWARD BURNEJONES & ENGRAVED BY WILLIAM MORRIS

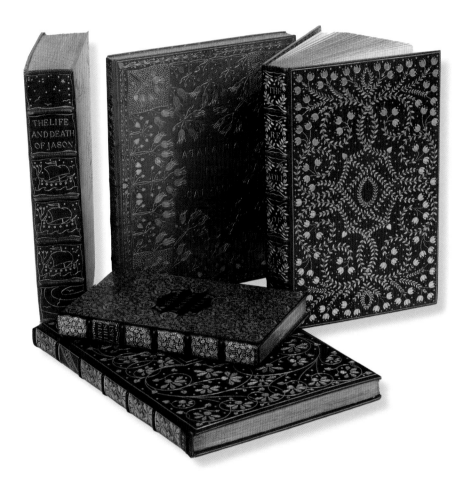

It is axiomatic that you cannot judge a book by its binding. You can, though, judge from it how greatly any particular volume was valued – and some of the fine bindings held by the Library are evidence that the books they cloak were, and are, valued very highly indeed. The collection ranges from lovingly crafted medieval bindings to imaginative works from the present day, while the work of the Conservation Centre ensures that the intricate skills of the binder are handed down to the next generation.

The first fine binding to be acquired by the Museum came in one of its foundation collections, that of Sir Hans Sloane. It is an embroidered cover that protects the fourteenth-century *Felbrigge Psalter*. Later even older examples were acquired, notably a jewelled binding on a German gospel book of the tenth or eleventh century. With the acquisition of the Royal Library came superbly tooled bindings on some of Henry VIII's books and Bibles, bearing the initials of the King and Catherine of Aragon, and of the King and Anne Boleyn. There are, too, bindings with the initials of his son Edward VI and later members of the royal family, including James I's eldest son Henry, a keen book collector who died at the age of 18. In the King's Library is a binding designed by the architect Robert Adam; a later purchase was one by another eighteenth-century architect, James 'Athenian' Stuart.

In 1868 Felix Slade, who gave his name to one of London's leading art schools, bequeathed his collection of bindings to the Museum, including

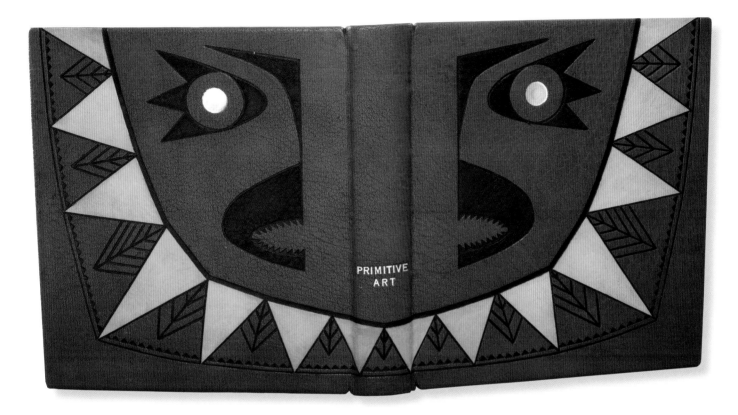

᠉ ABOVE

Trevor Jones's binding to
Panofsky's *Primitive Art*, 1958,
Henry Davis Gift collection.

a medieval example incorporating Limoges enamel and one made in Germany in 1722 out of tortoiseshell inlaid with silver and mother of pearl. The Cracherode collection provided many more early examples of the craft, but the richest treasure trove came in a gift from Henry Davis, a dedicated collector, in 1977. It comprises 890 English and European bindings covering all eras from the twelfth century to the twentieth. In 2007 the Library broadened the scope of its holdings in this area by purchasing the large collection of nineteenth-century bindings amassed by John Collins, a book dealer. Most of these were machine-made bindings of the kind that then covered popular literature. Modern hand-crafted bindings are also being acquired, including some from the early twentieth century by T.J. Cobden-Sanderson, a friend of William Morris, and more recently from craftsmen such as James Brockman and Sydney Cockerell.

Just as the machine age did not put an end to hand binding, nor did the coming of printing make manuscripts redundant. Authors still had first to produce their works by their own hand – and later by their own typewriters and word processors – before submitting them for reproduction. And they still allowed themselves second or third thoughts before deciding on the final shape of the work. These original drafts, with their deletions and emendations, along with the early proofs corrected by the author, became and remain valuable resources for those seeking to understand the creative process.

Hyperion Book 1st

Deep in the shady sadness of a Vale,
Far sunken from the healthy breath of Morn,
Far from the fiery noon, and ~~evening~~ Eve's one star,
Sat grey hair'd Saturn quiet as a Stone,
Still as the silence round about his Lair.
Forest on forest hung above his head
~~Like Clouds~~ ~~that~~ ~~whose~~ ~~bosoms~~ ~~thunderous bosoms~~
Like Cloud on Cloud. No stir of air was there;
~~Not so much life as what an eagle were,~~
~~Scarce spread upon a field of green said corn:~~
But where the dead leaf fell, there did it rest.
A Stream went voiceless by, still deadened more
By reason of his fallen divinity
~~Spreading a shade: if~~
Spreading a shade: the Naiad mid her reeds
Pressd her cold finger closer to her lips.

      Along the margin sand large foot marks went
No further than to where his feet had stay'd
And slept ~~without~~ ~~there since~~ a motion: ~~since that time~~
His old right hand lay nerveless ~~on the ground~~ listless, dead
Unsceptrd; and his ~~realmless~~ eyes were closd;
While his bow'd head seem'd listening to the Earth
His Ancient Mother for some comfort yet.

      Thus the old Eagle drowsy with ~~his~~ great grief
Sat moulting his weak Plumage never more
To be restored or soar against the Sun,
While his three Sons upon Olympus stood—

      It seem'd no force could wake him from his place
But there came one who, with a kindred hand
Touch'd his wide Shoulders, after bending low
With reverence, though to one who knew it not.
She was a Goddess of the infant world;
~~By her in stature the~~ tallest Amazon
Had stood a ~~little~~: she would have ta'en
Achilles by the hair and bent his neck,
Or with a ~~finger~~ Ixion's ~~toil~~

1

× Not so much life as on a summers day
Robs not at all the dandelions fleece:

CHAPTER ~ 7

On second thoughts . . .

'Genius is one per cent inspiration, 99 per cent perspiration'

~ THOMAS EDISON (1903)

WHICH READS BETTER: 'Just at the selfsame beat of Time's wide wings' or 'Upon that very point of winged time'? John Keats eventually plumped for the former as the first line of the second canto of his unfinished poem *Hyperion*, and most readers would, I imagine, agree that he made the right choice. So, surely, did Wordsworth, when he preferred 'I wandered lonely as a cloud' to 'I wandered like a lonely cloud', as the opening line of *Daffodils*, one of his best-loved poems. Manuscripts in the Library show precisely how the two poets changed their minds in the course of composition – although in Wordsworth's case the variant is in his wife Mary's handwriting, so it is possible that she initially made an error of transcription.

Even with the expansion of its functions in recent years, a core mission of the British Library remains that of safeguarding the nation's literary heritage. This it does by storing the books and journals that spill out from the minds of writers and, equally important, by recording the mechanics of the often punishing creative process. Among its

To the Printer 80
After the Poem (in the set under the title of "Moods of my own mind") beginning "The Cock is crowing" Please to insert the two following properly numbered & number the succeeding ones accordingly

~~I wandered like a~~

I wandered lonely as a Cloud
That floats on high o'er Vales and Hills,
When all at once I saw a crowd
A host of dancing Daffodils;
Along the Lake beneath the trees
Ten thousand dancing in the breeze.

The Waves beside them danced, but they
Outdid the sparkling Waves in glee—
A Poet could not but be gay
In such a laughing company:
I gaz'd—and gaz'd—but little thought
What wealth the shew to me had brought.

For oft when on my Couch I lie
In vacant or in pensive mood,
They flash upon that inward eye
Which is the bliss of solitude
And then my heart with pleasure fills,
And dances with the Daffodils.

Who fancied what a pretty sight
This Rock would be if edged around
With living Snowdrops? circlet bright!

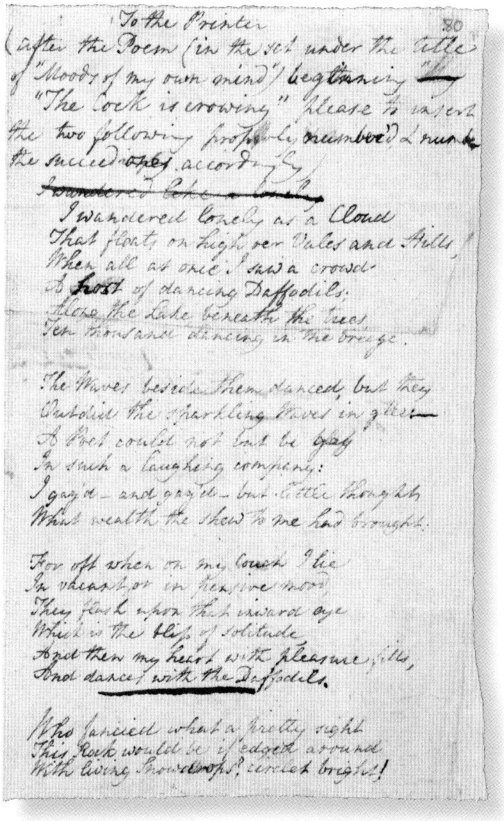

OPPOSITE
John Keats began to write his epic poem *Hyperion* in 1818, when he was 23. He abandoned it the following year, after he recognised the early symptoms of consumption – the disease from which he died in 1821. This is the first page of the manuscript, the many alterations indicating that he was struggling to find the right tone. Possibly this was why he failed to complete the poem, regarding it as a failure.

LEFT
Manuscript of Wordsworth's *Daffodils*, 1804.

RIGHT

Map of Coleridge's walks in the
Lake District, from one of his
notebooks, 1802.

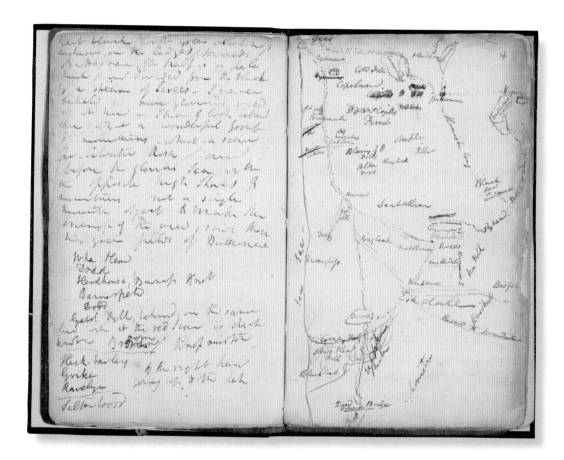

RIGHT

Map of Coleridge's walks in the
Lake District, from one of his
notebooks, 1802.

holdings are many autograph manuscripts showing the changes made before the final version was arrived at, sometimes with revealing notes scribbled in the margins. These are supported by letters and notebooks that give additional insights into the mood and intentions of writers struggling to bring their ideas to life. It all amounts to a virtual history of English literature.

The Keats material is rich and revealing. His *Hyperion* manuscript is scarred with words and lines that have been scratched out and replaced or restructured. Near the end of the second canto, the original

> Till suddenly a full-blown splendour fell'd
> Those native spaces of oblivion …

is amended and expanded thus:

> Till suddenly a splendour, like the morn,
> Pervaded all the beetling gloomy steeps,
> All the sad spaces of oblivion…

And in the second line of the third canto,

> Amazed were those Titans utterly,

Keats originally described the Titans as 'perplexed' – an alteration perhaps made to avoid repetition, since 'perplexed' occurs a few lines later on.

Then there are his touching letters to his younger sister Fanny. One was written when he had just finished writing *Endymion*, while she was at a boarding school. In it he declares that he wants to 'not only as you grow up love you as my only sister, but confide in you as my dearest friend'. He goes on: 'Perhaps you might like to know what I am writing about – I will tell you. Many years ago, there was a young, handsome shepherd who fed his flocks on a mountainside called Latmus. He was a very contemplative sort of a person and lived solitary among the trees and plains, little thinking that such a beautiful creature as the moon was growing mad in love with him.'

The Romantic poets are strongly represented in the Library's extensive collections of autograph manuscripts and letters. A large quantity of material relating to Samuel Taylor Coleridge was presented in 1951 by the Pilgrim Trust and has since been augmented. The 1951 acquisition included 55 of the poet's notebooks, containing jottings of ideas for poems and plays along with a description of a journey to Mount Etna in Sicily and maps that detail his exploration of some of the less accessible Lake District fells.

The Library also has a commonplace book in which Coleridge recorded his thoughts on religion, morals, literature and the events of the day, along with apt quotations from writers he admired. Here is an observation made in Bristol, where he was lecturing in 1813: 'People starved into war – over an enlisting place in Bristol, a quarter of lamb and a piece of beef hung up'. And this aphorism: 'When a man is attempting to describe another's character he may be right or he may be wrong, but in one thing he will always succeed – in describing himself'. There are jokes, too. After writing down a recipe for a seemingly disgusting wine (water, sugar, ginger, lemons and yeast) he adds a further 'Receipt for brewing wine: Get two strong faithful men bring proper instruments … break into a wine merchant's cellar and carry off a hogshead of best claret'. Some notes appear to be hastily recorded ideas for possible future poems or plays: 'A country fellow in a village inn, winter night, tells a long story – all attentive (except one fellow, who is toying with the maid). The countryman introduces some circumstance absolutely incompatible with a prior one – the amoroso detects it…'

Further aspects of Coleridge and his contemporaries are revealed in other parts of the manuscript collections. For lovers of literature who harbour a curiosity about the private lives of its practitioners, and of their contemporaries in other fields of endeavour, there are few greater delights than leafing through one of the many books of miscellaneous letters and papers, often collected by enthusiasts and bequeathed to the Library or sold on by their heirs. There is invariably some enchanting quirk or serendipitous insight just a few pages away.

Lady Charnwood assiduously amassed a fine haul of correspondence from A-list authors in the first half of the twentieth century, now bound together in eight volumes. At random, I chose to browse the volume identified prosaically in the catalogue as Additional Manuscript 70949. Here is Coleridge, in a letter to a friend in 1827, giving vent to authors' perennial complaints about the press: 'I could write a most edifying article on the effect and influence of newspapers on the intellectual and moral character of the English, especially of artists and authors.' He goes on to write of 'malignant slanderers' retailing 'some half-fact' that translates into 'a whole lie, and of the most fiendish character'. Like many represented in that volume, Coleridge takes a close interest in his health. He writes from Highgate in 1829, five years before his death, explaining to the librarian at the University of London that he had not appeared there as expected because of 'derangement of the bronchia with cough and excessive expectoration … accompanied with a depression so completely incapacitating me from all library effort'.

Ten years earlier Shelley, writing to his friend Leigh Hunt from Livorno, shared Coleridge's low opinion of the press: 'Ollier tells me that the *Quarterly* are going to review me. I suppose it will be a pretty morsel and as I am acquiring a taste for humour and drollery I confess I am anxious to see it.' As for health, it was not any symptoms of his own but the pregnancy of his wife Mary that was concerning him: 'One of our motives in going to Florence is to have the attendance of Mr. Bell, a famous Scotch surgeon. … I should feel some disquietude at entrusting her to the best of the Italian practitioners. The birth of a child will probably relieve her from some part of her present melancholy depression.'

The theme of ill-health is ubiquitous. James Boswell tells an acquaintance in 1790 that he fears his son might be suffering from chincough (whooping cough) because he has never previously had it. Horace Walpole, writing from Strawberry Hill in Twickenham in 1770, excuses a late reply to a letter on the grounds of 'a third fit of the gout in my left arm and hand', which made it hard for him to hold down the paper. The main purpose of that letter was to propose a bizarre scheme to organise a poetry competition in conjunction with a race meeting, 'to ennoble our horse racing, particularly at Newmarket, by associating better arts with the courses'.

The volume includes two telling items on the economics of authorship: a receipt from Oliver Goldsmith and a letter from Jane Austen. Goldsmith acknowledges a payment of 'five guineas for writing a short English grammar', while Austen writes in 1815 to her niece Caroline: 'I have just received nearly twenty pounds myself on the second edition of S and S [*Sense and Sensibility*], which gives me this fine flow of literary ardour.' That fine flow led to the publication the following year of *Persuasion*, the only one of her novels of which the Library has a portion of the autograph manuscript.

According to Robert Southey, the chance of earning anything at all from literary endeavour

BELOW
The heavily corrected
manuscript of Sir Thomas
Wyatt's poem on 'wrathfull love',
c. 1537–42.

is remote. Writing in 1839 to a Miss Nicholls of Islington, who has asked him to read her poems and recommend them to a publisher, he warns her, elegantly but unambiguously: 'You know not, Madam, of how little avail among publishers the opinion of an old author is in behalf of a young one; and how useless any opinion would be that the most experienced writer could give. It rarely happens in these times that a volume of poems obtains sale enough to cover the expenses, and authors who venture to publish at their own expense pay dearly for the disappointment which they are sure to meet with.'

On a more upbeat note, the volume includes two of the several manuscripts of Edward Lear's nonsense poems in the Library's possession. One is the comic but bleak *Lays of the Octapods*, with a few corrections, chiefly to improve the metre. The other is a characteristic limerick, with an appropriate illustration:

> There was an old man on a bicycle
> Whose nose was adorn'd with an icicle,
> But they said 'If you stop
> It will certainly drop
> And abolish both you and your bicycle'.

Among the earliest surviving autograph manuscripts with significant alterations is a love poem by the Tudor poet and courtier Sir Thomas Wyatt. There are crossings-out in each of its four verses, most of them so thorough that it is impossible to discern

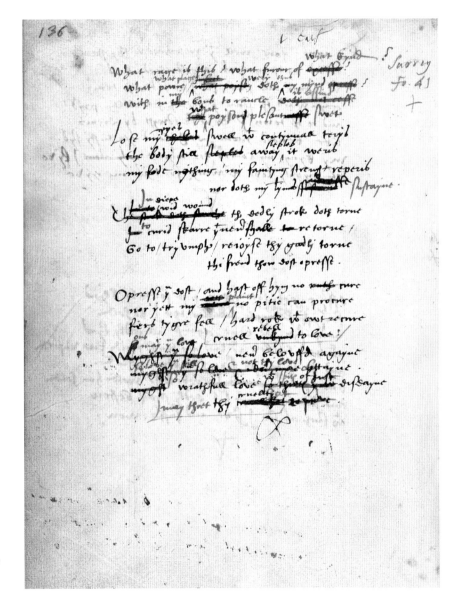

with confidence what his first thoughts were. None of the original manuscripts of Shakespeare's plays has been traced, probably because they disintegrated after heavy use by a succession of Elizabethan and Jacobean actors. All that the Library has in his handwriting is a signature on a mortgage deed, plus three pages from *The Play of Sir Thomas More* – a collaborative work from early in his career – that some believe to be in Shakespeare's hand. If so, the pages show that even the impeccable bard would alter or ruthlessly delete passages if he thought he had not got them quite right the first time. The manuscript of a play by Philip Massinger, a prolific contemporary, was discovered in a pile of rubbish in 1844. It is called *Believe as you List*, and in the margin the playwright has scribbled some stage directions: 'Enter taylor's wife, brown bread and a wooden dish of water'.

Autograph manuscripts by Ben Jonson, Shakespeare's fervent admirer, are almost as rare as those of Shakespeare himself: his personal papers were destroyed in a fire in his apartment in 1623. His fair copy of *The Masque of Queens,* written in 1608, escaped the blaze because soon after its performance Jonson had presented it to Prince Henry, the ill-fated eldest son of James I, and it was thus incorporated into the Royal Library. An accompanying dedication from the author heaps praise on the Prince, and is signed off thus: 'By the most true admirer of your Highness's virtues and most hearty celebrater of them, Ben Jonson.'

One of Jonson's most enthusiastic followers was Robert Herrick, who again is represented by only a single literary autograph – a poem he wrote when a Cambridge undergraduate, lamenting the death of John Browne, a leading figure at the university:

> For is there nothing can withstand
> The hand
> Of time, but that it must
> Be shaken into dust.

If the personal memorabilia of early Stuart writers are thin on the ground, that is not the case with the leading literary figure of the succeeding generation, the poet John Milton. Coleridge admired Milton, although he found his writings challenging, according to this entry in his commonplace book: 'A reader of Milton must be always on his duty: he is surrounded with sense; it rises in every line; every word is to the purpose. There are no lazy intervals: all has been considered.' Milton's own commonplace book is among the Library's holdings: a collection of profound thoughts and quotations, many in Latin, about governance and religion – although there are no quotations from the Bible. It spans the period from 1630, when Milton was 22, to 1650, when he held an administrative position in Oliver Cromwell's Commonwealth. Although he is counted a supporter of the Lord Protector, the entry illustrated opposite suggests ambiguity:

'The form of state is to be fitted to the people's disposition. Some live best under monarchy, others otherwise – which was the error of the noble Brutus

Milton's commonplace book, 1630–50.

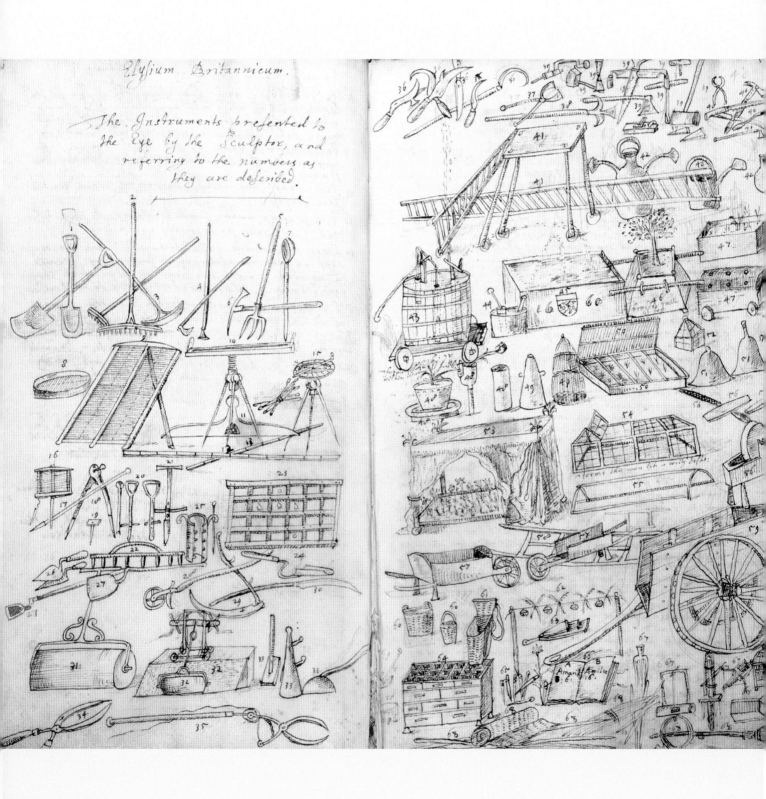

Elysium Britannicum.

The Instruments presented to
the Eye by the Sculptor, and
referring to the numbers as
they are described.

and Cassius who felt themselves of spirit to free a nation but considered not that the nation was not fit to be free. … They became slaves to their own ambition and luxury.'

John Dryden was another disciple of Cromwell, or at least for as long as such a stance seemed politic. The Library has the autograph manuscript of his *Heroic Stanzas*, written to commemorate the Protector after his death in 1658:

> His grandeur he derived from Heav'n above,
> For he was great ere fortune made him so,
> And wars, like mists that rise against the sun,
> Made him but greater seem, not greater grow.

However, after the Restoration of Charles II, echoing the Vicar of Bray, Dryden would write just as favourably of the new King.

Samuel Butler, on the other hand, was a consistently committed Royalist. The eponymous subject of his most famous poem, *Hudibras*, published after the Restoration, is a greedy and pompous colonel in Cromwell's army, whose 'brain outweigh'd his rage but half a grain'. He is also an extreme Presbyterian:

> For he was of that stubborn crew
> Of errant saints, whom all men grant
> To be the true Church Militant;
> Such as do build their faith upon
> The holy text of pike and gun;
> Decide all controversies by
> Infallible artillery.

The long poem – the Library has only part of the manuscript – was widely admired. Voltaire said he had 'never found so much wit in one single book'. Butler introduced phrases and concepts that remain current today, such as 'whys and wherefores', 'looking a gift horse in the mouth' and 'making the fur fly'. Another original saying was 'spare the rod and spoil the child', although the meaning was not as straightforward as it seems. The context makes clear that he was using the child as a metaphor for making love, and the phrase can perhaps be read as an argument for masochism or flagellation.

Not all seventeenth-century literature was about politics or religion. The diarist John Evelyn, whose archive was bought by the Library in 1995, had an impressively wide range of interests. The archive includes the original manuscript of his *Diary* along with extensive correspondence, including letters from such figures as his fellow-diarist Samuel Pepys, the carver Grinling Gibbons and Sir Christopher Wren. The manuscripts include a number of unpublished works, notably *Elysium Britannicum*, which would have been one of the earliest gardening manuals had it ever been published; but it exists only in manuscript form. Evelyn illustrated it with detailed drawings of recommended tools, some of them very like those in use today.

Gardening has been and remains a perennial theme of English literature. A century after Evelyn,

✤ OPPOSITE
John Evelyn (1620–1706) is best known as a diarist, contemporary with Samuel Pepys; but he was also a keen gardener and his archive contains the manuscript and pen-and-ink illustrations for an unpublished book about gardening, *Elysium Britannicum*. On this page he has drawn a selection of garden tools and features, some of them familiar to us today. The four-poster 'flower bed', halfway down the right-hand page, appears to be a visual pun.

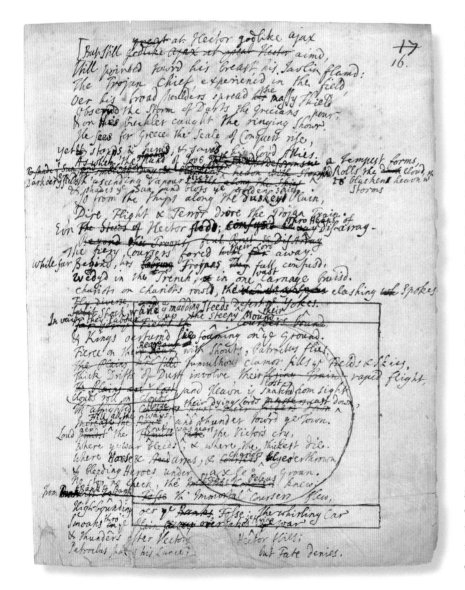

Rev. Gilbert White was an influential and much admired naturalist: his garden at Selborne in Hampshire remains a place of pilgrimage to this day. The Library has manuscripts of his annual *Garden-Kalendar* and later the *Naturalist's Journal*, covering between them the years 1751 to 1793. They contain meticulous descriptions of his gardening techniques, as well as notes on agriculture, natural history and the weather. White's calling as a clergyman is recorded in the autograph manuscript of a sermon on the text, 'For Godly sorrow worketh repentence to Salvation' (2 Cor. 7:10). He wrote it in about 1757, and the text is accompanied by a list of the places where he delivered it between then and 1792.

An earlier gardening enthusiast was Alexander Pope. Paper was expensive in the eighteenth century and the writers of that period would often use the backs of letters and other documents for their jottings. One particular page of Pope's draft for his translation of Homer's *Iliad*, bequeathed to the Museum as early as 1766, has been put to three separate uses. He composed the lines in 1720 on the reverse of a letter from the Duchess of Hamilton, then superimposed a geometrical pattern that appears to be a design for a flower bed in the garden of his new villa at Twickenham, which was occupying his mind at the same time. The detail of the translation reveals an author grappling to come up with the most telling form of words. His first draft of two lines went:

BELOW
One of Swift's letters to
'Vanessa', dated August 1714.

Swift o'er the fosse the immortal courses flew,
High-bounding o'er ye banks. The whirling car…

He adjusted this to read:

From bank to bank the immortal courses flew,
High-bounding o'er ye fosse. The whirling car…

The most fascinating surviving papers of Jonathan Swift, a close friend of Pope, are not drafts of his literary works but his letters to two women. Coincidentally both were called Esther, although he devised pet names for them. Esther Johnson, the daughter of a servant at the house where, as a young man, he was employed as a secretary, was his 'Stella'. They met in 1689, when she was eight, and remained close until her death in 1729, although precisely how close has not been definitively established. Esther Vanhomrigh, a later acquaintance, was 'Vanessa', contrived from the first letters of her surname and Christian name. A set of 65 letters that he wrote to Stella between 1710 and 1713 were published as *The Journal to Stella* in 1766, and a third of the originals are held by the Library. Although they contain much about high Tory politics, in which Swift was deeply involved, they are strewn with coy intimacies: he addresses Stella as his 'poo poo ppt' – poor poor poppet – and his already cramped writing tends to get smaller as he indulges in such nursery banter.

The 44 letters to Vanessa cover the period from 1711 to 1722, the year before she died. Some of them suggest that Swift was more than a little embarrassed by their relationship. One, dated 1714, written just before he was about to leave for Ireland, says that if he writes to her 'it will be always under a cover', and if she replies she should 'write nothing that is particular, but which may be seen, for I apprehend letters will be opened and inconveniences will happen'. Her reaction to these warnings was to stop writing and follow him to Ireland: not the outcome he sought or appeared to welcome.

Letters from authors' friends and acquaintances, written to third parties, can provide valuable insights into their character and state of mind. In 1756 Catherine Talbot visited the novelist Samuel Richardson, then 67, at his villa in Parsons Green. She wrote to a friend: 'Those who only know Mr. Richardson as an author do not know the most amiable part of his character. The villa is fitted up in the same style his books are writ. Every minute detail attended to, yet every one with a view to its being useful or pleasing. … One always sees there a succession of young women, and exceedingly elegant, well behaved, sensible young women, who improve and entertain his daughters … and every one calls him Papa.'

Another eighteenth-century novelist, Laurence Sterne, best known for *Tristram Shandy*, is represented in the Library by the manuscript of volume one of his last work, *A Sentimental Journey Through France and Italy*. Written in 1768, the year of his death, it is the earliest autograph manuscript

◆ BELOW
The beginning of the manuscript of Blake's epic poem *The Four Zoas*, including a drawing of the Goddess Vala, 1797.

of a novel among the Library's holdings. Although this seems to have been the copy that Sterne gave to the printer, it still contains a number of small, last-minute alterations and insertions.

Two highly valued literary manuscripts from the late eighteenth century, both now accessible digitally on *Turning the Pages* and online, are William Blake's notebook and Jane Austen's *The History of England from the Reign of Henry IV to the Death of Charles I*. Blake's book is full of surprises, both in the text and the many fine, powerful sketches. On a page marked 'Ideas' he has drawn a woman undressing to share a bed with a man, below which is the odd verse:

> When a man has married a wife
> He finds out whether
> Her knees and elbows are only
> Glassed together

On facing pages of the notebook, pages 29 and 30, are two versions of Blake's best-known poem, *The Tyger* ('Tyger! Tyger! Burning bright…'), written in 1794. The one on the left-hand page contains significant corrections, with some lines eliminated totally. That on the right is the final version, though without the fourth and fifth stanzas. Another important Blake manuscript in the Library is *The Four Zoas*, again interspersed with wonderfully atmospheric drawings.

While the portion of autograph manuscript of *Persuasion* is the most important of the Library's

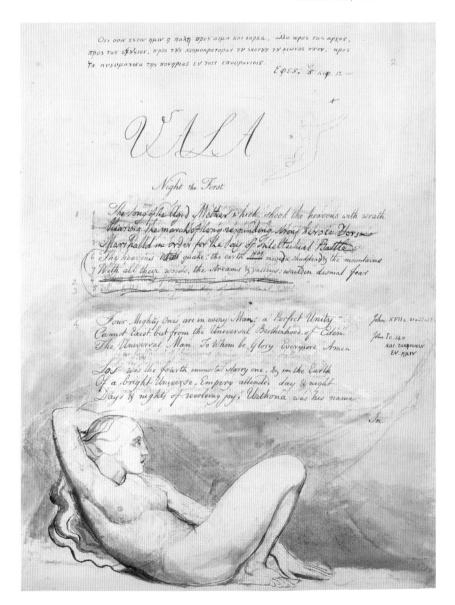

disgrace to humanity, that pest of society, Eliza-
-beth. Many were the people who fell Marty
to the protestant Religion during her reign;
I suppose not fewer than a dozen. She ma
-ried Philip King of Spain who in her Sisters
reign for famous for building Armadas. She died
without issue, & then the dreadful moment came
in which the destroyer of all comfort, the deceitful
Betrayer of trust reposed in her, & the Murderess of
her Cousin succeeded to the Throne. ——

Elizabeth ———

Elizabeth

Mary Q. of Scots

OPPOSITE

In 1791, when she was 15, Jane Austen wrote 'The History of England from the reign of Henry the 4th to the death of Charles the 1st. By a partial, prejudiced and ignorant Historian.' It was a witty parody of the current standard history books and has something in common

with *1066 and All That*, written 140 years later by W.C. Sellar and R.J. Yeatman. This is her autograph manuscript with roundel illustrations by her sister Cassandra.

BELOW

Charlotte Brontë's fair copy of *Jane Eyre*, 1847.

holdings relating directly to Jane Austen's novels, her *History of England* is a delight. The work is notable for a passionate defence of Mary Queen of Scots, whose execution was 'to the everlasting reproach of Elizabeth, her ministers and of England in general'. Indeed, Jane was impressed by all the Stuarts, remarking that she 'cannot help liking' James I and describing the ill-fated Charles I as an 'amiable monarch'. The work ends with a mellifluous dedication to her cousin: 'I commend to your charitable criticism this clever collection of curious comments which have been carefully culled, collected and classed by your comical cousin.'

Were there an award for the outstanding female novelist of the nineteenth century, Charlotte Brontë and George Eliot would vie with Jane Austen for the honour. The Library has a rich collection of autograph material relating to Charlotte and her sisters Emily and Anne, including drafts of novels and poems, as well as notebooks filled with childhood stories, verses and drawings. Most prized among them is the fair copy (the final manuscript) of *Jane Eyre*, Charlotte's best-known work, published in 1847. Although it was the second novel she wrote it was the first to be published. The manuscript is tidy and well set out, with few corrections: most of her significant second thoughts must have been incorporated into earlier drafts. There are some subtle changes, though. For instance, when Mr Rochester proposes to Jane, she asks him emotionally: 'Are you in earnest? Do you truly love me? Do you sincerely want me to be your wife?' That is the final form: originally the third question, neatly struck out, had a lot less resonance: 'Do you sincerely want me to marry you?'

George Eliot, on her death in 1879, bequeathed fair copies of most of her novels and poems to the British Museum. She had originally given them to the man who shared her life and at the beginning of *Adam Bede*, her first important work, there is a touching dedication to him: 'To my dear husband, George Henry Lewes, I give this ms. of a work which would never have been written but for the happiness which his love has conferred on my life. Marian Lewes. March 23, 1859.' Although she described him as her husband and assumed his surname they never married, because he already had a wife.

In 2000 the Library enhanced its material on Charles Dickens by acquiring about 300 letters and documents, many illustrating his often fraught relations with his publishers. It has no complete manuscript of any of his novels: in this category the holding is limited to only 22 heavily corrected leaves of Chapter 15 of *Nicholas Nickleby*. In it he has incorporated a letter supposedly written by Fanny Squeers, daughter of the headmaster of Dotheboys Hall, which he has amended to introduce the kind of spelling and grammatical errors that such a girl might be expected to make – 'nevew' for 'nephew' and 'took up by some stage-coach' instead of 'taken up…'.

Thomas Hardy was just as concerned to get the idiom of his characters right and his manuscript of *Tess of the d'Urbervilles* is as rich in second thoughts as Dickens's manuscripts. In one passage he converts standard English into West Country dialect. 'A show of himself' becomes 'A mommet of himself' and 'I want to tell her what has happened' is changed to ' … what *have* happened'. The Library also has Hardy's draft of his poignant 1926 poem, *A Reconsideration on my 80th Birthday*. In it, he changes the end of the first verse from:

> Never, I own, expected I
> A smooth life-thoroughfare.

to

> Never, I own, expected I
> That life would all be fair.

The papers of Hardy's prolific contemporary, Rudyard Kipling are scattered among institutions on both sides of the Atlantic. The Library has three important manuscripts – of *Kim, The Jungle Book* and *Just So Stories*, the latter including the author's own charming illustrations. The first two were bequeathed to the British Museum by his widow Caroline in 1939, together with manuscripts of poems and other writings covering the years 1900 to 1923. The manuscript of *Just So Stories* was bequeathed to the Library by his daughter, Elsie Bambridge, in 1976.

In 1925 Kipling had himself presented some of his autograph manuscripts to the British Museum

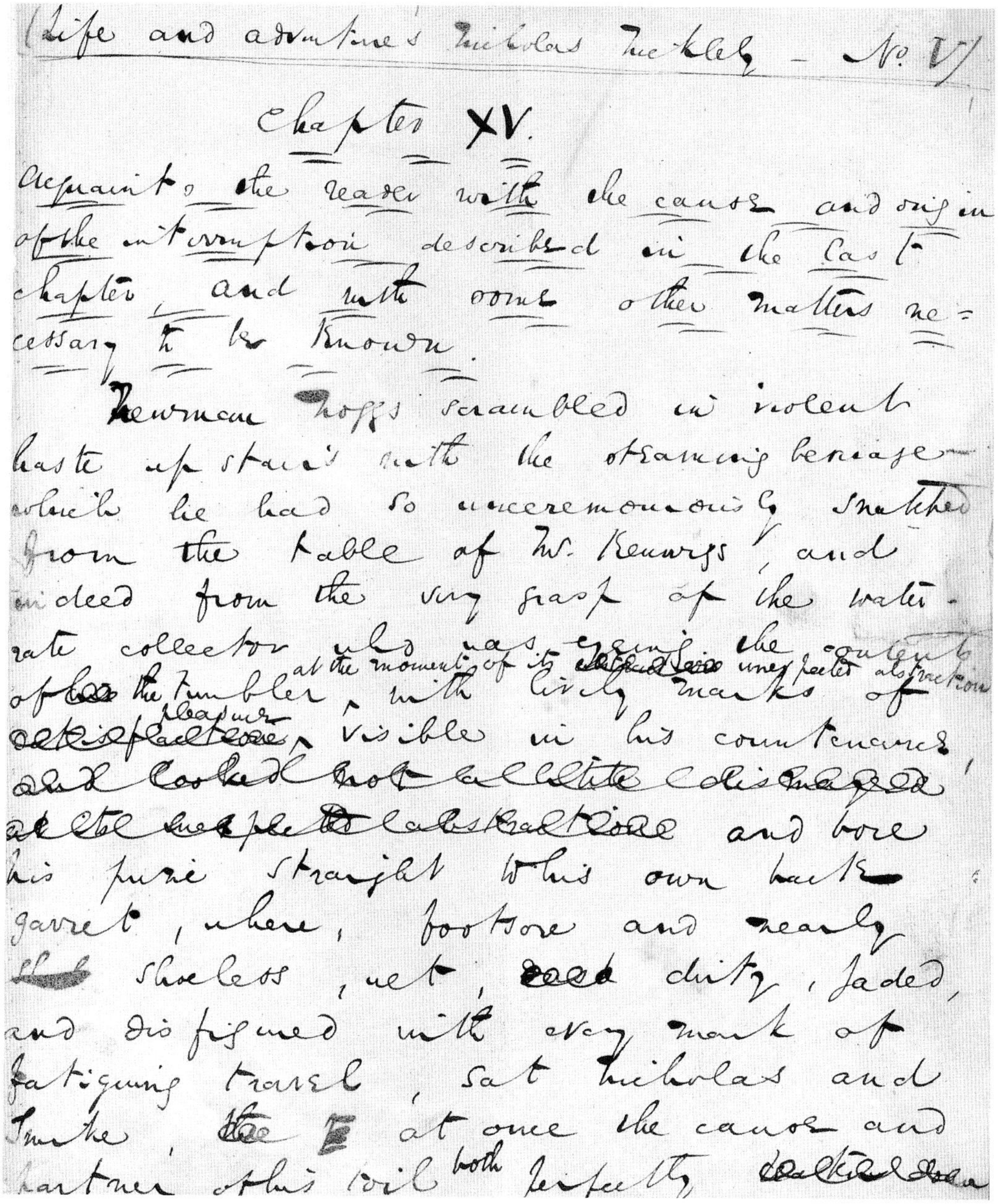

(Life and adventures Nicholas Nickleby – No. V)

Chapter XV.

Acquaints the reader with the cause and origin of the interruption described in the last chapter, and with some other matters necessary to be known.

Newman Noggs scrambled in violent haste up stairs with the steaming beverage which he had so unceremoniously snatched from the table of Mr. Kenwigs, and indeed from the very grasp of the water-rate collector who was eyeing the contents of the tumbler at the moment of its unexpected abstraction with lively marks of pleasure visible in his countenance, and bore his prize straight to his own back garret, where, footsore and nearly shoeless, wet, dirty, jaded, and disfigured with every mark of fatiguing travel, sat Nicholas and Smike, at once the cause and partner of his toil both perfectly

LEFT

A page of Dickens's manuscript of *Nicholas Nickleby*, 1838.

on condition that they should not be made available to researchers until after his death, which occurred eleven years later. Among other Kipling material in the Library is a draft of his poem *After*, written in July 1897 and published in *The Times* under the title *Recessional*. The poem is best known for the moving line 'Lest we forget—lest we forget!'). In the printed version of the work the final line reads: 'Thy mercy on Thy people, Lord', while in the original manuscript Kipling has struck out 'on Thy people' and changed it to 'and forgiveness', an amendment which would seem to have been subsequently dropped.

In 1999 an extraordinary discovery about an admired writer was made within a bundle of letters that had been in the Museum's and then the Library's possession since 1948. They were deposited by the sister of Phyllis Gardner, an art student who had a short but intense and secret love affair with Rupert Brooke, the young poet who died during the First World War. The parcel, donated on condition that it should not be opened for 50 years, contained about 50 love letters from the poet to Phyllis, as well as her 90-page narrative of their relationship, written after his death.

She tells how she had noticed him on a train from London to Cambridge and, struck by his good looks, drew a sketch and asked her Cambridge friends if they recognised who it might be. When she found out she bearded him at Grantchester and they began a relationship, although by her account she resisted his attempts at seduction: that is perhaps why he ended the affair before going off to war. Among the letters is his poem, *Beauty and Beauty*, clearly written for her:

> When Beauty and Beauty meet
> All naked, fair to fair,
> The earth is crying-sweet,
> And scattering-bright the air,
> Eddying, dizzying, closing round,
> With soft and drunken laughter;
> Veiling all that may befall
> After — after —

Phyllis never married, devoting her life instead to breeding Irish wolfhounds until her death, aged 49, in 1939.

Before those letters were discovered, it had been assumed that Brooke wrote *Beauty and Beauty* for a male friend. So letters and personal documents can alter profoundly our interpretation of works of literature: the most vital reason why, over the years, the British Library has been assiduous in collecting and preserving them.

∾ OPPOSITE

Rudyard Kipling provided his own illustrations for the original edition of the *Just So Stories*, published in 1902. One of the best known is this pen and ink drawing from *The Elephant's Child*, relating how the young elephant's trunk became elongated during a tussle with a crocodile. Before the encounter, Kipling relates, the elephant 'had only a blackish, bulgy nose, as big as a boot, that he could wriggle about from side to side; but he could not pick up things with it.' When he and the other elephants discovered how useful a trunk could be, they decided to adopt it.

we shall stick it out—
to the end but we
are getting weaker if
course and the end
cannot be far

It seems a pity but—
I do not think I can
write more—

R Scott

Last Entry—

For Gods sake look
after our people

CHAPTER 8

Making history

‘Events, dear boy, events.’

~ ATTRIBUTED TO HAROLD MACMILLAN
(1894–1986)

THERE IS MORE TO LIFE than literature. The British Library contains a wealth of documents that mark crucial events in the country's political and social history. Chief among them is *Magna Carta*, commonly regarded as the foundation stone of British democracy in that it imposed limits on the hitherto unfettered power of the crown. The Library has two of the four copies that survive from its original promulgation in 1215. Written on parchment in Latin, both came to the British Museum from the Cotton collection, though sadly one is now barely legible.

There is, too, the unique manuscript of the Articles of the Barons, the original demands that were incorporated into the charter, with its authentic seal. Accepted by King John under pressure at Runnymede, the charter contained so many clauses hedging his power – in effect decreeing that he could do nothing without the barons' approval – that he repudiated it within a month, sparking civil war. That he had influential support is confirmed by a letter from the Pope, customarily displayed alongside the charters, denouncing the attempt to limit the King's powers.

A manuscript of the revised, shorter version of *Magna Carta*, promulgated in 1225 under Henry III, was presented to the Museum in 1946 by Matilda Talbot, the former owner of Lacock Abbey in

OPPOSITE
One of the Library's most moving documents is the diary of Captain Scott, describing his disastrous expedition to the South Pole. He and his men reached the Pole in January 1912 but found that the rival Norwegian expedition had beaten them to it. This is the last entry he was strong enough to write: 'For God's sake look after our people' (see page 163).

BELOW
One of the Library's two copies of *Magna Carta*, 1215.

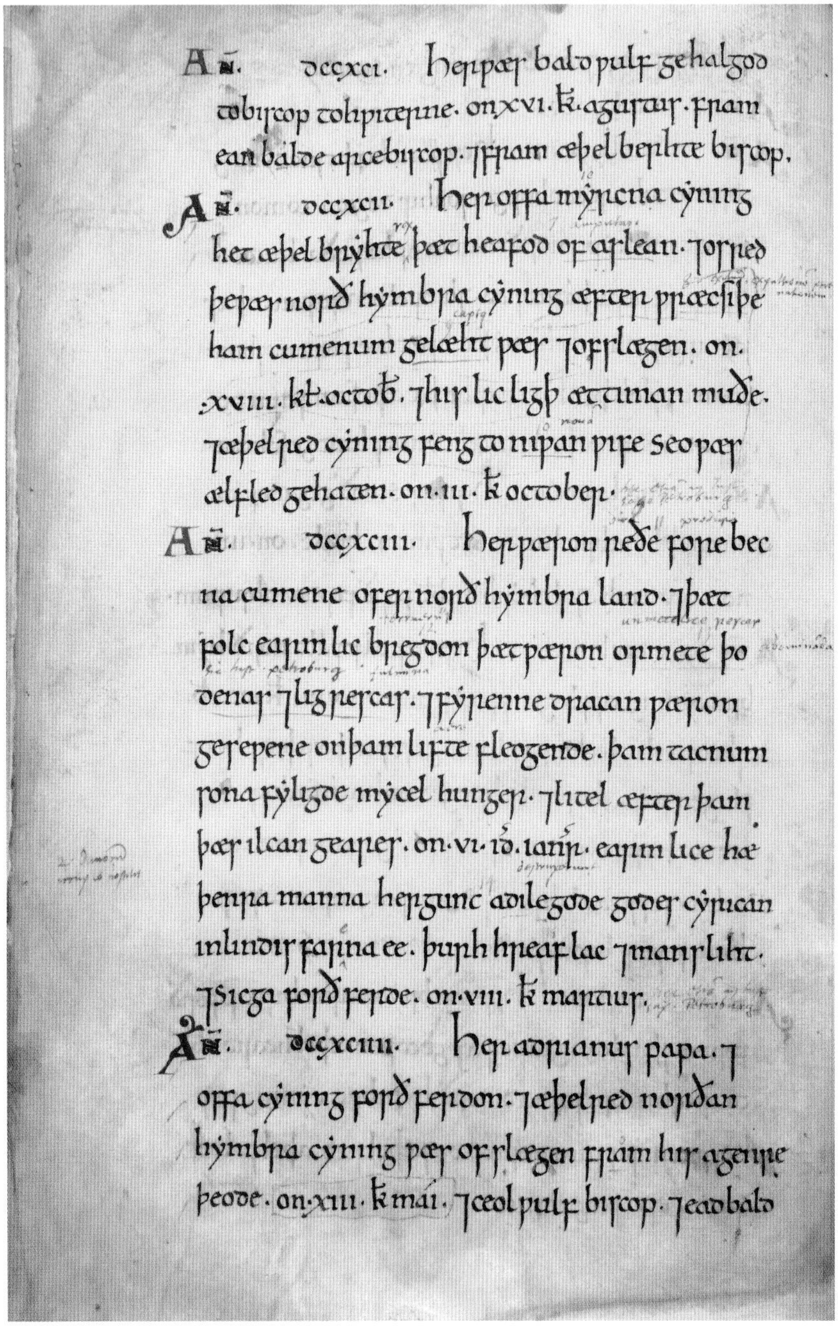

Wiltshire. The Abbey was founded in the early thirteenth century by Ela, Countess of Salisbury, whose husband William Longespee, the illegitimate son of Henry II, had been at Runnymede when the charter was sworn. Although shorn of the specific restraints on royal power, the later version retained the crucial principle for which *Magna Carta* is now best known:

'No free man shall be seized or imprisoned, or stripped of his rights or possessions, or outlawed or exiled, nor will we proceed with force against him, except by the lawful judgement of his equals or by the law of the land. To no one will we sell, to no one deny or delay right or justice.'

That affirmation of a person's right to freedom from arbitrary arrest and to trial by his equals is the basis not only of Britain's observance of human rights and the rule of law, but has also been an inspiration for key clauses in the American Bill of Rights and the Universal Declaration of Human Rights.

❀   ❀   ❀

Among the Library's earliest historical manuscripts are five copies, some incomplete, of the *Anglo-Saxon Chronicle*, the history of Britain between 60 BC and about AD 890, when the first version of the document was written during the reign of Alfred the Great. Covering a broader range of events than Bede's *Ecclesiastical History of the English People* (described in Chapter 5), it was distributed to

↦ RIGHT

A section of the *Genealogical Chronicle of the English Kings*, compiled about 1300.

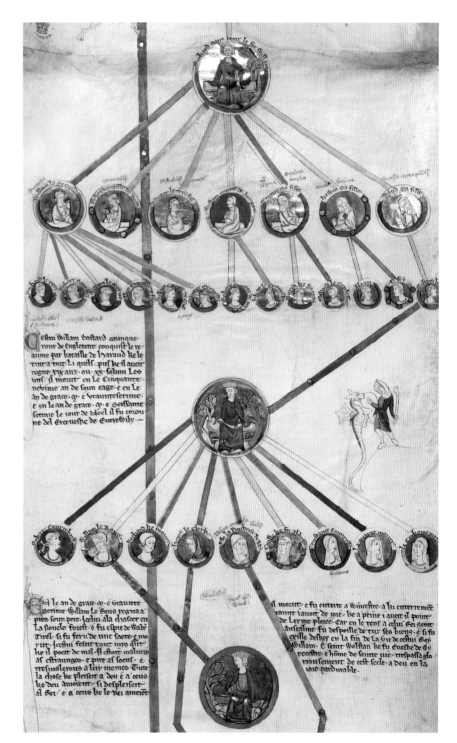

↦ RIGHT

A section of the *Genealogical Chronicle of the English Kings*, compiled about 1300.

monasteries, where scribes updated it until the middle of the twelfth century.

The power of the monasteries in the Anglo-Saxon and medieval periods was reflected in their large holdings of land, recorded in charters. The Library has a significant collection of them. The *Codex Wintoniensis* is a book of charters relating to the land acquisitions of Winchester Cathedral, founded as a monastery in the seventh century. Written in Latin and Old English, they date from 688 to the twelfth century, when the collection was probably compiled. Other Anglo-Saxon charters include a set from Evesham Abbey, founded in 700.

Some of the finest historical manuscripts were commissioned by monarchs to strengthen their claims to the throne. A parchment roll dating from around 1300 provides an illustrated genealogy of English kings, starting from Anglo-Saxon times, designed to show the legitimacy of the descendants of William the Conqueror – here given his earlier, less flattering soubriquet of William the Bastard.

The divide between history and literature is straddled by manuscripts that recount the story of King Arthur and the Knights of the Round Table, much of it surely legend. A lovely fourteenth-century copy of the French *Lancelot du Lac* is among the Royal manuscripts, having once belonged to Mary Bohun, wife of Henry IV. Better known is the unique manuscript of Sir Thomas Malory's *Morte d'Arthur*, written while he

Sir Thomas Malory's manuscript
of *Morte d'Arthur*, 1470.

was imprisoned in 1470. Malory was a Member of Parliament who became an outlaw, stealing sheep and cattle and robbing people with violence. He twice escaped from jail and fought for the Yorkists in the Wars of the Roses, before switching to the Lancastrians.

The Library is especially rich in documents that relate directly to the events and key personalities of the Tudor period. An account of the death of Henry VII in 1509 by Sir Thomas Wriothesley, Garter King of Arms, is illustrated with a picture of the deathbed scene, the fading King surrounded by his senior courtiers. A recent acquisition is an illuminated medieval prayer roll that belonged to Henry VIII before his accession and contains rare examples of his handwriting in that period. That it was once owned by him is confirmed by the appearance of his royal symbols at the top of the roll, including the Prince of Wales crowned ostrich feather. It shows that 25 years before his falling out with the Roman Catholic Church he was a devoted participant in its rituals. Not that he was any less pious after he had declared himself head of the Church of England. A psalter presented to him in 1540 by Jean Mallard, a poet and painter from Rouen, and dedicated by him to 'the most invincible King of England and France', contains marginal comments in the King's hand, in one of which he compares himself to the biblical King David. The book includes a portrait by Mallard of Henry with his jester, William Sommer.

The 'Great Matter' that initiated the rift with Rome was the King's desire to divorce Catherine of Aragon because of her failure to produce a male heir, and the whole painful process can be followed through documents in the Library. There is a poignant letter written to Thomas Wolsey in June 1518, in which Henry gives the news that Catherine is pregnant and that although it was not 'an ensured thing' he had 'great hope and likelihoods' of a

favourable result. In the event the child was stillborn.

When the British Museum inherited the Royal Library there came with it several books and manuscripts that Henry had garnered to support the argument that his marriage was never truly valid – because Catherine had been married previously to his late brother – as well as his claim to be the rightful head of the English Church. He prepared his case with immense diligence, getting officials and scholars to scour religious houses for any texts that might be useful, and to list them. The Library has the only one of those lists to have survived, *Tabula librorum de histories antiquitatum*, giving the titles of nearly a hundred books in monasteries in Lincolnshire: 37 are marked with a cross to signify that the King wanted to appropriate them. Henry made notes in the margins of some books, emphasising points that supported his case.

In 1530 his researchers presented Henry with a document called *Collectanea satis copiosa* (Sufficiently abundant collections), a digest of all the relevant manuscripts they had discovered, from which they had concluded that the King had supreme authority over both church and state. Henry was delighted and again wrote comments in the margins pointing out the most significant arguments. The Act of Supremacy of 1534 specifically cited the 'diverse sundry old authentic histories' that legitimised the break with Rome. The Library has a copy of the oath taken at Henry's coronation, apparently revised retrospectively in his own hand to make it

Miniature of Henry VIII and his jester, from *King Henry VIII's Psalter* by Jean Mallard, 1540.

The binding of this French translation of the Bible has been inscribed HA – Henry and Anne Boleyn.

clear that he was not subservient to the Pope. After divorcing Catherine he married Anne Boleyn, and one intriguing item in the King's Library is her book of hours, in which Henry wrote a flirtatious message to her in French: 'If you remember my love in your prayers as strongly as I adore you, I shall hardly be forgotten, for I am yours. Henry R. forever.' She replied in an English couplet:

> By daily proof you shall me find
> To be to you both loving and kind.

The fallout from this combination of high politics and frisky flirting is recorded in the last surviving letter that the ill-fated Sir Thomas More wrote to Henry. Once the King's most trusted advisor, More composed a set of congratulatory Latin verses on his coronation, which is also in the Library. But he opposed the break with Rome, urging Christians to continue to follow the old faith, and he boycotted Anne Boleyn's coronation. In this letter he sought, in vain, to persuade the King not to victimise him for his beliefs.

Many holdings illustrate the diplomatic and militaristic aspects of Henry's reign. His defeat of the Scots at Flodden Field in 1513 is recorded in the first known illustrated news pamphlet, called *True Encounter*. In 1520 Henry travelled to northern France to meet the French King Francis I at the Field of the Cloth of Gold: the detailed designs for the palatial, richly decorated tent that accompanied him have survived. From later in the reign comes

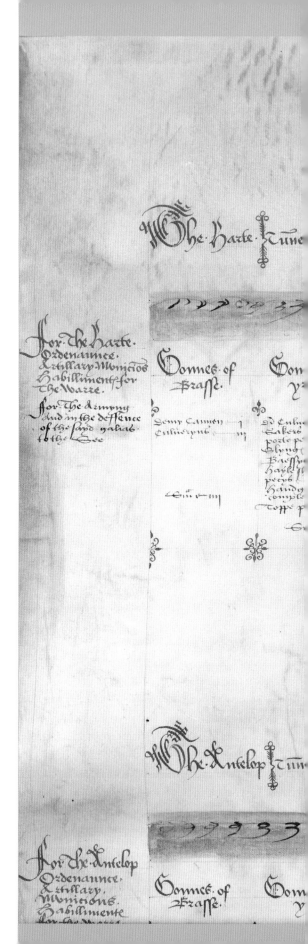

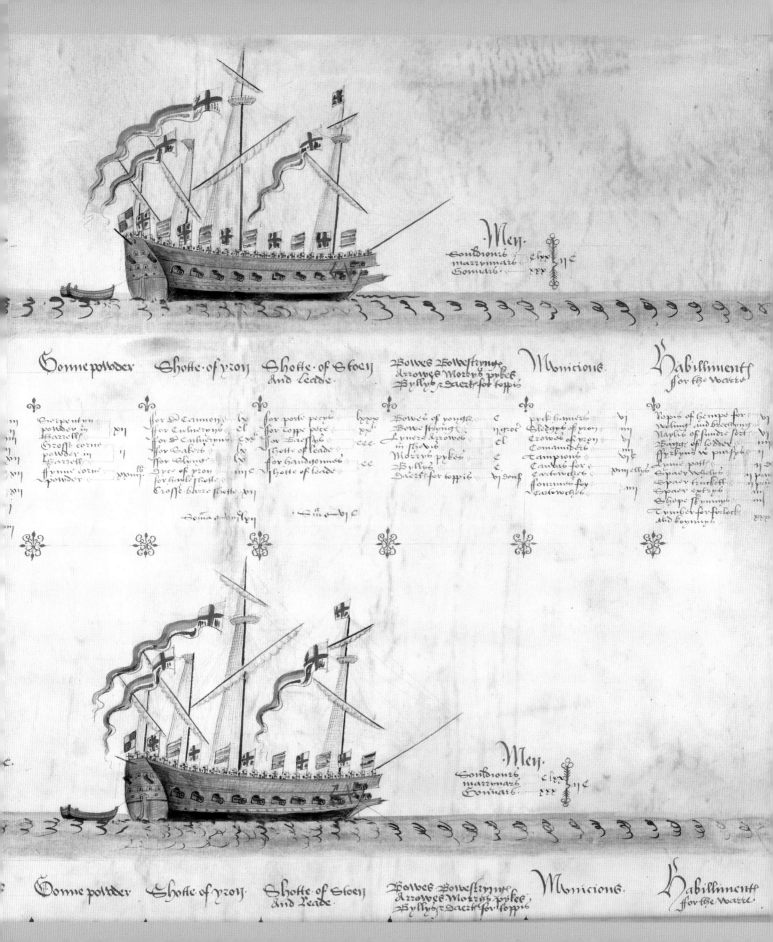

Men.
Souldiours
marynnars   CLXX iiijc
Gonnars   XXX

Gonnepowder | Shotte of yron | Shotte of Stoen and leade | Bowes Bowestrynges Arrowes Morysh pykes Byllys Dartes for toppis | Municions. | Habillments for the warre

Gonnepowder
Serpentyn powder in barrells
Grosse corne powder in barrell
Fyne corne powder

Shotte of yron
for Cannon
for Culveryng
for Culveryng
for Sakers
for Slynge
Dyes of yron for harke shotte
Crosse barre shotte

Shotte of Stoen and leade
for porte peces
for toppe pece
for Sacrys
Shotte of leade
for handgonnes
Shotte of leade

Bowes Bowestrynges Arrowes Morysh pykes Byllys Dartes for toppis
Bowes of yough
Bowe strynge
Lyvered arrowes in shefe
Morysh pykes
Byllys
Dartes for toppis

Municions
pyck hamers
Sledges of yron
Crowes of yron
Comaunders
Tampions
Tanckas for
Cartowches
Sounnes for
Cartowches

Habillments for the warre
Ropis of hempe for Welynge and breching
Naylis of sundre sort
Baggis of leader
Fyrkyns of pursh
Spare wheles
Spare turkell
Spare extrys
Shape stynnys
Tymber for forlock and boynnys

Men.
Souldiours
marynnars   CLXX iiijc
Gonnars   XXX

Gonnepowder   Shotte of yron   Shotte of Stoen and leade   Bowes Bowestrynges Arrowes Morysh pykes Byllys Dartes for toppis   Municions.   Habillments for the warre

the *Anthony Roll*, one of three illuminated rolls illustrating all the ships in the Royal Navy, presented to the King in 1546 by Anthony Anthony, one of his military aides. (The other two rolls were later presented to Samuel Pepys by Charles II and are in the Pepys Library in Cambridge.)

One of the most poignant Tudor documents is a letter written in 1553 by the future Queen Elizabeth to her 16-year-old half-brother Edward, who had succeeded Henry on the throne when he was nine but was now terminally ill with tuberculosis. In an admirably neat hand, but extremely florid prose, she explains that she had travelled from Hatfield to Greenwich to visit Edward at his sickbed but had been turned away. The letter begins: 'Like as a shipman in stormy weather plucks down the sails turning for better winds, so did I, most noble King, in my unfortunate chance on Thursday pluck down the high sails of my joy and comfort and do trust one day that as troublesome waves have repulsed me backward, so a gentle wind will bring me forward to my haven.'

She had been barred from his presence because the Duke of Northumberland, Edward's most influential advisor, had persuaded the young King to disinherit both Elizabeth and her half-sister Mary in favour of the Duke's daughter-in-law, Lady Jane Grey. Any meeting between brother and sister carried the risk that the plot, devised to ensure a Protestant succession, would be disclosed prematurely. In the event the Duke's scheme failed and Lady Jane Grey was executed the following year: the book that she took to the scaffold is among the Library's treasures, with marginal notes in her hand addressed to her father, the Duke of Suffolk, himself executed a few days later. The Catholic Mary became Queen, and on her death in 1558 was succeeded by Elizabeth.

The defeat of the Spanish Armada in 1588 was one of the key moments of Elizabeth's long reign, and the Library has two important documents that relate to it. One is a resolution to go to war with Spain, signed by the commanders of the English fleet, and the other a list of the Spanish ships, captured from one of them, annotated by William Cecil, Lord Burghley, the Queen's chief minister.

In 2011 the Friends of the British Library funded the purchase of a fascinating document that throws fresh light on this phase of English history. It is a proclamation in Dutch by Philip II of Spain, issued in 1569 after English 'pirate' ships had been attacking Spanish vessels and ports. Among the pirates' most daring acts had been to seize a ship carrying money to pay the Spanish soldiers fighting to put down a revolt in the Netherlands by supporters of William of Orange (William the Silent). The proclamation ordered all Spanish ships to be manned and armed sufficiently to thwart attacks by the pirates, and to counter-attack when necessary. It also banned any trade or other contacts with the English, and gave officers powers to search ships if they suspected them of breaching the embargo.

A feature of Elizabeth's reign was her vacillating relationship with Sir Walter Raleigh. Having once trusted him as an ally, she committed him briefly to the Tower of London for contracting an unsuitable marriage. Her successor, James I, imprisoned him there again in 1603 for alleged involvement in a plot against him, and eventually Raleigh was executed. The Library holds a wealth of manuscripts relating to him, many coming from Sir Hans Sloane's collection. One of them is a notebook that Raleigh kept during his second, longer incarceration containing, among other material, a list of some 500 books he was allowed to take to his quarters

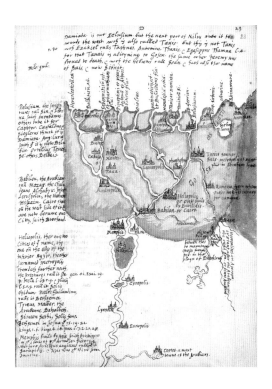

⮡ LEFT
Raleigh's notes for his *History of the World*, written while in the Tower, c.1603.

in the Tower of London, where he would have had plenty of time to read them. He also had the leisure there to write a pamphlet lauding the virtues of tobacco as a cure for headaches. Raleigh is credited with, or blamed for, introducing the addictive leaf to England from Virginia.

It might have been thought that the accession of James I, a professed Protestant but the son of a Catholic, would have stilled England's bitter religious turmoil, but it did not: the Gunpowder Plot of 1605 is evidence of that. As a result of the plot Parliament passed an act under which anyone suspected of Catholic sympathies had to take an oath of allegiance, recognising the King's absolute sovereignty. This provoked two letters from the Pope, and to answer them James, in 1607, wrote a pamphlet. *Triplici nodo triplex cuneus; or, an Apologie for the Oath of Allegiance against the two breves* [papal letters] *of Pope Paul V*. It detailed instances where the Pope had tried, illegally in James's view, to assert his authority over European monarchs. The Library has a copy of the first edition, with the King's handwritten emendations for the second edition.

Charles I, James's son, shared his father's unshakeable belief in the divine right of kings – a belief that was to prove his undoing in the face of a Parliament that sought to rein in what its members saw as the excesses of royalty. The ensuing Civil War ended in the King's defeat and his execution in 1649. The Library has a copy of the deathbed 'confession' of Richard Brandon, claiming that he was the

masked executioner who had wielded the axe. The document that best expresses the sentiments of the King's most determined opponents is *The Agreement of the People*, drawn up in the year of his death by the Levellers, a nationwide radical group, as the blueprint for a new constitution. The original is held by the Library. It sought to broaden the suffrage (although still excluding women), assure freedom of worship and reaffirm the basic rights set out in *Magna Carta*; but it was too extreme for Oliver Cromwell's Commonwealth and was never put into effect.

A rich source of information about the Civil War and its aftermath are the Thomason Tracts, a unique collection of more than 22,000 items printed between 1640 and 1661, gathered at the time of their publication by George Thomason, a London bookseller and friend of the poet John Milton. About a third of them are pamphlets and newsbooks, and many provide contemporary accounts of Civil War battles and political and religious developments, some with Thomason's handwritten comments. In 1762 George III bought them for £300 and presented them to the nascent British Museum. Thomas Carlyle called them 'the most valuable set of documents connected with English history'.

The Restoration of Charles II in 1660 was broadly welcomed by those who resented the Puritanical restrictions imposed by Cromwell's regime, but it was followed a few years later by two major disasters: the Great Plague of 1665 and the Fire of London

BELOW

Pamphlet from the English Civil Wars, part of the Thomason Tracts collection, 1647.

THE
World turn'd upfidedown:
OR,
A briefe defcription of the ridiculous Fafhions
of thefe diftracted Times.
By T.J. a well-willer to King, Parliament and Kingdom.

London : Printed for *John Smith*. 1647.

the following year. They are movingly described in
the many editions of Samuel Pepys's diaries in the
Library's possession, but some of the most evocative
mementoes come from the ephemera of the times –
the leaflets and billboards that attracted the attention
of citizens because they reflected their concerns.
One typical piece in the Library's rich collection of
such material is a handbill advertising 'A famous
and effectual medicine to cure the plague' – a kit
consisting of red powder, ointment, cordial water
and plasters – along with a list of people allegedly
cured through using it. It is offered at 'an easy price.
… very little more than what they cost making'. As
for the Great Fire, the most vivid evidence of the
devastation that it wrought comes in the map of the
city drawn by Wenceslaus Hollar in its immediate
aftermath (see page 176).

Charles II died in 1685 with no legitimate
children and was succeeded by his brother James II,
whose Catholicism reignited politicians' mistrust
of the monarchy. As a result, in 1688 Parliament
offered the throne jointly to James II's daughter Mary
and her husband William of Orange, the Dutch
head of state, whose army ousted James from power.
Pamphlets issued by both William and James sought
to justify their actions. The one favouring William
begins: 'It is both certain and evident to all men
that the public peace and happiness of any state
or kingdom cannot be preserved where the laws,
liberties and customs established by the lawful
authority within it are openly transgressed and

TO CURE THE
PLAGUE.

And having (through Gods blessing) cured these several Persons under written,
(and above fifty more,)I thought it my duty to publish it abroad in the World,
for the benefit and good of others; And have put an easie price on the medicines (very little more then what they cost making) for it is my chiefest aim
to do good, and not to get gain; For I thank God I can very well subsist without it, and truly I dare say through Gods blessing, and with careful looking unto, not ten in one hundred will miscarry.

The names of those as have been Cured.

Henry Contelloe, and five in his Family, living   Four Milk-women,
  in New-market.   Mrs. Joan's Daughter,
Rich. Pearce, his Wife and   Mrs. Brown,   In Coven Garden.
  his Nurse,   in Bridges street.   Mrs. Carter,
Mrs. Muncross,   Mrs. Adkings.
Ann Pole,   Ambo. Basket-field in Grase-Inn.
Mary Baget,   John Brown,
Andrew Baget,   Eliz. Contelloe,   in Stanop street.
Eliz. Egenhead,   In St. Gile's-   Mary Waight, in Bedford-Bury.
Margret Sanders,   Five more in White-hart-yard in the Strand.
Ann Ksmner, and her   Sixteen more in Chequer-Ally at Westminster.
  Nurse.   12. more in Church-head-Ally in Fetter-lane.

Now followeth the MEDICINE.

The red Powder. 1s.   IF any one is infected, and finds themselves ill, then presently let them (without delay) take
this powder, and then to bed and sweat carefully three hours; And if they are dry, make a
Posset with Sage, or Sorrel, and Dandilion, and so drink freely in their sweat, or afterwards, and be sure after your sweat you keep your self warm; And if any swelling appear,
beware of drinking any Beer or Ale, hot or cold, but keep your selves to the above-said Posset-
drink, or Beer, or Ale boyled with a crust of brown Bread, with one blade of Mace and two
Cloves. Put the Powder in a Spoon, with a little Bear or Posset-drink, and so take it.
  Also this Power is excellent good against Small-Pox, Fevers, Agues, and Surfeits; and if it
be for a Child, then take but one half of this Powder.
  Then when you are out of your sweat, and well rubbed and dryed, then take a spoonful of

ague Water. 2s.   this cordial water, if the party be sick, take one spoonful every four hours, if well, do not wast it.
  And if you find any pain in your heads after your sweat, then presently apply two of these

Plasters. 2d.   Plasters to your Temples, which will give you both ease and rest, and if your pain continues,
then shift every twenty four hours.

Salve. 1s.   And if you find any Risings in any part of your body, then take some of this Salve out of
the Pot, and spread it on Ships-leather, and then lay it to the Sore or Swelling, which Plaster
will both ripen, break it, and heal it; the first Plaster, keep it on as long as you can, and when
the Sore is broken, then dress it twice every day.
  But in case the distemper break out into a Vomiting and Looseness, or Griping in the Belly,

Cordial Water for   then take of this Cordial water every three hours two spoonful, untill you find ease, and in
griping. 2s.   case you are a dry, drink Mace-ale, not too sweet.
  Also here is a most excellent water for a sore mouth, either for Canker, Thrush, or a sore

1s.   mouth by reason of a Feaver, being a little warmed, and with a cloth garble the mouth, and
let one drop or two down.
  An infallible Powder for Men, Women, or Children, troubled with Convulsion-fits, Falling-

1s.   sickness, or fits of the Mother, taken with a little Black Cherry water fasting in a morning. If
the Children be very young, then divide the Paper of Powder into three parts, and for middle aged Children take one half, and for Men and Women the whole Paper.

  The Medicines are to be had at Mr. Leonard Sowersby, a Book-seller next to Turn-stile neer the Dukes Play-
house, by the Church-yard wall. At Mr. Heywoods house, next door to the Green Dragon in Alderman-bury, o-
ver against Adel-street. At Mr. Owens at the Holy Lamb in Islington. At Mr. Goodlaks at Trinity house at Stepney.

annulled: more especially where the alteration of religion is endeavoured.' The one supporting James, for its part, explains why he has gone into exile so as to be out of reach of one who 'invaded my kingdoms without any just occasion given him for it'. But he promises to be 'within call whensoever the nation's eyes shall be opened'.

From the mid-seventeenth century, with Parliament challenging the monarch's supreme power, British political life underwent a radical change. Differences were settled through argument rather than by brute force, with wit and satire replacing the sword and musket as weapons of choice, particularly at election time. Many of the most wounding sallies were in verse: the Thomason Tracts include about 600 political poems from the Cromwellian period, some of them savage. From half a century later, the Library catalogue lists more than 40 poems or songs criticising Sir Robert Walpole, the first British Prime Minister.

Another way for historians to gain insights into the ebb and flow of political fortunes is to study the archives of the politicians and aristocrats who held sway over the country for centuries. Because the National Archives does not purchase the personal papers of statesmen or other key public figures, the British Library is a major resource for this kind of material. It is voluminous: the papers of the Victorian Prime Minister William Gladstone, for instance, occupy 750 volumes. Other significant politicians whose papers can be found here include

Sir Robert Peel, Lords Liverpool and Aberdeen, and Arthur Balfour.

In 1985 the Library acquired the Althorp Papers, 2855 volumes and boxes detailing all aspects of the life and activities of the powerful Spencer family from the fifteenth to the twentieth centuries. The Library already owned material relating to the Spencer-Churchills, including the first Duke of Marlborough, the hero of Blenheim, and his son-in-law, Charles Spencer, third Earl of Sunderland. The prize memento of Blenheim is the note that the Duke scribbled in pencil to his wife Sarah on the back of a tavern bill: 'I have no time to say more but to beg you will give my duty to the Queen, and let her know her army has had a glorious victory'.

The advent of daily newspapers at the beginning of the eighteenth century laid the foundation for the style of political discourse we indulge in today. The British Museum began collecting them almost by accident. The Thomason Tracts contained a quantity of newsbooks, giving largely domestic news, and corantos, specialising in despatches from abroad; but these were published irregularly. The Library now has an almost complete run of the *London Gazette*, the oldest British periodical still being published. It began life as the *Oxford Gazette* in November 1665, because the King and court had decamped to Oxford to escape the Great Plague. After 23 issues it moved its base the following

February to the capital and became the *London Gazette*, which it remains, still an outlet for official information and announcements.

It was not until 1818 that the Museum's collection of news-related material really took off, with the purchase of 700 bound volumes, dating from 1603 to 1817, from the estate of the Rev. Charles Burney. They included a copy of issue number one of London's first daily paper, *The Daily Courant* of 11 March 1702. Four years after acquiring the Burney collection the Museum began to collect copies of every newspaper published anywhere in Britain. Since 1712 the publishers had been required to supply copies to the Stamp Office, where newspapers were taxed, and in 1822 it was agreed that these copies should be passed after three years to the British Museum and stored at Bloomsbury. In 1869 the legal deposit legislation under the Copyright Act was broadened to include newspapers, which henceforth were delivered direct to the Museum. Today they are submitted to the Newspaper Library, where large numbers of overseas titles are also held.

In 1932 the collection was moved to Colindale, where some volumes were destroyed in wartime bombing. Today the Library's newspapers fill 665,000 bound volumes and parcels, embracing 52,000 titles and occupying around 32 kilometres of shelving, with microfilm rolls taking up another 13 kilometres. Soon they will be transferred to the new facility at Boston Spa, although major newspapers and journals will by then be available at St. Pancras

✑ LEFT

Issue number one of *The Daily Courant*, 1702.

in digital form or on microfilm. And as newspapers provide more and more of their content online, the Library is finding ways of capturing and storing their electronic output as well.

The press does not only record history but can sometimes help to shape it. Through the years the

DROPPING THE PILOT.

proprietors and editors of national newspapers have exercised a powerful influence on government policies, as well as on the reactions of the general public to those policies. These influences can be traced through the archives of such powerful men as Lord Northcliffe, the former Alfred Harmsworth, who founded the *Daily Mail* in 1896 and was a pioneer of mass-market newspapers. His enormous archive, amounting to 245 volumes, includes letters to and from senior politicians, among them Arthur Balfour and Winston Churchill. It illustrates, too, the influence that Northcliffe exerted on the policy of his newspapers through his enthusiasm for innovations such as motoring and aeronautics: the *Mail* sponsored races involving both. Other influential journalists whose papers are held by the library include Wickham Steed, editor of *The Times* from 1919 to 1922, and C.P. Scott, editor of the *Manchester Guardian* for more than 57 years until he retired in 1929 at the age of 83. He is remembered for his much-quoted dictum: 'Comment is free but facts are sacred'.

A recent acquisition is a complete archive of the satirical magazine *Punch*, from its foundation in 1841 to its demise in 2002. The archive includes original material and correspondence from scores of writers, artists and public figures, along with the celebrated table on which contributors carved their initials when attending editorial lunches. It affords unique insights into the published copies of the magazine held in the Newspaper Library. *Punch*

was not only a prolific source of information on prevailing attitudes on a variety of social issues, but its powerful political cartoons provide an engrossing commentary on the history of its times.

There are occasions, too, when the newspapers themselves become an integral part of the story. The Library has a run of 165 copies of the 'special siege slip' editions of *The Mafeking Mail*, 'issued daily, shells permitting' during the siege of Mafeking between November 1899 and June 1900. It is written with the stiff-upper-lip nonchalance to be expected of the Victorian military under stress, as in this terse front-page notice from a December edition: 'We are sure we represent the whole of Mafeking when we offer most hearty congratulations to Captain Wilson and Lady Sara Wilson on her ladyship's safe arrival in our tight little garrison after her experience with the Boers.' By this deadpan little note hangs a tale of

great derring-do. Sara Wilson, a cousin of Winston Churchill, was the first female war correspondent, appointed by Alfred Harmsworth to cover the war after the Boers captured the *Daily Mail*'s staff man. Accompanied by her maid, she left the comparative safety of Mafeking to tour behind enemy lines until she, too, was duly captured; but she soon returned to the besieged town in a prisoner exchange for a horse thief.

Other newspapers published at times of conflict include the *Ladysmith Bombshell*, from a second South African town besieged at about the same time. Only eight issues appeared: the Library has four of the originals and the rest in facsimile. Then there is *The Kangaroo Out of His Element*, published on board the troopship *Afric* as it brought members of the Australian Imperial Expeditionary Force to Europe in October and November 1914. Many of the Australians lost their lives at Gallipoli.

⊛   ⊛   ⊛

Through newspapers and magazines, researchers can follow intricate details of the nation's story in words and, since the invention of photography, in pictures. But that does not devalue the significance of the actual documents through which history was made. One of great historic and military interest is Nelson's first draft of his tactics for defeating the French and Spanish fleets, written 12 days before the Battle of Trafalgar in October 1805. It is in the form of a memorandum to his second-in-command, Admiral Collingwood, datelined '*Victory*, off Cadiz, 9 October, 1805'. The plan was to draw up the fleet in two lines of 16 ships each, with eight of the fastest forming an advanced squadron. It was a resounding tactical success, even though it resulted in Nelson's death – Collingwood's report of which to the Admiralty is also in the collection.

Ten years later the French army under Napoleon was decisively defeated by the Duke of Wellington at Waterloo, and the Library has an equally poignant document celebrating that victory: Wellington's autograph draft of his despatch to the Secretary of State for War describing his triumph in detail. 'The enemy repeatedly attacked us with a large body of infantry and cavalry, supported by a numerous and powerful artillery: he made several charges with the cavalry on our infantry, but all were repulsed in the steadiest manner. … Our loss was great, as your lordship will perceive by the enclosed return; and I have particularly to regret his Serene Highness the Duke of Brunswick, who fell, fighting gallantly, at the head of his troops.' There are smudges on the paper that some believe to have been made by Wellington's tears. The fair copy of this draft, signed but not written by Wellington, is in the National Archives at Kew.

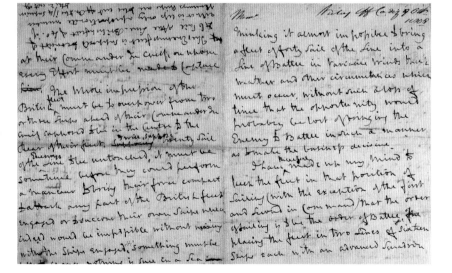

⊰❦ BELOW

Nelson's first draft of tactics for the Battle of Trafalgar, October 1805.

A further testament to the horrifying effects of war is in letters from Florence Nightingale, who went out to Scutari in the Crimea in 1854 to organise nursing care for the many British soldiers wounded or taken ill there. Writing to Sidney Herbert, the Secretary of State for War and one of her principal supporters, she describes the appalling conditions she found and her difficulties in recruiting properly qualified nurses.

Among many holdings relating to the First World War is the original of the 'backs to the wall' memorandum written by Field-Marshal Haig, Commander-in-Chief of the British armies in France, in April 1918. It ends: 'Many amongst us now are tired. To those I would say that victory will belong to the side which holds out the longest. The French army is moving rapidly and in great force to our support. There is no other course open to us but to fight it out. Every position must be held to the last man: there must be no retirement. With our backs to the wall and believing in the justice of our cause each one of us must fight on to the end. The safety of our homes and the freedom of mankind alike depend upon the conduct of each one of us at this critical moment.'

From the Second World War comes the draft of the ultimatum from Lord Halifax, the Foreign Secretary, delivered to the Germans after their invasion of Poland in September 1939. Halifax has made several emendations to the text, but the message comes across clearly: unless the German

To be checked 161

On the instructions of H.M. Principal Secretary of State for Foreign Affairs, I have the honour to make the following communication.

Early this morning the German Chancellor issued a proclamation to the German Army which indicated clearly that he was about to attack Poland.

At   this morning the German Chancellor issued

Information which has reached His Majesty's Government in the United Kingdom and the French Government indicates that German troops have crossed the Polish frontier and that attacks upon Polish towns are proceeding.

If this information is correct it appears to the Government of the United Kingdom and France that by their action the German Government have created conditions (viz. an aggressive act of force against Poland threatening the independence of Poland) which call for the implementation by the Governments of the United Kingdom and France of the undertaking to Poland to come to her assistance.

I am accordingly to inform Your Excellency that unless the German Government can immediately satisfy His Majesty's Government in the United Kingdom that these reports are unfounded, or in the alternative are prepared to give His Majesty's Government satisfactory assurances that the German Government has suspended all aggressive action against Poland and are prepared promptly to withdraw their forces from Polish territory, His Majesty's Government in the United Kingdom will without hesitation fulfil their obligations to Poland.

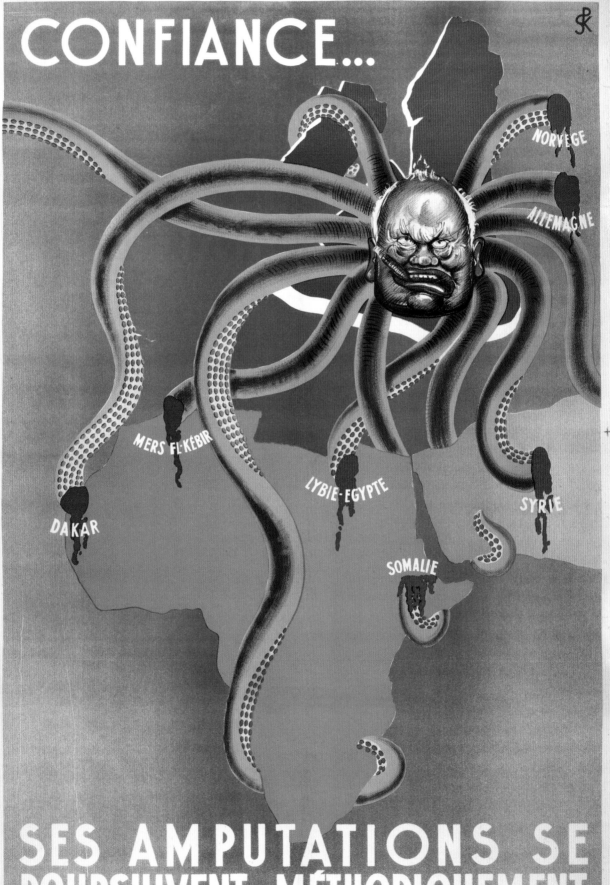

army withdraws, the British Government 'will without hesitation fulfil their obligations to Poland'.

Heroism is not confined to wartime. Captain Scott's Antarctic diary (see page 144) begins in November 1911, in the early optimistic days of the expedition, when he discusses such subjects as the ponies' reluctance to eat the oil cake provided: 'Chinaman and Jehu will not go far, I fear'. Things start to go badly wrong in December: 'Miserable, utterly miserable. We have camped in the "Slough of Despond". The tempest rages with unabated violence.'

When he discovered that they had been beaten by the Norwegians, he kept his dignity in the face of adversity, writing: 'It is a terrible disappointment and I am very sorry for my loyal companions.' Then comes the dreadful return journey in atrocious weather, and his companions begin to die of cold and exhaustion. Captain Oates deliberately walks to his death in a blizzard, announcing that he might be gone for some time. Scott's writing becomes weaker and weaker until his final entry: 'For God's sake look after our people.' But just before that he found time to write a 'message to the public' at the back of the diary: 'The causes of the disaster are not due to faulty organisation, but to misfortune in all risks which had to be undertaken.'

Scott and his companions were brave men who knew the dangers and forfeited their lives in the cause of furthering our knowledge of the most remote parts of the world. Exploration is one of mankind's basic instincts: the Library's collections of maps and topographical material, described in the next chapter, record its history.

❧ OPPOSITE
This Second World War propaganda poster was produced by the Vichy regime in France on 1942. It portrays Winston Churchill, the British Prime Minister, as a cigar-chomping octopus, spreading his tentacles to parts of North Africa that were formerly within the French or Italian sphere of influence, as well as into Germany and Scandinavia, but having them amputated by the Axis powers. The fortunes of war would eventually be reversed.

CHAPTER 9

Finding our bearings

'So geographers, in Afric-maps,
With savage-pictures fill their gaps;
And o'er unhabitable downs
Place elephants for want of towns.'

～ JONATHAN SWIFT, *ON POETRY* (1733)

THE BRITISH LIBRARY'S collecting policy recognises no chauvinistic constraints. Since its inception as part of the British Museum, it has gleaned material from all corners of the world, in almost every known language, reflecting the founders' intense curiosity about the universe whose true extent was only then being revealed. Nowhere is this better illustrated than in the unrivalled collection of maps and globes. The 2010 exhibition *Magnificent Maps* was the most popular the Library had until then mounted. The over-arching theme was that maps are not mere geographical records, or tools for navigating seas and highways, but frequently contain a political message. They might celebrate recent territorial gains or manipulate traditional boundaries to depict areas that rulers aspire to control, even if they do not actually do so. And the mystique of cartography persists: newspaper editors know that if they print a map that assigns disputed territory to a specific nation, there is bound to be a protest from other parties to the dispute.

The earliest known map that depicts the British Isles with any degree of accuracy was drawn in Canterbury in the first half of the eleventh century, shortly before the Norman Conquest. It is almost certainly based on a map drawn centuries earlier

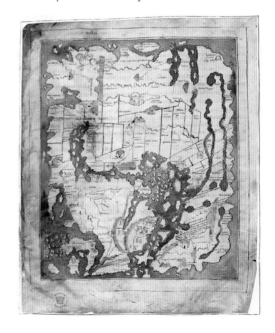

⚘ OPPOSITE

The Library's cartography collections include around 100 globes.Outstanding among them is the Chinese globe made in 1623 by two Jesuit missionaries, Manuel Dias and Nicolo Longobardi, who signed it in their Chinese names of Yang Manuo and Long Huamin. Painted in lacquer on wood, it is the earliest surviving terrestrial globe made in China, but broadly reflects the Western rather than the Oriental view of the world. However, one of many inscriptions refers to terrestrial magnetism, the force that makes compasses point north – a concept that was accepted in China long before Sir Isaac Newton observed it later that century. This globe is believed to have been displayed in the Imperial Summer Palace, near Beijing, for many years.

⚘ LEFT

The *Anglo-Saxon World Map*, first half of eleventh century. The British Isles are in the bottom left-hand corner.

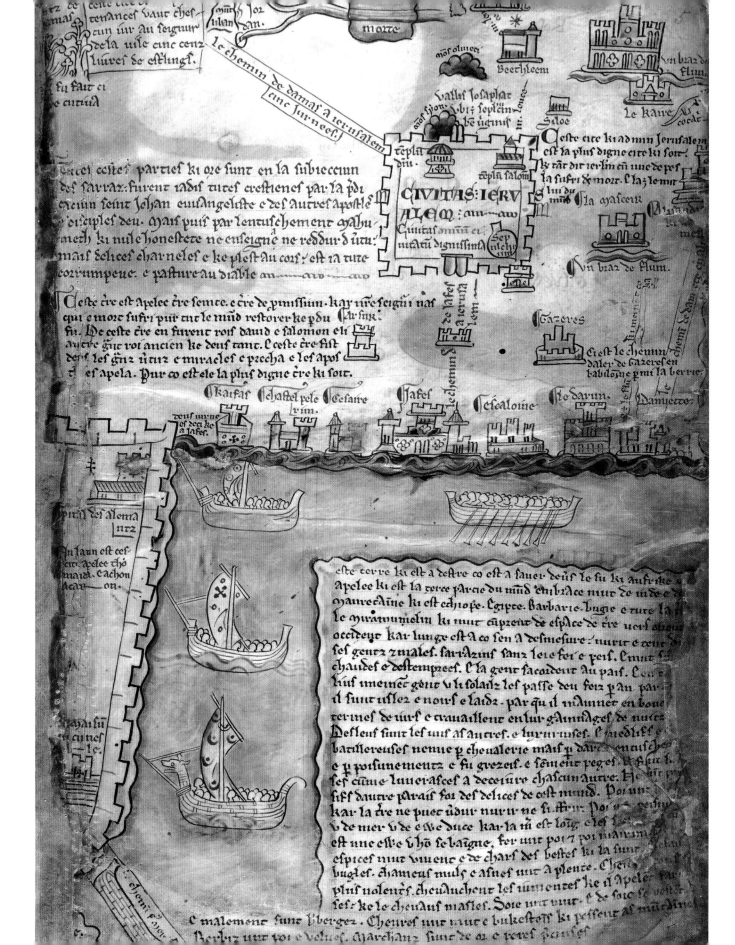

by the Romans showing the provinces of their empire, including 'Britannia'. Like most maps of its period it has east at the top: the British Isles are placed at bottom left. The coastline is depicted with commendable accuracy, given that precision in cartography was impossible until the development of triangulation and trigonometry in the fifteenth and sixteenth centuries. London, Winchester and Dublin are clearly marked, as are the boundaries of the Saxon kingdoms. Known as the *Anglo-Saxon World Map*, it came to the Library in Sir Robert Cotton's collection, the source of many rarities – including four maps of Great Britain drawn by the historian Matthew Paris in about 1250.

Matthew Paris's maps, which have north at the top in what is now the conventional manner, are the earliest that survive with recognisable geographical details conveying a few physical features. Major towns are mostly shown as miniature crenellated structures, with Windsor Castle elegantly straddling the Thames. Some 250 towns, rivers and ranges of hills are named, many spelled in ways to excite etymologists: Wales is 'Wallia', Snowdon 'Snaudun' and Norfolk 'North Folk', although 'Sufolck' is closer to its present-day form. Hadrian's Wall is drawn as a line of battlements, as is the less durable Antonine Wall to its north, built by Antonius Pius, Hadrian's successor. Thanet in Kent is shown as the island it then was and the southwestern spur of Cornwall is allowed to extend into the left-hand margin (enlarged to indicate the importance of the Cornish

tin industry). Both vertical margins contain notes of the countries to be found to the east and west of the British Isles.

Matthew Paris, born about 1200, was a monk at St. Albans Abbey with influential connections at the court of Henry III. His most important achievement was to write *Chronica Major,* an attempt to list all significant events in the world from its creation until 1259, the year of Paris's death. At the beginning of the manuscript is a map of the route from London to Jerusalem, probably designed as a spiritual guide for monks making a virtual pilgrimage within the confines of their monastery. It is a colourful piece of work with lively images including camels, boats, and churches, culminating in a depiction of Jerusalem surrounded by a crenellated wall.

The *Psalter World Map*, created at Westminster in about 1265, is so called because it is sandwiched between the pages of a book of psalms of the same date. It is circular, with east at the top, and shows the three known continents – Europe, Asia and Africa – encircled by sea. The map embraces religious as well as topographical themes: for instance there are depictions of Noah's Ark, Adam and Eve, Bethlehem and the sun and moon, shown with trees growing on them. It is small, about the size of an octavo book, and was almost certainly drawn by a skilled miniaturist, possibly the one who illustrated the psalter itself. Many of the map's details are barely perceptible to the naked eye but, remarkably, its original colours have survived down the centuries.

Some 200 years later Fra Mauro, a Venetian monk, drew a map of the known world (still missing out America and Australia) at the behest of the Signoria, the Venetian council, to celebrate the extent of their empire and the achievements of Marco Polo, the thirteenth-century Venetian explorer. The Library has a meticulous copy of this map, made for the East India Company in 1804. It has south at the top and contains a mass of illustration and a written commentary that evaluates the claims made by explorers and others about the attributes of distant lands. Unlike earlier medieval maps there are few religious references: Fra Mauro was concerned above all with factual

✤ BELOW
Map of the British Isles from
the *Queen Mary Atlas* by Diego
Homem, 1555.

and geographical accuracy. The Garden of Eden is depicted, but it appears beyond the map's borders, with no attempt to locate it in the real world.

By the sixteenth century the existence of the Americas had been confirmed by Spanish and Portuguese explorers. The most splendid early printed map that celebrates their discovery was commissioned in 1562 by Philip II of Spain from Diego Gutiérrez, a specialist chart maker. Only two copies of the map, magnificently engraved by Hieronymus Cock of Antwerp, are known to exist: one is at the British Library, the other at the Library of Congress in Washington. While the Americas take centre stage, Spain, the British Isles and northwest Africa are shown at top right. The illustrations reflect Europeans' sense of wonder at the exotic species that lived there. There are parrots, monkeys, swordfish and, in the African sector, rhinoceros and lions. We see mermaids, sea monsters, cannibals in Brazil and giants in Patagonia. King Philip is portrayed as Neptune, being carried above the Atlantic towards his new dominions.

In about 1555 Philip's wife, Mary I of England, commissioned an atlas from Diego Homem, a Portuguese map maker. It is believed that she intended it as a gift for her husband, but she died before it was completed. It includes South America – although the area south of Argentina is labelled 'Terra incognita' – and here, too, are colourful illustrations of its people and wildlife. The most intriguing detail of the atlas occurs on the map of England and Wales,

Detail showing Plymouth from the map of coastal defences commissioned by Henry VIII, 1539.

superimposed with Mary's and Philip's coats of arms. Philip's arms have been scratched out – some believe by Elizabeth I, Mary's successor, who despised Philip and eventually defeated him through the rout of the Armada in 1588.

Mary's father, Henry VIII, had been fascinated by maps, especially those that could be put to practical use. Knowing that his break with Rome would place him in conflict with many of Europe's Catholic rulers, his priority was to strengthen his country's defences. With this in mind, in 1539 he instructed

Thomas Cromwell, the Lord Great Chamberlain, to institute a survey of the whole coast. Cromwell deputed local people to do the initial research and send it to Greenwich Palace, where the details were incorporated into maps for presentation to Henry. The King was so delighted with the results that he displayed them in Whitehall Palace. Of the sections that survive in the Library, the most impressive is the view of the coast from Exeter to Land's End, measuring ten feet from end to end and packed with intricate detail. Proud sailing ships crowd the sea, while on land there are depictions of houses, castles and churches, one perched precariously atop St. Michael's Mount. That the map was put to practical use is shown by annotations made in about 1541, recording where the fortifications had been strengthened. Other surviving sections of the survey cover Dorset, Essex, Suffolk, Dover and Calais – then part of Henry's domain.

Maps of the world were sometimes drawn as two separate circles. An example is contained in another book presented to Henry by the eager-to-please Jean Mallard, the donor of the psalter described in Chapter 8. This second gift was his adaptation into verse of *Les Voyages Avantureux*, a French navigator's account of his search for the Northwest Passage. (The double-hemisphere technique continued in the seventeenth century: on a page of a scrapbook compiled by the bookseller John Bagford, incorporated into the Harley Library, are pasted three such maps dated 1601, 1628 and 1688.)

The Flemish cartographer Gerardus Mercator is acknowledged to be the father of modern map-making. He is best known for the projection, named after him, that first appeared on his world map of 1569 – a method of translating the earth's curved surfaces to two dimensions. Until very recently it was the standard method for depicting the world. Mercator's maps differ from earlier ones in that there are comparatively few illustrations and a much greater emphasis on geometric and scientific accuracy – none of Swift's 'elephants for want of towns'.

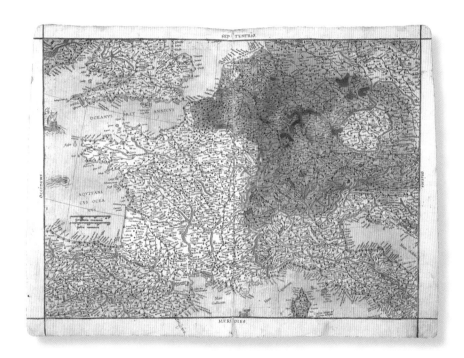

ABOVE
Map of Europe from the
Mercator Atlas of Europe, 1572

In 1997 the Library, with the aid of the Heritage Lottery Fund, bought the *Mercator Atlas of Europe*, compiled in about 1572 and containing the only surviving example of his innovative wall map of Europe, published 18 years earlier. In 1564 Mercator produced a detailed map of the British Isles in eight copper-engraved sheets, together measuring 3ft. by 4ft., showing west at the top, scaled at 14 miles to the inch. It appears in segmented form in the *Atlas of Europe*. The belief that this map partly derives from a survey of England and Wales commissioned by Mary I in the 1550s is supported by the omission of any reference to the Protestant bishoprics created by Henry VIII. Although it marks a radical advance on earlier printed maps, it contains several inaccuracies, sometimes confusing the names of counties with those of villages. Many of these errors were corrected in the more impressive map of England published by Mercator's son in 1595. It features the names of scores of towns and villages that we can recognise today, usually with their Latin spellings: Sussex, for instance, is 'South Saxia' and Kent 'Cantium'.

The first comprehensive survey of England and Wales was conducted in the 1570s by Christopher Saxton, a land surveyor from Yorkshire, commissioned by William Cecil, Lord Burghley, Chief Minister to Elizabeth I. Burghley recognised that accurate maps were a key to efficient governance and state security. Saxton's first map, of Norfolk, was printed in 1574, and within four years the whole country had been covered in 34 maps in a range of scales, the largest being of his native county.

In 1579 they were put together in an atlas, dedicated to the Queen. The Library owns the unique surviving set of trial proof copies sent to Burghley for his approval. His annotations, aimed at making the maps more useful to him, can be seen on virtually every map. Later, probably under James I, the volume was incorporated into the Old Royal Library, presented to the British Museum in 1757. John Speed, one of the most celebrated English cartographers, drew on Saxton's work for his 1611 *Theatre of the Empire of Great Britaine*, a book of maps of the British Isles, county by county, adding detailed town plans as well as descriptive text. His maps have been reproduced countless times and are displayed in many homes today.

In addition to maps, the Library has about a hundred globes in its collection, dating from the seventeenth century onwards (see page 165). Maps and globes representing the galaxy of stars and planets, in so far as it was then possible to observe them, became popular in the sixteenth century as aids to navigation. In 1596 the Elizabethan mathematician John Blagrave included a detailed star chart in his *Astrolabium Uranicum Generale*, which he subtitled 'a necessary and pleasant solace and recreation for navigators in their long journeying'. It was designed to be used in conjunction with the astrolabe that Blagrave had developed to calculate the distances of stars from the earth. Andreas Cellarius, a German cartographer and schoolteacher based in Holland, who has an asteroid named after him, produced the most elaborate celestial atlas of the seventeenth century, the *Atlas Coelestis*, or *Harmonia Macrocosmica*.

The celestial atlas compiled by Sir John Flamsteed, the first Astronomer Royal and the guiding spirit behind the foundation in 1675 of the Royal Observatory at Greenwich, was not published until 1729, ten years after his death. In this meticulous work, based on his observations from Greenwich, he listed 2,935 stars – three times as many as had been named in the previous standard work on the subject, by the sixteenth-century Danish

LEFT
Christopher Saxton's *County
Map of Hertfordshire*, 1577.

astronomer Tycho Brahe. The numerical system that he used to identify the stars, the Flamsteed designations, is still in limited use. One globe of special interest depicts the moon, based on the surface visible from Earth. It was made by the artist John Russell in 1797.

Back on *terra firma*, one of the most photographed objects in the Library is the *Klencke Atlas*, a set of wall maps bound as a volume more than five feet tall, presented in 1660 to Charles II by a Dutch merchant, Johannes Klencke, to mark the Restoration. By contrast, another map of the

The German-born cartographer
Andreas Cellarius (1596–1665)
produced the remarkable
Atlas Coelestis in 1660. In this
image he draws the Pacific and
Antarctic regions as if seen
from a point in space, showing,
as was his custom, some of
the creatures that inhabit the
regions seemingly floating above
them. It appears to have been
primarily a work of imagination
rather than the product of his
astronomical researches.

The *Duke's Plan* of New York,
1644.

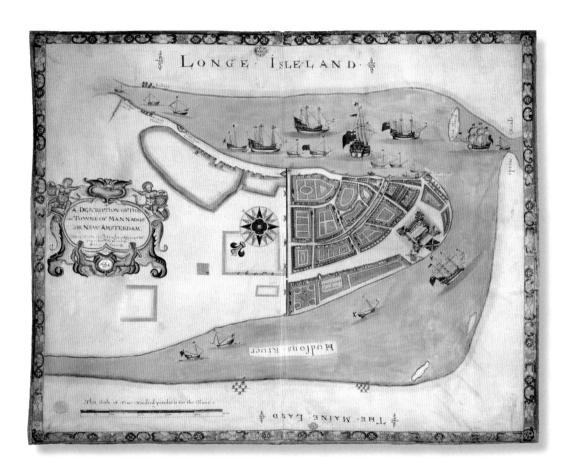

same period that is frequently reproduced covers not much more than a square mile of ground. It is the *Duke's Plan* of New York, drawn in 1664, the year that the British took New Amsterdam from the Dutch and changed its name to honour the Duke of York. It shows clearly that all the inhabited part of the city lay south of the wall that ran along the line of what is now Wall Street, with the few houses arranged around formal gardens. The *Duke's Plan* had been part of George III's topographical collection that was moved into the British Museum in 1828. It contains around 300 maps and views of North America among 50,000 from all parts of the world, dating from 1540 to 1824.

Wenceslaus Hollar (1607– 77) was an artist and etcher from Prague who settled in England in 1637. Late in his career he became known for his maps of London. This one, drawn just after the Great Fire of 1666, shows how the city was devastated by the flames. Sir Christopher Wren used this map as the basis for his plan – never fulfilled – to design an entirely new street pattern on the ashes of the old city: the Library has a copy of Wren's diagram of his proposals.

The Library has superb holdings of maps of London, founded on the collection made in the mid-nineteenth century by Frederick Crace – an interior decorator who worked for the Prince Regent, later George IV, in the Royal Pavilion in Brighton and in Windsor Castle, and rose to become one of London's Commissioners of Sewers. Crace's collection of about 1200 maps and views of the capital and its suburbs, dating from 1570 to 1860, was acquired by the British Museum in 1878. Today the views are still held by the Museum: the Library has inherited the maps, graphically documenting the remorseless spread of the city over the centuries. While the collection includes many large rolls and wall maps, some are simply small plans cut from rent books. A number portray development projects that were never fulfilled and others, naturally enough, relate to drainage systems.

The Library's global and historical range was expanded significantly in 1982 when it was given custody of the old India Office Library, initially established by the mighty East India Company. Founded in 1600, the Company was for more than 200 years one of London's most powerful financial institutions; it attracted several notable employees including the writers Charles Lamb and Thomas Love Peacock and the philosopher John Stuart Mill. Although its library was not formally inaugurated until 1801, its records, books, paintings,

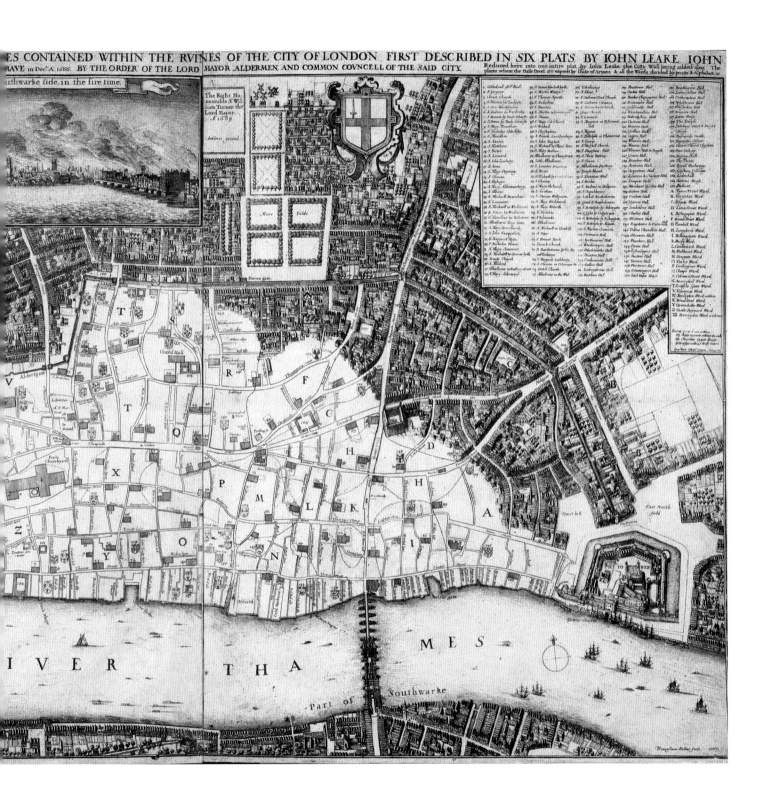

maps, journals and other artifacts go back to the Company's earliest years. It pursued a vigorous policy of acquiring indigenous art and literature until its political control of India ceased in 1858. That was when the India Office was established to take over its responsibilities and records, as well those of the Board of Commissioners for the Affairs of India (more commonly known as the Board of Control), created in 1784. In 1867 both the India Office Library and the British Museum were given the right to requisition any book published in India.

When India, Pakistan and Burma gained independence in 1947, the India Office became redundant and its library was taken under the wing of the Commonwealth Office, later the Foreign and Commonwealth Office. It is a treasure trove of information and art works from and about those three nations, and it encompasses material from southeast and central Asia, the Middle East and parts of Africa where the East India Company had commercial interests. The library amounts to more than a quarter of a million volumes, boxes and objects. Official archives are complemented by about 300 collections of private papers and over 3000 smaller deposits that provide a revealing and sometimes moving testament to the British experience in India. Among the most fascinating are almanacs, year books and ephemera that include the books of rules (strictly enforced) of expatriate clubs, programmes of dramatic societies and books with advice for newcomers on clothing, local conventions and cookery.

Some of the original furniture, paintings and sculpture from the East India Company's London headquarters in Leadenhall Street remained in the Foreign Office complex in Whitehall after the India Office was abolished, but many items are now housed at St. Pancras. By the entrance to the Asian and African Reading Room on the third floor are busts of some of India's Governors-General, officials of the East India Company and senior military figures. Inside, on the high walls above the document issue desk, hangs the cream of the art collection. The oldest painting is a portrait of Nakd Ali Beg, who came to London in 1626 claiming to be the ambassador of the Shah of Persia. This claim was disputed by Sir Robert Shirley, who claimed that *he* was the rightful ambassador. Nakd Ali Beg was sent back to Persia, but was so upset that he poisoned himself on the voyage. The painting is by Richard Greenbury, official portrait painter to Henrietta Maria, Charles I's queen.

In the liveliest – and most gruesome – of the pictures on display, James Atkinson, a surgeon and hobby painter, portrays the hook-swinging festival of Charakpuja in 1831. Hook-swinging was a rite of penance undertaken to appease Hindu gods at times of trouble such as famines and epidemics, and discouraged by British officials because of its assumed barbarity. The picture shows a vertical pole on which two horizontal cross-pieces are fixed in such a way that they will revolve slowly, with penitents attached at each end by hooks that

pass through holes carefully made beneath their shoulder-blades – an extreme form of body-piercing. In the picture three penitents are already swinging, with a fourth preparing himself, and a large crowd has gathered to watch.

Most of the other paintings on show are of bejewelled Indian potentates, some depicted by local artists and some by British visitors. An exception is the picture of Robert Clive ('Clive of India') receiving a donation from the Nawab of Bengal to his fund for disabled servicemen and military widows. The sentimental composition shows Clive gesturing towards two disabled soldiers, while in the background a widow comforts her bereaved children. It was painted in 1772 by Edward Penny, the first professor of painting at the Royal Academy. The East India Company initially paid him £150, but he complained that this was an insult to a painter of his standing, so they came up with an extra £60 to make his fee 200 guineas.

The India Office collection contains thousands of beguiling images of the sub-continent, many more than can be displayed. At random I selected *The Tranquil Eye*, a book of eight watercolours by Col. Robert Smith of the Bengal Corps of Engineers. It records a journey down the Ganges that he took in

❧ ABOVE LEFT
James Atkinson's painting of the hook-swinging festival of Charakpuja, 1831.

❧ ABOVE RIGHT
The granary ('gola') at Bankipur near Patna in Bihar, watercolour by Col. Robert Smith, *c.*1830.

1830, just before he left India after 25 years of service. He paints elaborate mosques, temples and palaces, with dhows in full sail on the river and cows grazing by its bank. Indian folk paintings from the nineteenth and twentieth centuries are an especially charming feature of the collection, which also includes hundreds of fascinating photographs, some recording historic occasions: one set shows the headquarters of the *Times of India* in Bombay in 1898, when the paper was celebrating its 60th anniversary.

For students of Indian history there is material in abundance. Official despatches to and from the British Viceroys paint a vivid picture of the shifting priorities of the colonial power. There are documents recording the Indian Mutiny of 1857, including personal letters from some of the soldiers sent to suppress it, while the slow march to independence and partition is traced in communications to and from British and Indian leaders, as well as from the United States President Franklin D. Roosevelt, who took a keen interest.

The India Office Library is not the only source of material relating to the sub-continent. The purchase of the papers of Lord Lytton in 2004 added depth to the collection. Viceroy from 1876 to 1880, he tried to cement the imperial relationship between India and Britain, executing Disraeli's policy of having Queen Victoria proclaimed Empress of India at a durbar in Delhi in 1877. His papers display a dismissive attitude to the Indian middle class, with their 'shallow English education': an attitude that strengthened their desire

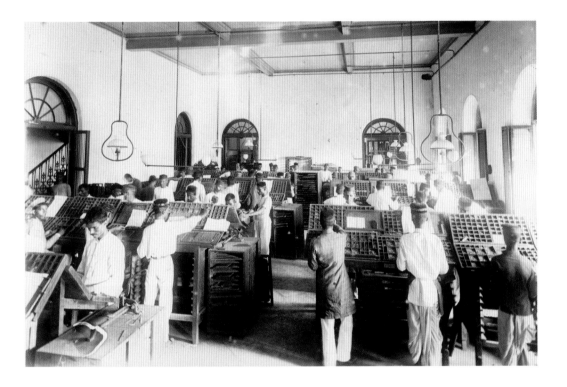

The composing room of the *Times of India* in Bombay in 1898.

The *Hyakumantō darani* or *Million pagoda charms*, eighth century AD.

to throw off the British yoke. Lytton introduced a regulation by which the publishers of newspapers had to put down a deposit which would be forfeited if they printed seditious material, and his attempt to solve the perennial problem of Afghanistan by turning it into a client state resulted in the Second Afghan War in 1878.

While the incorporation of the India Office collection means that the Library's Asian holdings are weighted towards India and Pakistan, there are also treasures from other parts of the continent, notably a wealth of manuscripts, drawings, maps and printed items from both China and Japan. The collection of Japanese antiquarian books is invaluable to students of printing, since they include works that pre-date the introduction of the craft to Europe. The oldest – possibly the earliest printed documents to have survived anywhere – are eight *Hyakumantō darani* ('Million pagoda charms') printed in the eighth century AD on the orders of Empress Shōtoku (718–70). Examples of Japanese woodblock printing from the twelfth to the sixteenth

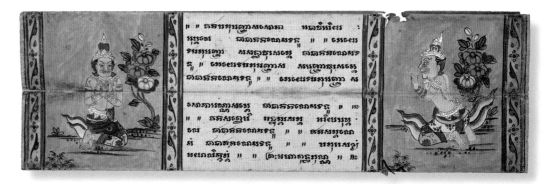

centuries were among 900 Japanese and Korean books bought by the Museum for £300 in 1884. They came from the collection of the diplomat and bibliophile Sir Ernest Satow, who served in Japan for many years.

From Thailand comes a late eighteenth-century illuminated manuscript, in the form of a folding book, of *Ten Birth Tales of the Buddha*, a standard religious text. Buddhists believe that their god experienced 547 previous lives before being born as the Buddha, and the birth tales illustrate the last ten of them. A fine nineteenth-century version of the tales was bought by the Library from the estate of Henry Ginsburg. Curator of Thai material for 30 years until his death in 2007, Ginsburg's expertise and enthusiasm made an enormous contribution to the quality of the collections. In 2004 some Thai lacquer manuscript boxes and cabinets were donated by Doris Duke's Southeast Asia Art Collection, and two are on display outside the Asia and Africa Reading Room.

Remarkable items from Africa include around 800 Ethiopic manuscripts dating from 1400 to 2000, and early printed books. Some were donated by the Church of England Missionary Society while others had a less benign provenance: the largest single acquisition was of 349 manuscripts taken from the Emperor Theodore's capital at Magdala by a punitive expedition in 1868. (Stung by his defeat, and unwilling to face capture, the Emperor shot himself with a pistol that had been presented to him by Queen Victoria.) One especially rare Ethiopian manuscript is in the Nubian language. The Library also has 11 Swahili manuscripts, mostly religious and mainly from Kenya, in Arabic script, ranging in date from the 1890s to the 1970s.

The Australian and New Zealand collections go back almost to the Museum's foundation. The private library of Sir Joseph Banks, the naturalist and long-serving President of the Royal Society, contained 16,000 books and was donated to the British Museum in 1827, seven years after his death.

Among the material are accounts of the voyages of the initial explorers of the South Pacific in the 1770s, including Captain Cook, whom Banks accompanied on the *Endeavour*. Cook's journal is also in the Library, written in his own hand and providing a more vivid account of his adventures than could have been gleaned from any second-hand report. He tells of one incident where, to test rumours of cannibalism among islanders, he orders his men to cook part of a corpse found on the beach and offer it to a native – who, sure enough, devours it enthusiastically. Cook's copy of Bougainville's *Voyage autour du monde* (1771) includes a map on which Cook has traced his own route.

There is much material that brings to life the early days of the penal colony at Botany Bay and its evolution into New South Wales, including the transcript of the court-martial that followed the Rum Rebellion in Sydney in 1808, in which the Governor, William Bligh, was deposed. The Library has one of only three known copies of the first book printed in Australia, *The 1802 New South Wales General Standing Orders*. It was acquired by the Museum in the 1860s from F.F. Bailliere, a Melbourne publisher and bookseller, who supplied it with many early books and journals.

✦ RIGHT
The Eureka Stockade by Raffaello
Carboni, 1855.

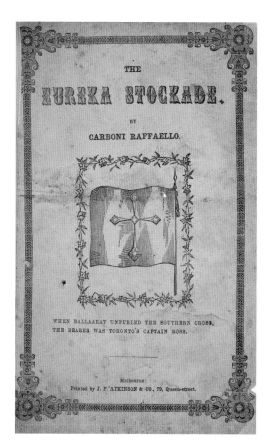

THE
EUREKA STOCKADE.

BY
CARBONI RAFFAELLO.

WHEN BALLAARAT UNFURLED THE SOUTHERN CROSS,
THE BEARER WAS TORONTO'S CAPTAIN ROSS.

Melbourne:
Printed by J. P. ATKINSON & CO., 79, Queen-street.

Leaflets and booklets document how emigration
to Australia was officially encouraged from the 1820s.
At the same time New Zealand was being settled by
Europeans, and early publications from there include
translations of parts of the Bible into the Maori
language, the first of them appearing in 1835. The
earliest known Australian novel was Henry Savery's
Quintus Servinton, published in Hobart, Tasmania,

in 1831 and bought by the Museum in 1839.
Another historic volume acquired from Bailliere
is an original 1855 edition of *The Eureka Stockade*,
the account by the Italian revolutionary Raffaello
Carboni of the previous year's Eureka rebellion. This
seminal event in Australian history was a revolt by
diggers in the Victorian goldfields against the high
cost of a mining licence, which they saw as blatant
exploitation by the authorities. In the ensuing battle
more than 30 people were killed. Carboni's book is an
extraordinary document, written in broken English
and beginning with this apology:

'NOTA BENE
In person I solicit no subscription – in writing
I hereby ask no favour from my reader. A book
must stand or fall by the truth contained in it.
What I wish to note is this: I was taught the English
language by the Very Reverend W. Vincent Eyre,
Vice Rector of the English College, Rome. It has
cost me immense pains to rear my English up to
the mark; but I could never master the language
to perfection. Hence, now and then, probably to
the annoyance of my readers, I could not help
the foreign idiom. Of course, a proper edition,
in Italian, will be published in Turin. I have
nothing further to say. Carboni Raffaello. Prince
Albert Hotel, Bakery Hill, Ballaarat, Anniversary
of the Burning of Bentley's Eureka Hotel, 1855.'

In fact he had a great deal further to say. 'I
undertake to do what an honest man should do,
let it thunder or rain. He who buys this book to
lull himself to sleep had better spend his money in

❧ BELOW
The first Bible translated into a
native American language, 1663.

grog. He who reads this book to smoke a pipe over it, let him provide himself with plenty of tobacco – he will have to blow hard. A lover of truth – that's the man I want – and he will have in this book the truth, and nothing but the truth. Facts, from the "stubborn-things" store, are here retailed and related – contradiction is challenged from friend or foe. The observation on, and induction from the facts, are here stamped with sincerity: I ask for no other credit. I may be mistaken: I will not acknowledge the mistake unless the contrary be proved.'

❧   ❧   ❧

The first book in English known to have been written and printed in North America was *The Bay Psalms Book*, a selection of psalms translated from Hebrew, produced in Massachusetts in 1640. The Library has a copy of the second printing, as well as of the first Bible translated into a Native American language, which appeared in 1663. They are part of one of the richest collections of American printed books outside the United States – a collection that continues to grow rapidly. It is especially strong in the publications of university presses, learned societies, museums and research libraries, as well as Government documents, and there is useful material on the history of American printing and publishing.

Much that relates to the colonial period came, like the maps, from the British Museum's foundation collections. Sir Hans Sloane, for instance, had

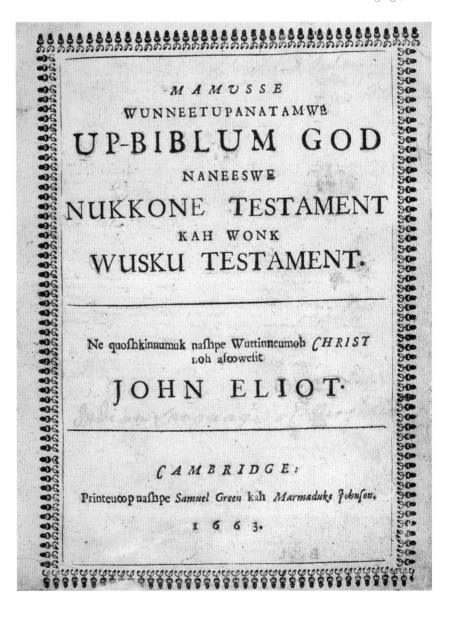

The first Bible translated into a native American language, 1663.

'The Black Man's Lament; or How to Make Sugar by Amelia Opie, 1826.

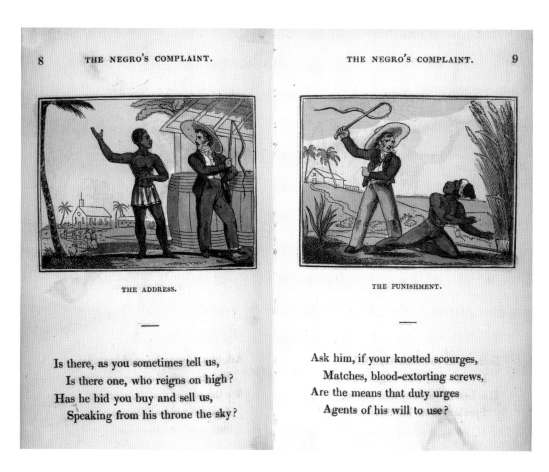

amassed a set of early issues of the *New England Courant*. A key historical document is the manuscript of George III's 1775 proclamation for suppressing rebellion and sedition. After independence the pace of American acquisitions slowed, until in 1846 Antonio Panizzi despatched Henry Stevens to 'sweep America' for suitable material. As a result of his efforts, more than 12,000 volumes were added in the ensuing decade. In 1867 the Library of Congress reported that 'the most complete collection of books relating to America in the world is that now gathered on the shelves of the British Museum'. The legal deposit requirement was extended in 1886 to cover American books distributed in Britain.

In 1858 Stevens secured for the Museum a collection of 780 single issues of American newspapers and magazines. Some early newspapers from across the Atlantic came as part of the Burney collection and many others, dating from the seventeenth to the nineteenth centuries, can now be consulted on microfilm, in a collection covering some 700 titles. Black newspapers held by the Library include the *Liberator* and the *Black Panther*: it also has the *Cherokee Phoenix*, published from 1828 in English and Cherokee.

The extensive material on slavery features a copy of President Lincoln's proclamation on emancipation, signed by the President himself. The final draft of 1863 is held in the US National Archives, but several commemorative editions quickly followed it; the Library's is one of 48 copies sold at a fair to raise funds for wounded soldiers in Philadelphia in 1864, which Lincoln attended. Typical of the literature that highlighted the iniquities of the slave trade is *The Black Man's Lament; or How to Make Sugar*, a poem written in 1826 by Amelia Opie, with powerful illustrations. It tells the story of an African man's capture by traders, his journey to the Caribbean on a slave ship and how he was forced to work on the sugar plantations. This verse states the basic theme:

> That mill, our labour, every hour
> Must with fresh loads of cane supply;
> And, if we faint, the cart-whip's power
> Gives force which nature's powers deny.

CHAPTER 10

Lend me your ears

> ❛Be not afeard: the isle is full of noises,
> Sounds and sweet airs that give delight
> and hurt not.❜
>
> ∽ SHAKESPEARE: *THE TEMPEST* (1611)

MUSICAL MANUSCRIPTS and printed scores had been a strong presence in the British Museum library since its foundation, but were not given their own dedicated catalogue until 1842. The earliest examples date from the tenth century and others come from the library of Henry VIII, indicating his and his queens' musical tastes. There are, too, autograph manuscripts from most leading classical composers, as well as a few non-documentary extras such as a tuning fork that once belonged to Ludwig von Beethoven (and was later presented by Gustav Holst to Ralph Vaughan Williams). From more recent times material relating to the Beatles, the 1960s pop group, is on long-term loan to the Library: when on display, it is invariably surrounded by a cluster of enthusiastic admirers of all ages.

Among the most celebrated medieval holdings is the manuscript of the much-performed *Sumer is icumen in*, believed to have been written at Reading Abbey in the thirteenth century. A song for up to six voices, it has two sets of words – the familiar celebration of the season in Middle English,

along with a religious lyric in Latin. It came to the Library as part of the Harley collection in 1753, and is unique in that no other version of the song has been traced. The *Old Hall Manuscript*, meticulously written out by a scribe in about 1420, is one of the earliest surviving collections of English part music, mostly settings of common texts used in the Mass. A composer of one of the settings is named as Roy Henry, thought to be Henry V. This was the Library's first major purchase after its separation from the British Museum in 1973; it was bought from St. Edmund's College at Old Hall in Hertfordshire for £68,000.

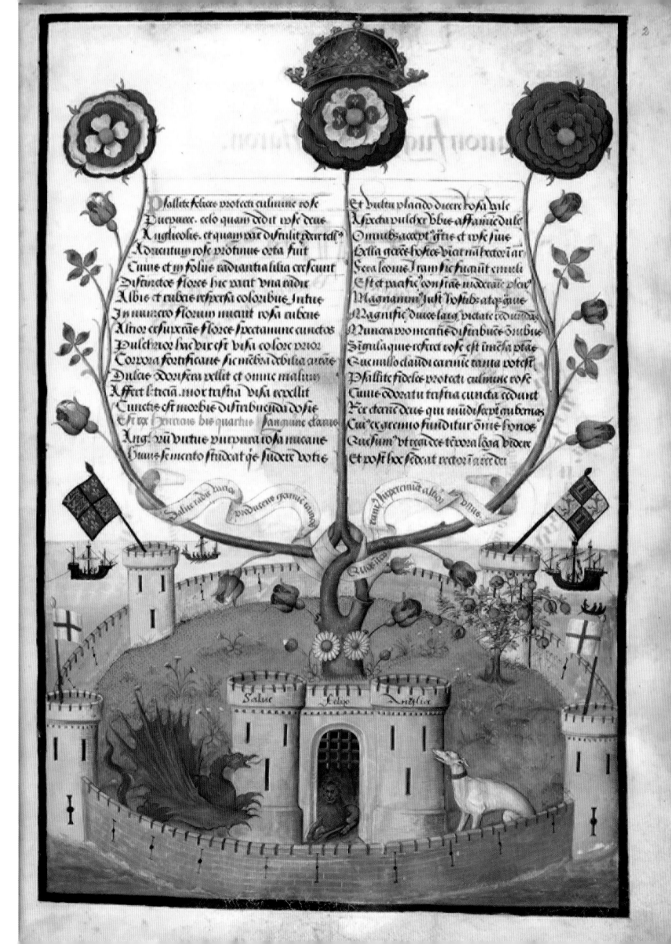

⌀ OPPOSITE

This is the title page of a set of motets composed for Henry VIII during his marriage to Catherine of Aragon. The allegorical image features a crowned Tudor rose, celebrating Henry VII's unification of the houses of York and Lancaster. Below to the right, beneath the flag of Aragon, is a pomegranate tree – a heraldic symbol of Catherine's family. The garden where the two trees grow is symbolic of England, secure within high fortified walls.

⌀ LEFT

The acquisition in 2006 of *My Ladye Nevells Booke*, dating from 1591, added significant strength to the Library's collection of historic music manuscripts.

From the sixteenth century comes a setting of the Lady Mass (a mass in honour of the Virgin Mary) contained in four volumes whose bindings are inscribed with the arms of Henry VIII and Catherine of Aragon. It was composed by Nicholas Ludford, a musician in the royal chapels. Another of Henry and Catherine's books is a score of *Salve radix*, a complex composition in which each of two voice parts is written in a circular band surrounding a Tudor rose. On the first page is a picture of a castle, the English and Spanish flags flying proud from its towers. The Latin words pay tribute to the anticipated flowering of the Tudor dynasty, with the first line translated as: 'Hail, root, bringing forth stems of different colours from your shoot'.

Forward to the next century: here the highlight of the music collection is Henry Purcell's large manuscript volume of anthems and welcome songs, including *My heart is inditing*, the anthem he wrote at 26 for the coronation of James II in 1685. A boy

chorister at the Chapel Royal and later an organist there, Purcell was an admired composer in the baroque style then coming into fashion. His best-known work is the opera *Dido and Aeneas*, while his arrangement of *Lillibulero*, a traditional Irish song, is played several times daily on the BBC World Service, introducing the news.

In the year Purcell wrote *My heart is inditing*, Georg Frederic Handel and Johann Sebastian Bach were born in Germany; but since Handel spent most of his productive life in London and became a British subject in 1727, he is regarded as an English composer. After his death all Handel's surviving manuscripts were presented to George III, a great admirer of his music, and retained by the Royal Family until 1957, when Queen Elizabeth II donated the Royal Music Library to the British Museum. They include the draft score of his majestic, much-performed *Messiah*, written in 1741 and given its première in Dublin the following year.

The music of both Handel and Purcell was featured at the Spring Gardens at Vauxhall, established just

❧ LEFT
The Hallelujah chorus from
Handel's *Messiah*, 1741.

❧ BELOW
The Grand Walk at Vauxhall
Gardens, engraved by E. Rooker.

after the Restoration in 1660. In the early eighteenth
century the Gardens were enjoying their heyday as
Londoners' principal means of temporary relief from
the pressures of the teeming, polluted city; a venue for
outdoor performances and celebrations. A sample of
the songs heard there comes in a 1737 compilation
called *The Musical Entertainer*, with eye-catching
engravings by George Bickham Jr. Many of the lyrics
celebrate pleasures such as hunting and drinking,
while a few are dedicated to the venue itself. This is
Rural Beauty, or Vauxhall Gardens:

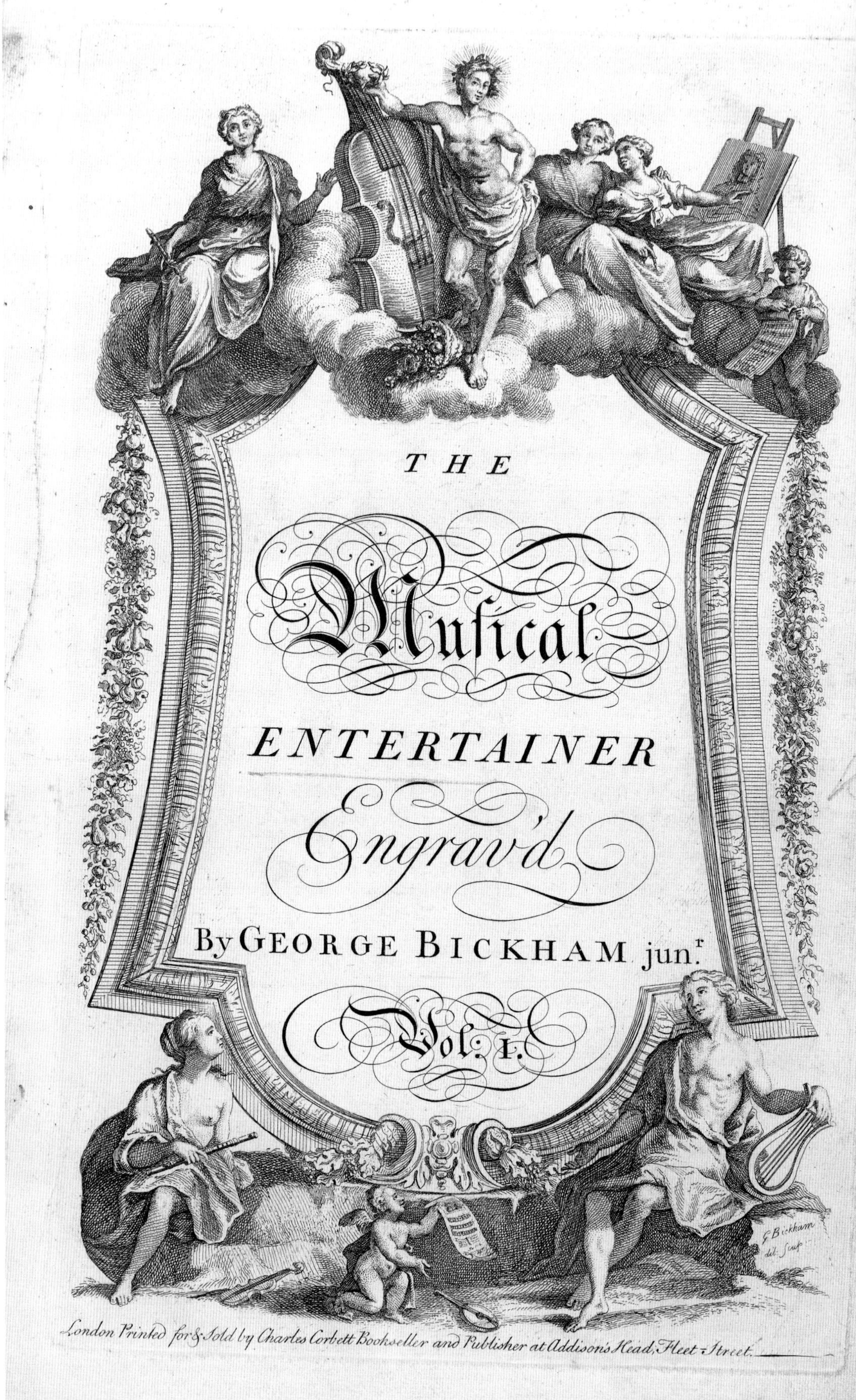
THE
Musical
ENTERTAINER
Engrav'd
By GEORGE BICKHAM jun.r
Vol. I.
G. Bickham del. Sculp.
London Printed for & Sold by Charles Corbett Bookseller and Publisher at Addison's Head, Fleet-Street.

RIGHT
Title page of *The Musical Entertainer*, 1737.

Lo! What splendors round us darting
Swift illume the charming scene;
Chandeliers their light imparting
Pour fresh beauties o'er ye green.

In contrast, a sad ballad laments the Gardens'
annual winter closure:

The sun now darts fainter his ray,
The meadows no longer invite;
The wood nymphs are all tript away,
No verdure cheers sweetly the sight.
Then adieu to the pastoral scene
Where harmony charm'd with her call:
Where pleasure presided as queen
In ye echoing shades of Vauxhall.

By the turn of the century the songs performed
at Vauxhall were becoming less lyrical and more
raucous – approaching the style of the music
halls that would come into fashion during Queen
Victoria's reign. In 1801 James Hook compiled
*A Collection of Favourite Songs sung at Vauxhall
Gardens*, copies of sheet music bound in a single
volume. The lyrics come in three basic categories.
Women singers would give tongue-in-cheek advice
about how to handle men, while men tended to be
more romantic, lauding the charms of their loved
ones. Here's Rosemund Mountain, wife of the leader
of the Vauxhall orchestra:

Silly men, not to know when we wheedle and
    tease
We have only one wish, that's to do what we
    please.

The repertoire of both sexes also included patriotic
numbers, singing the praises of the armed forces,
such as these, performed by Mrs. Franklin:

May George rule our hearts, may his fleets rule
    our shore,
And Britons be Britons till time is no more.

And again:

Give me the lad who braves the sea,
Defending Britons, guarding me,
A sailor is the lad for me.

Back in the calmer world of the classics, Bach is
represented in the Library by the manuscript of *The
Well-tempered Clavier*. It contains all but three of his
second set of 24 preludes and fugues, compiled in
1742 but not published until after he died in 1750.
Most of the pieces were written out by the composer
himself, but a few were copied by Anna Magdalena,
his second wife. Of the three missing scores one is
in Berlin, but the other two have not been traced.

In June 1765 the violinist Leopold Mozart visited
the British Museum with his children, including
nine-year-old Wolfgang, already recognised as a
prodigy. Leopold presented the Museum with his
young son's first publications, the violin sonatas op.1
and 2, and Wolfgang composed a special motet, *God
is our refuge*, which was to remain his only setting of
English words. Another prized Mozart item is the
thematic catalogue that he compiled meticulously

The composer Wolfgang Amadeus Mozart (1756–91) first met his cousin Maria Anna Mozart in her native Augsburg in 1777, when she was 19. For a while they conducted a romance and in this affectionate letter he included a drawing of her. In 1779 she stayed with him in Salzburg for nearly three months, but subsequently their relationship cooled. Maria Anna lived until she was 82 and although she never married she had a daughter, fathered by a cleric.

Pages for 24 February to 24 April 1788 from Mozart's thematic catalogue.

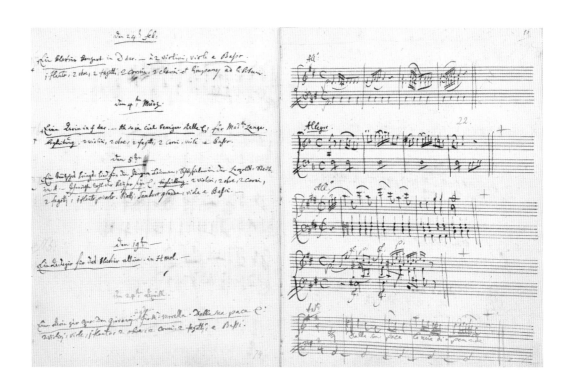

from 1784 until his death in 1791, to bring order to his dazzling and exhausting programme of performance and composition. In it, he listed the date and title of the works, the instruments they were composed for and, in the case of operas, the singers who appeared in the first performance. On a facing page he jotted down the notations for the opening bars.

The catalogue was one of many important documents relating to musical history donated to the Library in 1986 by the heirs of Stefan Zweig, an Austrian Jewish writer. Zweig fled Nazi persecution in 1934, after Adolf Hitler had refused to attend an opera by Richard Strauss because Zweig had written the lyrics. He moved to England, becoming a British subject, then relocated to Brazil, where he committed suicide in 1942. He had begun to collect musical and literary autograph manuscripts while at school in Vienna, and over the years he and his heirs built up one of the world's great collections. In 1957 the family presented the thematic catalogue to the British Museum on loan, eventually transferring ownership of the whole collection to the Library.

It includes autograph scores by Bach, Beethoven, Wagner, Mahler, Debussy and others, as well as many literary manuscripts. Among the musical highlights are the manuscript of Maurice Ravel's *Bolero*, as he arranged it for a piano duet, and Franz Schubert's setting of *An die Musik*, a poem by Franz von Schober. Schubert originally wrote the music

fig: I. Kopf

Engel

fig: III. Nasen   Spitzen fig: II

fig: VI.

fig: IV. Brust: Halb fig: V

Wann und wann eine seine Vorstellung an ihrem Herrn Herdern
= bringen in so: Herderbringer — Nemlich an den der sich
die Mühe geben hat ihnen zu machen, und den Künsten
die ihnen hat ihnen lernen. Adieu — Adieu — Engel.

Meine Vetter giebt ihnen seinen Onckelschen Seegen.
und meine Schwester giebt ihnen seinen Cousinschen Kuss.
und der Vatter giebt ihnen das was er ihnen nicht geben darf.
Adieu — Adieu — Engel.

in 1817, when he was 20, and revised it in 1827, a year before he died (possibly of syphilis). It is one of more than 600 songs he wrote in his short life, many performed frequently to this day.

The Zweig collection was not confined to manuscripts. Other intriguing items include a portrait of Schubert, painted two years before his death, and Mozart's contract of marriage to Constanze Weber, his landlady's daughter, in 1782 – a match that Leopold Mozart initially opposed. The contract is essentially an early form of pre-nuptial agreement,

laying down that the bride would contribute a dowry of 500 guilder, which the groom would make up to 1500 guilder, and this would constitute a fund to be paid to the surviving partner when one of them died.

Well before the Zweig treasures came its way, the British Museum was assiduously augmenting its collection of musical manuscripts. In 1881 it bought more than 400 volumes from Julian Marshall, a writer about music (and tennis). The star item is a volume of Ludwig van Beethoven's sketches for his *Pastoral Symphony*, dating from 1808 when, at the age of 38, he was already profoundly deaf. Like many of his manuscripts, the sketches provide evidence of his meticulous, even obsessive working method: they are littered with crossings-out and insertions where Beethoven had second and third thoughts about a particular phrase, providing an insight into the processes that led to the final versions of a great composer's works.

The holdings on Beethoven and other musical titans were further strengthened in 2002 when the Library raised £1million by public subscription, plus a grant from the Heritage Lottery Fund, to buy the archive of the Royal Philharmonic Society, which had unique links with the composer. The Society commissioned Beethoven's *Ninth Symphony* in 1822 and two years later the manuscript arrived in London, with a dedication to the Philharmonic Society on its title page. It is now one of the Library's most important musical possessions. In 1827, when Beethoven was impoverished and dying, the Society sent him £100 – a gift that George Bernard Shaw judged to be 'the only entirely creditable incident in English history'. The composer offered to write another symphony, the projected *Tenth*, as a gesture of thanks; but it remained unfinished when he died.

Among the 270 autograph scores in the Society's archive is that of Mendelssohn's First Symphony, as well as the performance scores of some of his overtures, on which he made handwritten changes. There is also a treasure trove of letters from composers including Berlioz, Brahms,

Dvořák, Debussy, Liszt, Wagner, Sibelius and Rachmaninov. The man who conducted the first London performance of Beethoven's *Ninth*, at the Philharmonic Society's Hanover Square rooms, was Sir George Smart, one of its founder members. At his death in 1867 Smart bequeathed his musical collection to the British Museum, including his diary, in which he recorded meeting Beethoven at a dinner in Vienna in 1825: 'He was in the highest of spirits. We all wrote to him by turns, but he can hear a little if you halloo quite close to his left ear.'

❧ ABOVE
A page from Beethoven's sketches for his *Pastoral Symphony*, 1808.

Of the many collections of private papers of figures in the world of music, Sir George's are among the most fascinating. A poignant memento of another nineteenth-century German composer, Carl von Weber, is the score of his opera *Oberon*, composed at the invitation of the Royal Opera House, Covent Garden, where Sir George was Musical Director. Weber came to London in April 1826 to conduct his own new work, and just five weeks after the performance he died of tuberculosis, aged only 39, at Sir George's London home.

The Smart bequest includes a large number of programmes, mainly of concerts that Sir George conducted in London and at festivals across the country. On many he wrote comments – not always complimentary – on the performances. At an Edinburgh concert in 1824 the harpist, Mr. Pole, was 'nervous, therefore hurried the first solo'. In Bath in 1833, during a West Country tour that Sir George was organising but not conducting, much of the programme 'went beautifully … very effective' and, best of all, several performances were 'encored'; but one new ballad was dismissed as 'a failure – obliged to change for Bristol'. A further irritation at Bristol was that, before the railways brought about a standardisation of time throughout the British Isles, the clocks there showed a different time from that in London. A stickler for noting exactly when items in the programme began and ended, the conductor wrote that he would persist in using London time because 'the Bristol time is slower'.

⊰◦ BELOW
Catherine Stephens, from
Oxberry's Dramatic Mirror.

Taken together, Sir George's diary and the annotated programmes provide a lively and intimate picture of the classical music scene of the 1820s and 30s, when he was its dominant figure. There is the recurring nightmare of lead singers cancelling at the last minute, usually pleading illness. A repeat offender was Catherine Stephens, the most famous soprano of the time, her 'full, rich, round, lovely' voice greatly admired – but with a notable exception. Sir George records that when she sang for George IV at Brighton in 1821, the King expressed his disappointment. Such was her reputation, though, that engaging her added gloss to any programme; yet it was a calculated risk, for she appears to have been just the kind of singer whose behaviour gave prima donnas a bad name.

Stephens clearly found Edinburgh especially harmful to her health, cancelling performances there in 1819 and again in 1824 –the latter being the ill-starred concert at which poor Mr. Pole had made a mess of his harp solo. In Norwich in 1827 she 'came to the hall so ill that she was obliged to return', but she was better the next day and redeemed herself by volunteering to join in the semi-chorus in part two of Handel's *Messiah*, although she was not scheduled to sing in that act. Sir George fawned on her, noting in the programme that this was 'very kind of Miss Stephens', and there were other occasions when he found it politic to butter her up. At a London concert in 1827, for example, he noted that she was 'encored for all her songs', and the following year he reported

MISS STEPHENS,
AS
ROSETTA.

with relief that she had arrived 'in very good time' for her appearance – despite having had to hotfoot it from Covent Garden, where she was singing in a version of *Aladdin*. Stephens's subsequent history confirms that she was a lady who knew her own mind: shortly after retiring at 41 she married the Earl of Essex, then over 80. He died a year after the marriage and, with her days of stardom – and of ill-health – behind her, she spent another 40 comfortable years as the dowager countess.

Absent singers were not the only cause of what Sir George termed 'derangement' – having to alter the running order at the last minute to accommodate the foibles of the performers. In one of the annual concerts he organised in London for the New Musical Fund for the Relief of Decayed Musicians he had booked an Italian married couple, the soprano Giacinta Toso and her husband Giovanni Puzzi, a horn player. When Sra. Puzzi saw that her solo was scheduled immediately after her husband's, she insisted that the order be changed. Sir George complied, placing two other pieces between them, and vented his exasperation by writing 'Fantasio!!!' in the margin of the programme.

The high point of his concerts for the New Musical Fund came in 1831, when Niccolo Paganini, the legendary violin virtuoso, made a guest appearance. 'Between the acts I rehearsed with Sr. Paganini in a room below stairs – the air *The Carnival at Venice* which I accompanied alone with him after his intoductory prelude. He played

after Mrs. Knyvett's song. [She was Deborah Travis, wife of the singer and composer William Knyvett.] He came on without his violin to bow his thanks but was encored – when he began his variations on the same air without any prelude.'

Among the strongest elements of the Library's musical collections are twentieth-century British autograph scores. Counted among them, although composed in 1899, is Edward Elgar's *Variations on an Original Theme (Enigma)*, in which he attempts musical portraits of his wife, his friends and himself, laced with lively humour. It was the first work to gain him popular recognition, even though only his friends were able to interpret the coded references. Elgar's daughter bequeathed most of her father's manuscripts to the Library, but the never-completed draft score for his third symphony was presented by the BBC, which commissioned the work. It is a fascinating manuscript, and includes a charming photograph of the composer with his dog.

In 1969 the widow of Sir Henry Wood, creator of the Promenade Concerts, gave his archive to the British Museum. Three years later Imogen Holst, daughter of Gustav Holst, donated a large collection of her father's manuscripts. After Benjamin Britten died in 1976 the Library was allocated 30 of his scores under the Acceptance in Lieu scheme, to offset death duties. These are now on permanent loan to the Britten-Pears Library at the Red House in Aldeburgh, Suffolk, where Britten and the singer Peter Pears lived.

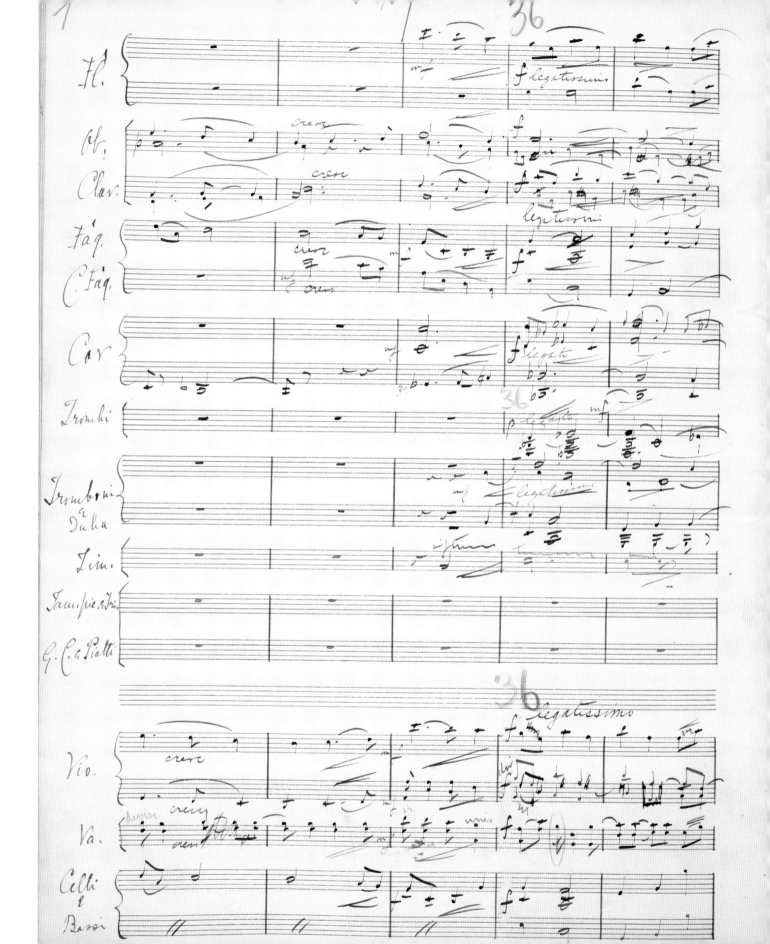

Sir Michael Tippett sold most of his autograph manuscripts to the Library in his lifetime, using the proceeds to establish the Michael Tippett Musical Foundation, providing grants to support young musicians and composers. He drafted his scores in pencil and there are frequent emendations until his final – or in some cases not quite final – intentions are expressed in ink. The scores amount to 150 volumes; far fewer than the 316 volumes of the manuscripts of Sir Peter Maxwell Davies, acquired from the composer between 1993 and 2007, or the several hundred volumes of Ralph Vaughan Williams' papers, presented by his widow. More recently the Library has acquired the manuscripts of many living composers, including Gavin Bryars, Brian Elias, Steve Martland, John McCabe and Robert Saxton, as well as papers of performers, conductors, musical administrators and publishers.

The collection of printed music comprises more than 1.6 million publications. In the nineteenth century the Museum acquired music alongside printed books, by legal deposit and purchase, but had never systematically bought the works of such household names as Mozart, Haydn and Beethoven. In 1946 the Trustees were offered the music library of Paul Hirsch, a German Jewish industrialist who had transported it from Frankfurt to England not long before the Second World War. The collection was acquired in its entirety, providing the Museum with first editions of much of the repertoire that is fundamental to modern concert life. Since then the Library has been active in acquiring printed music, filling gaps in its holdings and purchasing new editions from all over the world. There is also a substantial collection of music periodicals, from nineteenth-century journals such as *The Musical World* to current magazines, along with posters and playbills.

The development of digital technology means that visitors to the Library can now listen to many compositions as well as reading the scores. In 1983 the Library took over the British Institute of Recorded Sound and it now holds over a million discs and thousands of tapes as well as some historic cylinders from the 1880s – soon after Thomas Edison invented the first machine that could record and reproduce sounds.

The British Museum began collecting aural material in 1905, starting with the voices of statesmen, poets and actors. Music entered the collections a few years later, but there was no thought-out acquisitions strategy. The Museum relied almost totally on donations from record companies, which included early recordings by Francesco Tamagno, Dame Nellie Melba and Enrico Caruso, as well as the non-musical voices of celebrities such as the Russian writer Leo Tolstoy and the explorer Ernest Shackleton.

There was, however, no enthusiasm in the Museum for building a comprehensive collection, so a separate organisation, the British Institute for Recorded Sound, was established in 1955, with its headquarters in Russell Square. This was the time when 78rpm shellac discs were being replaced by 45rpm and 33rpm vinyl, so a timely appeal to the public to donate their old 78s resulted in many thousands of records being added to the then sparse holdings. Nothing was rejected: there were donations of music from all over the world, as well as recordings of speech and wildlife sounds. By the time the Library took it over, the Institute had moved to larger premises in South Kensington: the Archive is now located beneath the Conservation Centre at St. Pancras.

Although the legal deposit obligation does not extend to sound recordings, most British record companies donate copies of their records when they are released, so that they are available to be heard at the Library. Thousands of foreign recordings are also held, as well as concerts and other performances broadcast by the BBC since its inception in 1927, many never made available commercially. Although for some years the BBC did not keep recordings of all its output, an enthusiast named Kenneth Leech recorded significant concerts off-air, including the Promenade Concerts: the Library now has his collection. Another enthusiast, Brian Head, donated the recordings he had made of broadcasts by the choir of King's College Chapel in Cambridge.

From 1963 the Sound Archive made its own recordings of important BBC broadcasts. There is,

too, a wealth of material from the Glyndebourne Opera House, the Royal Opera House in London and the festivals at Edinburgh, Aldeburgh, Cheltenham and Bath. The Voice of America radio station donated hundreds of tapes of concerts by the New York Philharmonic and other leading orchestras of the

BELOW
A late 1890s Edison phonograph for recording sound.

United States, along with performances by the New York Metropolitan Opera between the 1940s and the 1960s. Several musicians and conductors – among them the late Sir Charles Mackerras – donated their own collections of recordings to the Library.

In 1909 the Gramophone Company of London sent a recording engineer on a journey of some 5000 miles in the southern regions of Tsarist Russia, to record the traditional music of the people. He came back with 1200 remarkable recordings, which the company donated to the British Museum. Among many other unique and historic items is a tape of Igor Stravinsky experimenting with a revised version of his *Symphonies of Wind Instruments* with musicians in a Hollywood film studio in 1948. Taped talks by Elisabeth Schwarzkopf, Yehudi Menuhin and other famous musicians are also preserved in the Sound Archive. Popular music is not neglected: indeed, the Archive has one of the most wide-ranging collections in the world, ranging from the inevitably crackly voices of the stars of Edwardian music hall to the latest digitally mixed chart-toppers. These are supported by pop videos and recordings made at important concerts and festivals.

Queen Victoria is the first British monarch whose voice is on record. In 1888 at Balmoral she tried out an early recording device: some 40 words survive on a wax cylinder, but few are comprehensible and not everyone accepts that it is the Queen speaking. All her successors' broadcasts to the nation, at Christmas and at times of national emergency, have been preserved. Florence Nightingale can be heard appealing for funds to aid distressed former members of the Light Brigade, 'my dear old comrades at Balaclava'. The Library also has a recording of Alfred, Lord Tennyson, from his home in the Isle of Wight, reading his poem about the Light Brigade's debacle, as well as his less well-known *Charge of the Heavy Brigade*.

Moving into the twentieth century, there are recordings of major poets such as W.H. Auden and W.B. Yeats reading their work. Plays written specifically for BBC Radio by the leading playwrights of the day can be heard, along with landmark performances of Shakespeare and other classic plays by great actors. From the world of science, Albert Einstein attempts to explain to laymen his pivotal equation, $E=mc^2$; and his speech on attaining US citizenship in 1940 has also been preserved.

The Library's 2010 exhibition *Evolving English*, chronicling how the language had developed over the centuries, relied heavily on voice recordings from the Sound Archive to chart changes in dialects and usage over the twentieth century. Visitors were invited to give samples of their own voices to provide research material for future generations.

The depth of the Library's sound collections has been increased by the National Life Stories project, launched in 1987. Notable personalities from many walks of life are interviewed at length, with the aim of providing a detailed record for posterity of the texture of contemporary life. Each set of interviews is themed around a specific profession or activity. Among groups represented are architects, artists, authors, booksellers, publishers, craftspeople, scientists and workers in a number of industries such as oil, fashion, the press and the wine trade. Sometimes specific firms are singled out: an oral history of Tesco, the supermarket chain, is being compiled under the National Life Stories banner. Interviewees are asked intimate questions going back to their childhood and family background, their schooling and their professional and domestic lives.

Although the guidelines are the same across all categories, each project is organised separately. With Authors' Lives, for example, an advisory committee, chaired by the novelist Penelope Lively, listed 100 leading British writers to be targeted by a dedicated interviewer. Most of them agreed to take part. The interviews ran into several sessions lasting about 15 hours on average, with some coming to nearly double that: among the longest were those with the biographer Michael Holroyd, the playwright and novelist Michael Frayn and Penelope Lively herself. In some cases the subjects have stipulated that the interviews should not be published in their lifetime, but from those that have been released it is clear that they amount to a significant account of how the world of literature has responded to the rapid social and technological changes of the early twenty-first century.

Not all the voices to be heard in the Sound Archive are human. There are more than 160,000 recordings of 10,000 species of birds, mammals, amphibians, reptiles – even fish and insects. Many of them have been donated to the Library by enthusiastic naturalists and bird-watchers, who recorded them in the wild, and there are also sounds obtained from zoos and farms. It was in 1969 that Patrick Sellar, secretary of the ornithology section of the London Natural History Society, suggested that the British Institute of Recorded Sound should institute a wildlife section. The recordings are popular with nature-lovers and many have been transferred to CDs, including such arcane compilations as the sound of birds mimicking other birds. (How can you tell?) They also have a practical purpose in the entertainment media: producers of films and plays, especially radio plays, use them to establish rural settings. Other countryside sounds, such as rainforests, waterfalls and thunder, form part of the collection, and there are historic recordings made by Ludwig Koch, a pioneer in this field, who introduced radio listeners to nature's aural joys in the years following the Second World War.

CHAPTER 11

The appliance of science

✎ OPPOSITE

As well as being a supreme artist, Leonardo da Vinci (1452–1519) was a pioneer scientist and mathematician. His notes, recording his many interests and experiments in geometry, mechanics and much else, including investigating the flight of birds, were bound into several volumes after his death. The drawings are accompanied by notes in Italian, in his characteristic mirror handwriting, reading from right to left. In the seventeenth century one notebook was owned by Thomas Howard, Earl of Arundel: it was given to the British Museum library in 1831.

❛As respects the great contrivances and inventions which have conferred so much power and wealth upon the nation, it is unquestionable that for the greater part of them we have been indebted to men of the humblest rank.❜

～ SAMUEL SMILES, *SELF-HELP* (1859)

THE LIBRARY'S STRONG scientific holdings have their roots in the most important of the collections that the British Museum acquired at and soon after its foundation – those of Sir Hans Sloane, Sir Robert Harley, Thomas Grenville, George III and the naturalist Sir Joseph Banks. All contained a wealth of practical books about exploration, discovery, natural history and medicine, ranging from medieval times to the burgeoning developments in physics, chemistry and biology of the eighteenth and early nineteenth centuries. Since then, with the enforcement of legal deposit, the Library has built a comprehensive store of books covering developments in all aspects of science, including social science.

In 1966 the Museum took over the former National Library of Science and Invention, based on the Patent Office Library created in 1855 by Bennet Woodcroft, who effectively invented the present system for registering patents in Britain. The NLSI

was established not only as a resource for scientists, but also as a tool for inventors and manufacturers considering applying for patents, enabling them to discover what other products or blueprints existed in their field. It acquired historic works by and about the early pioneers of observation and experimentation, now incorporated into the appropriate categories of the British Library's collections.

The Library has many first printed editions of such thinkers as Aristotle, Plato, Pliny the Elder, Ptolemy and Archimedes. Among the manuscripts is *Poeta Astronomica*, a collection of writings about astronomy and related subjects compiled about 1200. It once belonged to the priory of Rochester Cathedral, becoming part of the Royal Library on the dissolution of the monasteries. Notes written on the manuscript are believed to have been the work of Patrick Young, librarian to James I.

Medieval cautery, from a
twelfth-century medical tract.

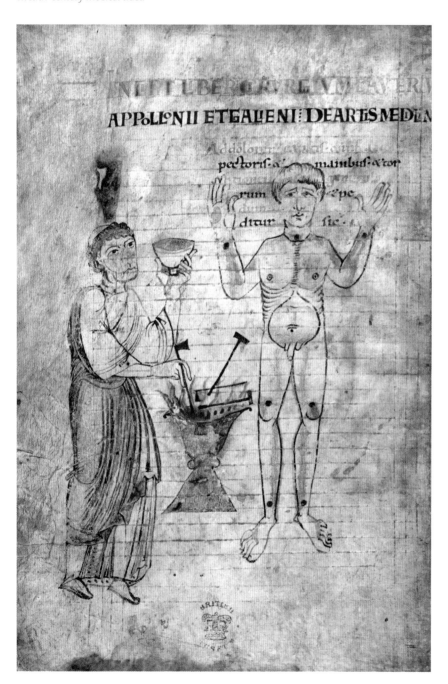

The medieval belief that the movements of
the stars influence events on Earth resulted in
the publication of numerous astrological charts
and almanacs. Several depict the human body,
with annotations revealing which parts of it were
thought to have been affected by which signs of the
zodiac. Books and manuscripts about early medical
practices were much sought after by eighteenth-
century collectors. Because Sir Hans Sloane was a
physician, his collection included many works on
medicine, and through the words and illustrations
in its manuscripts we can follow the progress of
medieval health care.

An image from the early twelfth century
demonstrates the practice of cautery – the
application of a hot iron to specific parts of the
body that are pinpointed on the diagram. This
technique was used to treat a variety of internal
and external disorders (and is still employed today
in sophisticated surgery, but with more advanced
instruments). Another manuscript, compiled
some 400 years later, depicts the gentler process of
cupping: applying a heated cup to the skin to ease
the flow of blood around the body. From the late
twelfth century come gruesome images of a doctor
performing basic surgery – removing cataracts by
poking a needle in the sufferer's eye or gouging
out haemorrhoids with a knife, using a clawed
instrument to separate the victim's buttocks. A later
manuscript, not in the Sloane collection, shows a
range of crude tools for carrying out this and other

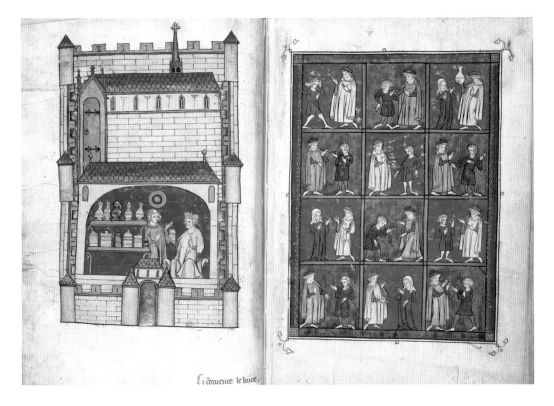

✦ LEFT

Apothecary shop and medical
consultations from a fourteenth-
century French manuscript.

ſi comuence le liure.

operations in the same region of the body, with
unsettlingly detailed diagrams of how and where
the instruments should be inserted.

A book made in Amiens in the fourteenth
century includes 48 equally stark illustrations of
consultations between physicians and patients,
whose symptoms include vomiting, fainting and
what appear to be head lice. From the same work
comes a vivid depiction of an apothecary's shop
and an extraordinary diagram that purports to

reveal the workings of an eye. Most striking of all
are two fifteenth-century English manuscripts,
each showing 17 positions of a foetus in the womb,
some involving twins – presumably intended as
handbooks for midwives. Sloane, ever eager to
supplement his learning, also owned a 53-volume
set of medical dissertations submitted at Leiden
University in the Netherlands between 1593 and
1746. The volumes are bound in white vellum and
each holds between 20 and 75 documents.

Sir Robert Harley's collection, too, is rich in early medical works, including three fifteenth-century manuscripts compiled by doctors that list the names of their patients, their illnesses and the prescribed remedies. Thomas Fayreford worked principally in the West Country in the early years of the century, treating men, women and children ranging from aristocrats and clergymen to artisans and tradespeople. One of the most common female ailments was what he termed 'suffocation of the womb': at that time many women's health problems were thought to originate from disorders of the uterus. Other conditions included a variety of fevers, as well as injuries such as burns and fractures. Fayreford's remedies were a mixture of rudimentary science, surgery and superstition: as well as prescribing herbal solutions and other medicines, he would recite healing 'charms' in the hope of hastening a cure. To this record of his medical activities he attached manuscripts of cures gleaned from a variety of sources.

John Crophill, a decade or two younger than Fayreford, operated in Essex as a part-time doctor, his main occupation being bailiff of Wix Priory. He also included charms in the mix of remedies offered to his patients, who came principally from the labouring class. His manuscript ranges wider then Fayreford's, including notes on cookery, astronomy and alchemy, as well as some verses addressed to five local women.

The third of the Harley manuscripts naming patients and recording their prescriptions is anonymous; but the document is of special interest because many of those treated by the author were members of the courts of Edward IV and Richard III, including the Kings themselves. Some compound medicines bear the names of the distinguished figures for whom they were prescribed: there is, for instance, a 'Preservative of Richard', thought to be a safeguard against plague. A prescription written for Edward IV, to neutralise the effects of poison, provides evidence

Crowsfoot, a cure for a dog bite, from a twelfth-century herbal.

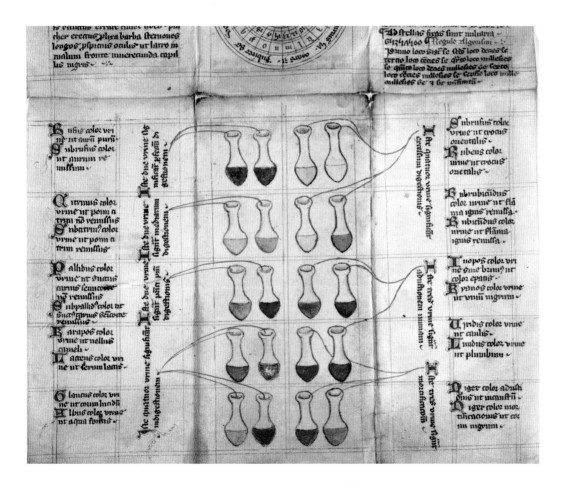

⌐ LEFT

Diagnosis by urine, from a
Physician's folding almanac,
c. 1406.

of the turbulence of the age. Harley also had earlier
medical manuscripts: one from the twelfth century
features a dramatic image of a dog biting an
unfortunate man's leg, along with a drawing of the
herb crowsfoot, then the remedy of choice for such
bites. There is, too, a useful colour chart of urine
samples in purpose-made flasks that vary little
from those seen in hospitals today. Notes alongside
the drawings indicate the illnesses suggested by the
various shades of yellow.

By the sixteenth century, hitherto accepted
theories about astronomy and the natural sciences

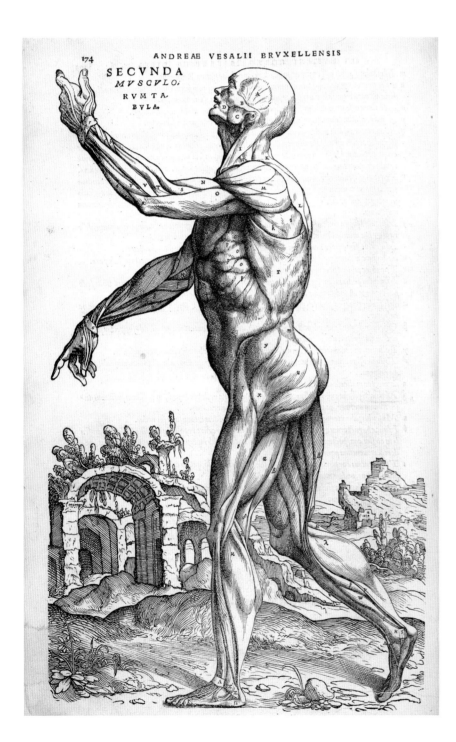

were being questioned and challenged by such as
Nicolaus Copernicus, Galileo Galilei and Leonard
Fuchs, who wrote what is thought to be the first
scientific description of plants. In 1544 Andreas
Vesalius, a Belgian anatomist, published *De
Humani Corporis Fabrica*. This ground-breaking
description of the structure of the human body is
notable for accurate illustrations by artists who had
clearly been present at autopsies and could depict
the structure of muscles and other body parts with
unprecedented accuracy. So great was the impact
of the book that Vesalius was appointed physician
to Charles V, the Holy Roman Emperor; but the
anatomist died in 1564 in a shipwreck while on
a pilgrimage to the Holy Land. In 1628 William
Harvey took medical science a stage further when
he revealed his theories about the circulation of
blood, and an early edition of his treatise is in the
Library's collection, in addition to one of the largest
collections of his papers.

Sir Joseph Banks's collection includes the book
that no botanist of his era could be without: Carl
Linnaeus's *Systema naturae*, published in 1735,
which proposed the system of plant classification
still in use today. The most striking item visually is
Elizabeth Blackwell's *A Curious Herbal*, two volumes
of illustrations of medicinal plants, originally
published in weekly parts between 1737 and 1739.
On his copy Banks made a number of notes about
the plants illustrated.

Apart from their intrinsic beauty, the engravings

☙ BELOW

A dandelion, from Elizabeth Blackwell's *A Curious Herbal*, 1737–39.

are fascinating because of the bizarre circumstances of their creation. In 1728 the Scots-born Elizabeth Blachrie, then 28, married Alexander Blackwell who, during careers as an unqualified doctor and later as a printer, ran up large debts and was sent to prison. Elizabeth undertook her plant engravings, using samples from the Chelsea Physic Garden as her models, to raise enough money to keep herself and their child. She had been trained as an artist before her marriage, and from her brief career as a doctor's wife she knew that there would be a market among apothecaries for an up-to-date herbal incorporating plants recently introduced from the Americas and elsewhere, such as tobacco and sassafras, an aromatic dried root.

After she had completed the drawings she took them to the debtors' prison, where Alexander identified the plants and composed a page of medical text for each one. She then engraved the copper plates and coloured the engravings. With the money she earned from the herbal Elizabeth was able to buy Alexander's release; but his incarceration had not reformed him. More debts were incurred, until in 1742 he abandoned his family and went to Sweden as court physician. There he became involved in political intrigue and was hanged for treason in 1748. Elizabeth died ten years later.

Among the more arcane of the early scientific works is Benjamin Franklin's pamphlet *Observations on smoky chimneys, their causes and cure, with*

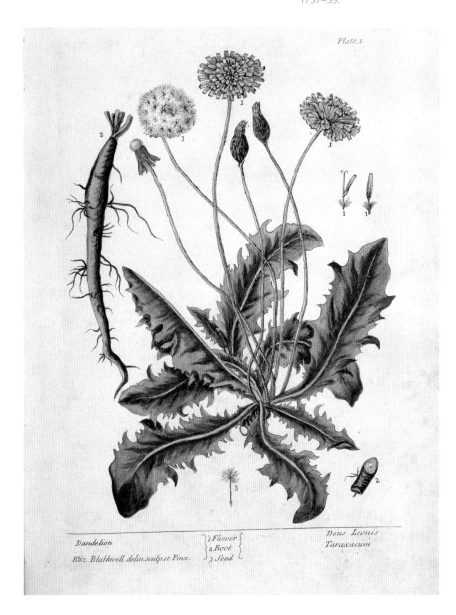

Dandelion

Eliz. Blackwell delin. sculp. et Pinx.

{ 1 *Flower* {
  2 *Root*
3 *Seed* }

Dens Leonis
Taraxacum

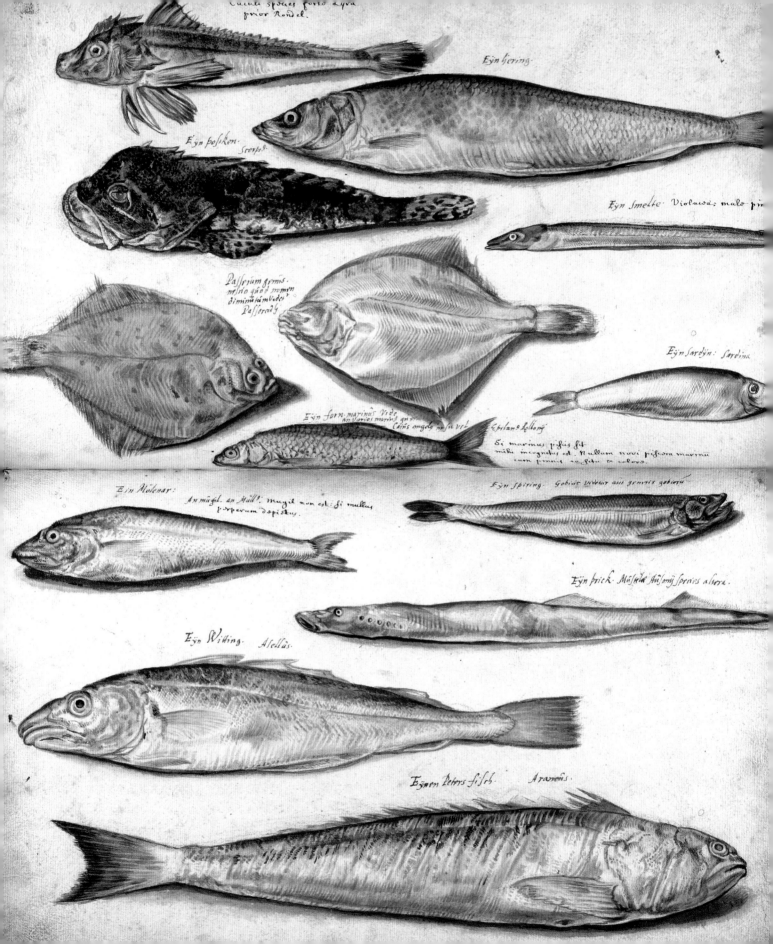

Cucula species forte aqua
prior Rondel.

Eyn hering.

Eyn poſiken.
Scorpis

Eyn Smelte· Violaua: malo pir

Passerum genus.
neſcio quod nomen
diminutum Vides
Paſſeraly

Eyn Sardijn· Sardina

Eyn ſorn marinus Vide
an Varias marina qu
Cuiis angels naſu Vel

Epiland kelkory

Si marinus piſcis ſit
mihi incognitus eſt. Nullum noui piſcem marinu
cum pinnis ea ſitu et colore

Ein Molenar:
An mugil. an Mull·. mugil non eſt· ſi mullus
perperam depictus

Eyn Spiring· Gobius Videtur aut gentis gobiorū

Eyn brick· Muſtela Auſonij ſpecies altera.

Eyn Witting· Aſellus.

Eynen Peters fiſch· Araneus.

considerations on fuel and stoves, illustrated with proper figures, published in 1793, three years after his death. It is a reminder that Franklin was a scientist as well as a statesman and printer. The pamphlet is the transcript of a letter he wrote in 1785 in response to an enquiry from Dr Jan Ingen-Housz, the physician to the Holy Roman Emperor in Vienna. Franklin wrote the letter while on a sea voyage – clearly a long voyage, because the pamphlet runs to 38 wordy pages.

The central message is that, in order to get smoke to rise through the chimney, rather than being diffused over the room being heated, there has to be a constant flow of fresh air. Franklin illustrates this with complex experiments involving a pipe filled with tobacco, a decanter of water, a glass tube, a quill and a filament of silk – quaintly illustrated at the back of the booklet. But how to get air into the room without making it cold, thus defeating the purpose of the fire in the grate? Franklin gives as an example a custom that he says prevailed in Iceland for some years: the islanders built their front doors low and constructed a gallery above them 'wherein the women can sit

✺ OPPOSITE
John Ray (1627–1705) was the leading English naturalist of his era, an archetypal polymath with a broad range of interests and expertise. He wrote important works on botany and zoology – including innovative attempts to classify plants and creatures into species – as well as on travel, theology and the use of language. This page is from the manuscript of his *History of Fishes*, published in 1686 with the support of the Royal Society, of which he was a leading light.

✺ LEFT
Equipment used by Benjamin Franklin in inventing a stove, from his *Observations on smoky chimneys*, 1793.

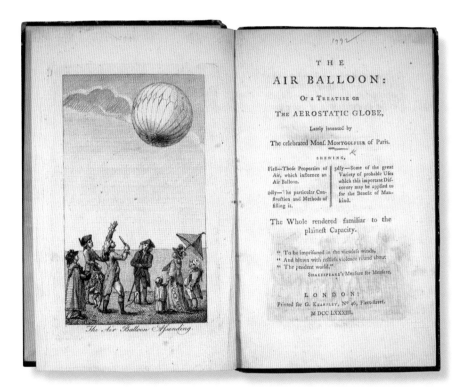

and work and the men read or write etc'. The air warmed by the fire rose to the gallery while the cold air admitted when the door opened, being heavier than the warm air, did not rise above the door.

The illustrations at the end of the pamphlet include several relating to a stove that Franklin invented. It was immensely complicated and building it would be a severe challenge even to those adept at putting together today's self-assembly furniture. There is, too, a letter to Franklin from Dr Thomas Ruston, a surgeon who had worked in both Britain and America. He wanted to follow up their discussion of smoky chimneys at dinner the previous evening. Ruston quoted a version of what was apparently a popular couplet:

A smoky house and a scolding wife
Are (said to be) two of the greatest ills in life.

Another pamphlet typifying the restless quest for knowledge that fuelled the Industrial Revolution is *The Air Balloon: or a treatise on the aerostatic globe lately invented by the celebrated Mons. Montgolfier of Paris*, published in 1784. At the front is an image of a balloon ascending, and the anonymous author quotes from Shakespeare's *Measure for Measure*:

To be imprisoned in the viewless winds,
And blown with restless violence round about
The pendant world…

The invention of a device that would allow men to emulate birds and escape the fate of being rooted to the ground, where the Creator had apparently consigned them, was rightly seen as a significant scientific advance. The introduction of the air balloon, wrote the author, 'in a very few ages back would have filled the world with amazement and wonder, and perhaps have sent the inventor to his grave with ignominy and disgrace'. He explains that the essential property of air is its elasticity, which enables it to be compressed and expanded. 'This property seems peculiar to air, there being no other elastic fluid in nature yet discovered.'

One method of making air light enough to power a balloon is, he maintains, to mix oil of vitriol with water and iron filings; but that makes it impossible to control and could end in a nasty accident. Montgolfier's method was to burn wet straw 'and by carrying a quantity of this fuel with him (in a little gallery constructed round the balloon, for the purpose of feeding it) he can ascend or descend at pleasure'. The author describes Montgolfier's flight in Paris the previous October, when he ascended to 1650 ft. ('more than four times higher than St. Paul's'):

'The gardens about Paris appeared to them like bouquets and the people passing and re-passing "like so many mites in a cheese", according to one passenger.' The author presages the eventual development of air travel by reporting that some people are experimenting with winged devices; but he believes that the main use of balloons will be for observation rather than travel, in particular for spotting invaders arriving by sea. 'During sieges they may be rendered particularly useful, by observing the works of the enemy and of course rendering them ineffectual.' Had balloons been deployed during the American War of Independence, he surmises, they could have prevented 'the debilitated and humiliating state of Great Britain'.

The progress of the Industrial Revolution can be charted by looking at copies of the 1769 patents for Richard Arkwright's 'water frame', which enabled cotton to be spun in large quantities on a single machine, and the original design of James Hargreaves's Spinning Jenny, which advanced the technique further. Shortly afterwards James Watt perfected the steam engine. This not only changed our way of life, but also did much to develop the system of acquiring patents to establish the rights of inventors, through a series of court cases in which Watt and his partner Matthew Boulton successfully protected their intellectual property.

A century later Michael Faraday achieved a comparable advance in his taming of electric power. The Library has the deposit copy of his *Experimental Researches in Electricity*, three volumes of papers that he read to the Royal Society, published in 1839, 1844 and 1855. In his introduction he makes an eloquent philosophical statement about scientists

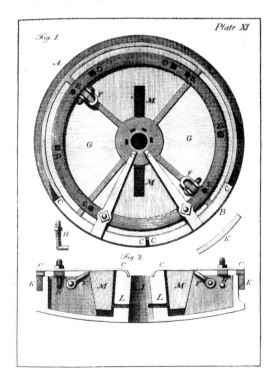

⟨ LEFT
Plate from James Watt's handbook on his steam engine, showing a plan and cross-section of the engine piston, *c*.1780.

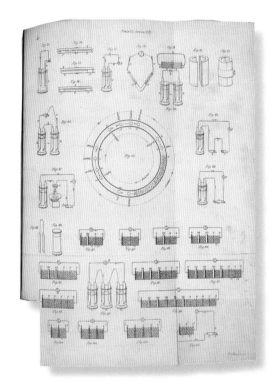

and their mission: 'Although I cannot honestly say that I *wish* to be found in error, yet I do fervently hope that the progress of science in the hands of its many zealous cultivators will be such, as by giving us new and other developments, and laws more and more general in their applications, will even make me think that what is written and illustrated in these experimental researches belongs to the by-gone parts of science.'

Well before the end of the nineteenth century, electricity and steam power had become established features of everyday life. A vivid idea of the impact of these developments can be gleaned from a remarkable collection of ephemera – advertising posters, sales catalogues, theatre programmes and such – acquired by the British Museum in 1895. It had been amassed by Henry Evans, a conjuror and ventriloquist born in south London about 1832. He performed under the stage name of Evanion; thus the material is known as the Evanion Collection.

Evans's father was a caterer with strong links to the world of popular entertainment. For some years he sold food and drink at Vauxhall Gardens and had a spell as landlord of the Black Prince pub in nearby Kennington. There it was that Henry, as a boy, began entertaining customers with conjuring tricks. He began his professional career at 17, playing in theatres and music halls all over Britain. By the 1860s he was sufficiently well established to be invited to perform for the royal family, and he later became friendly with Harry Houdini, the American escapologist and another enthusiastic collector of theatrical ephemera.

Evans's collection initially concentrated on playbills and posters connected with show business. Conjurors predominate, but there are bills for plays by J.M. Barrie and Jerome K. Jerome, while Marie Lloyd and Dan Leno are among famous music hall artists represented. There is a poster for Barnum's Circus, another for a roller-skating rink in Stockwell

BROEKMAN'S CIRCUS
AND GREAT MONKEY THEATRE,
THE "DUKE'S," HIGH HOLBORN.

GRAND CHRISTMAS
PANTOMIMIC STEEPLECHASE

 Executed by Ponies, Monkeys, Bears, Stags, Elephant, Goat, Dogs and Poodles.

NEVER BEFORE WITNESSED IN LONDON.

1876 7

EIGHTY FOUR-LEGGED ARTISTES
Will take part in the Performance.

EVERY DAY AT 2 & 7.

GENERAL REPERTOIRE FOR WINTER SEASON:

COMIC DINNER PARTY of EIGHT MONKEYS, and the Waiter "JOE."

The Wonderful MONKEY ACRO-BAT on the SLACK ROPE.

The extraordinary Monkey "LENA," on the Tight Rope, a la Blondin.

The Comical Adventures of the Derby by SIX MONKEYS IN THEIR CARRIAGE DRAWN BY POODLES.

The Highly-educated Dog, "Avarino."

Promenade de Madame Pompadour.

BOTTLE PYRAMID, a la LEVANTINE, executed by the Wonderfully-Trained GOAT, DINORAH.

The Wonderful Thoroughbred and BEST TRAINED PONIES IN THE WORLD, ALY and EMIR, in their Extraordinary Leaps over objects Six Feet High.

GRAND PAD ACT, by the Wonderful Equestrian Monkey, JACO.

LEDDY, the most highly Trained and only MUSICAL PONY in the World.

GRAND ACT DE MANAGE, executed by the famous Monkey MUMMY, (25 Years on the Stage) riding the Pony NEGRO.

Grand Voltige a la Richard.

The Astounding Performances of the AFRICAN ELEPHANT, ZARA

The Ponies MONTROSE and AIDA in their Extraordinary Evolutions.

Introduction of FOUR HIGHLY-TRAINED THOROUGHBRED PONIES.
(The whole world challenged to produce their equal).

The Hungarian CZIKOS POST, executed by the Monkeys JOE and HAN, on Seven Ponies.

The Destruction of DELHI, executed by DOGS and MONKEYS.

PRICES:—Private Boxes from 10s. to £2 2s.   Orchestra Stalls, 4s.   Dress Circle, 3s.   Boxes, 2s.   Pit, 1s.   Gallery, 6d.
Children Half-price (Gallery excepted).   Schools and Large Parties liberally treated with.

WALTER SMITH, "Bloomsbury Steam Printing Works," 61 & 62, High Street, W.C

and several for freak shows: S. Watson's American Museum of Living Curiosities in Oxford Street boasts the stoutest lady in the world, a woman with two heads, a man with no arms or legs and a kilted couple billed simply as 'Australians'. An advertisement for 'Harvey's Midges' promises a sight of people less than two feet tall. There are freak animals, too: another show boasts a giant cart horse, a sheep with four horns, a pony only 26 inches high and monster rats, larger than hares, 'recently captured after desperate resistance to men and dogs'. A flyer from the 1830s records the recent arrival of two giraffes at Surrey Zoological Gardens, with the kudos of having been visited by Queen Victoria.

A typical theatre notice describes the bill at the Canterbury Theatre of Varieties, near Waterloo Station, in December 1886, for five nights only: 'Testo, the Herculean American gymnast, will nightly perform his astounding feat of pulling against the united strength of two horses and defy them to move him, no matter how big they may be. … Onri, in her marvellous lightning descent by the hair of her head. First appearance of the wonderful Belgian giant (8 ft. high) Alfredo Devartos (24 years of age).'

Soon Evans broadened the collection to include material about commerce in general, with advertisements and catalogues for food, patent medicines, machinery, furniture and household goods. He was a regular user of the British Museum library, mainly to consult books on conjuring, and

in 1895 he approached Dr Richard Garnett, Keeper of Printed Books, with a view to selling part of his collection to the Museum. Garnett, who could see that the material would be valuable to social historians, agreed to buy about 5000 items. Because the price was less than £20 he did not have to get the permission of the Standing Committee – which was fortunate, because the majority of its members did not approve of broadening the Museum's remit to embrace the acquisition of ephemera.

Most of the items are from the second half of the nineteenth century – in other words contemporary with the adult Evans. A few, though, are rather older. A poster issued by the Theatre Royal in Hull in April 1801 illustrates the turn-of-the-century hunger for scientific knowledge:

'Mr. Lloyd from London will read a course of astronomical lectures illustrated by the new dioastrodoxon, or grand transparent orrery, 21 feet in diameter, assisted by upwards of 40 changes in appropriate classic scenery. … The lecturer presumes that the novel, varied and sublime spectacle he has now the honour for the first time of introducing in this town, will be highly grateful to his friends and be found worthy the attention and patronage of an enlightened, liberal and discriminating public by rendering astronomical truths so perspicuous that even those who have not so much as thought on the subject may acquire clear ideas of the economy and harmony of the planetary system. Every attention will be paid to unite pleasure with instruction.'

The rapid rate of technological advance in Victorian Britain is recorded in advertisements for innovations that in a few years would be taken for granted, such as Barrett and Elers's screw-top bottle for beer and other beverages. 'These screw bottles are opened with a turn of the fingers; are not shaken as in uncorking; and the whole, or any portion of the contents, may be poured out without disturbing the sediment.' There are advertisements for novelties such as sewing machines, bicycle lamps, horse-drawn reapers and mowers from Canada and a Carry-All tricycle for tradesmen as an alternative to the horse and cart. Numerous medical potions and remedies are promoted, many making claims that would not be acceptable today: 'Oh doctor, must my darling die?' 'There's very little hope, but try Scott's Emulsion.'

Familiar products launched in that period include Vaseline. 'It is not too much to say that no other article, introduced during this century, has received such unanimous recommendation', declares an advertisement, which lists a number of subsidiary products that have long vanished: Vaseline hair tonic, Vaseline concoctions for the throat and pulmonary complaints and Vaseline boot polish. A flyer records the change of name of Johnson's Fluid Beef to the more marketable and more enduring Bovril.

The 1884 catalogue of Hawkey's Furnishing Warehouse includes images of the elaborately designed chairs, sofas and chaises longues that we now regard as typically Victorian, fetching high prices in the auction rooms. By contrast, an advertisement for Fenby's wooden camp furniture, including deck chairs, shows strictly practical pieces and contains a vivid description of part of the high-tech manufacturing process: 'When this machine is fed by two lads the pieces of wood leave the machine like a rapid and continuous flight of rockets, and a wooden butt or target is found necessary to stop them from being shot to an inconvenient distance in the factory.'

Advertisements for gadgets that apparently failed to establish themselves in the market include one for a mechanical saddle replicating the action of riding a horse. It is said to quicken circulation, rouse torpid livers and mitigate hysteria, insomnia, gout and rheumatism. An early typewriter that has no keyboard but requires the user to turn a disc until the correct letter is reached can be had for ten shillings and sixpence. A ball-pointed pen – not a modern ballpoint but a conventional pen with a rounded end to the nib – is said to represent the greatest improvement in the manufacture of steel pens since they were introduced: 'They are suitable for writing in every position, never scratch or stick in the paper, hold more ink and last longer. By them bad writing is abolished, as they are adapted for all.' And in case the message needed reinforcing:

> The Ball-Pointed Pen is the pen of the age.
> 'Tis used by the banker, the merchant, the sage;
> The Editor joyfully shouts from his den,
> 'Eureka! I've found it, the Ball-Pointed Pen!'

❧ LEFT
Advertisement for ball-pointed pens, c.1888.

In 2006 the Library decided to launch a hands-on approach to its exhaustive material on patents by opening the Business and Intellectual Property Centre (BIPC). Its purpose is to support entrepreneurs, inventors and small businesses by providing access to its comprehensive collections of business and intellectual property databases and publications, as well as offering free advice to people on how they can start and run businesses. It incorporates the London search facility for the UK Patent Office. An 'inventor in residence' helps novices steer their way through the maze of regulations and gives tips on market research, copyright and sources of funding, allowing them to turn their ideas – if sound enough – into reality. And the Centre runs a series of talks and discussions under the heading 'Inspiring Entrepreneurs'.

Some may doubt whether this is a proper role for a national library; yet the men whose collections formed the basis of the British Museum library were themselves eager for knowledge not just for its own sake, but also for the profitable uses to which it could be put. Books are not simply sources of enlightenment and intellectual pleasure: they also serve as powerful tools in the pursuit of business.

The Centre attracts a noticeably different clientele from the other Reading Rooms. Where traditional Library users are, for the most part, either soberly dressed scholars or confident young Ph.D. students fully wired for sound, the business tyros are typically younger than the former and older than the latter. They are casually dressed – often in T-shirts – outgoing and eager to communicate. The anteroom of the BIPC Reading Room is set up as a venue for networking, with armchairs where people can sit and talk, racks of business newspapers and magazines to read and a small exhibition of successful new products launched by the Centre's alumni.

It is an impressive display. Of those inventions whose path to production was eased by the Centre, one of the most succesful is the Anywayup Cup, an unspillable drinking vessel for toddlers. Mandy Haberman was visiting a friend's house when a child spilt blackcurrant juice over the carpet. That inspired her and a fellow inventor to design a cup with a lid that obviates spillage, while still allowing the toddler to drink from it. Few households with young children are now without the device – and because she learned at the BIPC about her intellectual property rights, Ms. Haberman was able to launch a successful legal action against foreign companies proposing to copy her design.

Other products whose originators benefited from the Centre's facilities include a self-warming baby feeding bottle; a device to allow bicycles to be parked securely alongside street signposts;

❧ BELOW

The Anywayup Cup and its inventor, Mandy Haberman.

the Wiggly Wigglers line of ecological garden accessories; a popular brand of pomegranate juice; and a range of children's chairs and tables that double as toys, accompanied by a related story book. One client praised the Centre as 'an intoxicating mix of inspiration and information under one roof'.

The inaugural inventor-in-residence, Mark Sheahan, is the President of the Institute of Patentees and Inventors. He was named Inventor of the Year in 2004 for designing a plastic lid that opens if you just squeeze it – a solution he came up with after his mother complained that her arthritis made it hard for her to open tins of shoe polish. It can be used on containers for a wide range of products. He attends the Library for two full days a month, and such is his reputation that there is always a wait of several weeks before hopeful inventors can schedule an hour-long meeting to benefit from his advice.

'The idea has to be good to begin with, but an idea isn't enough,' he says. 'You have to be businesslike if you're going to make money from it. Being an inventor is a tough journey. There are occasions when people come here and I almost have to reinvent the idea. I understand what they're trying to achieve, but it's not actually manufacturable, at least not at the right cost. I enjoy it: I like meeting people with spirit who want to change their lives.'

The likes of Sir Robert Cotton, Sir Robert Harley and Sir Hans Sloane would, if they were to visit the BIPC today, no doubt be surprised to see this particular manifestation of how the national library has developed over the centuries since it was but a glimmer in their eyes – surprised, but surely not disapproving. For all of them were generous in sharing their expertise, their experience and the resources of their bookshelves with people whose curiosity matched their own: people with spirit who wanted to change their – and other people's – lives.

CHAPTER 12

Tales of the unexpected

‘Surprises are foolish things. The pleasure is not enhanced and the inconvenience is often considerable.’

∽ JANE AUSTEN, *EMMA* (1816)

⅗ OPPOSITE

William Henry Fox Talbot (1800–77) was a pioneer photographer who invented the calotype process of making prints from negatives. In 1845 he published a volume of photographs entitled *The Pencil of Nature*. This example, *The Ladder*, photographed at Lacock Abbey, his home in Wiltshire, is the only one that includes people. In 2006 the Library was given Fox Talbot's archive, including the notebooks in which he described many of his experiments.

IF YOU WANTED, for whatever reason, to consult a 1992 edition of *Chelsea Calling*, the primitively produced fan magazine – or fanzine – of Chelsea Football Club, you would not necessarily think first of going along to the British Library. Yet there you would find it, in a collection of fanzines purchased by the Library in 1999. Moreover, to look at it you would be made to take it to the supervised desk in the Rare Books and Music Reading Room designated for 'special materials', because fanzines are highly collectable and flimsy with it.

The Library is brimful of such surprises. Many visitors to its principal exhibition in the winter of 2009 discovered for the first time that it has an impressive collection of photographs, dating from the very origins of photographic techniques. In 2006 its holdings in this area were greatly strengthened with the gift of the Fox Talbot Collection, an extensive archive of photographs, correspondence, manuscripts and research notes from William Fox Talbot, the photographic pioneer.

Some of the best early photographs are among the 200,000 from the India Office Library collection, depicting people, wildlife, buildings and landscapes in India and other parts of Asia from the middle of the nineteenth century until India's independence in 1947. They cover a broad spectrum of life and society in the subcontinent, from royal visits to picnics, amateur dramatics to colourful street scenes.

They embrace, too, nearly all the early methods of capturing images for posterity. The daguerreotype, where the image is preserved on a metal plate, was the first viable photographic process. Through it we can today look at a marvellously atmospheric portrait of a British officer in the Indian army, posing with his sword, white gloves and bristling moustache, taken by John William Newland, a much-travelled daguerreotypist, in Calcutta in the 1850s.

At around the same time John Murray of the Bengal Medical Service was using the calotype process, patented by Fox Talbot in 1841, to photograph some of the great monuments of India, including the Taj Mahal.

⅗ BELOW

Chelsea Calling fanzine.

❧ ABOVE
Daguerrotype of a British Officer
in the Indian army by John
William Newland, 1850s.

❧ RIGHT
The Taj Mahal by John Murray,
calotype negative, 1850s.

In 1855 the Indian administration sent a diplomatic mission to Burma. Among the participants was Linnaeus Tripe, an officer in the Madras army and a keen photographer, who took more than 200 pictures on paper negatives.

Some ten years later another prolific photographer of Indian buildings was Edmund David Lyon. He used the glass negatives which by then had superseded earlier techniques, and it was their capacity for producing unprecedentedly sharp images that inspired the growth of amateur photography, persisting through a steady series of technical advances to this day. Lyon was commissioned by the colonial government to

LEFT
Ruins of the North Taku Fort in the Second Opium War, by Felice Beato, 1858.

record the traditional architecture of Madras and Bombay, and several hundred of his pictures are in the collection. In 1858 Felice Beato, one of the first photographers to specialise in scenes of war and its resulting devastation, went out to record the Indian rebellion and subsequently the Anglo-French campaign in China in 1860. His image of North Taku fort in north-east China, just after its capture, shows the bodies of its defenders draped among the ruins – bringing home the grim reality of conflict to those who had no first-hand experience of it.

Since then, wars have proved irresistible to photographers. The weight and bulk of the early equipment at first prevented them from recording battles, but they were quickly on the scene to photograph the consequences. Roger Fenton was the most notable of them in the Crimea (1853–56), while Mathew Brady, Alexander Gardner and a team of talented colleagues produced some evocative work in more than 8000 images of the American Civil War, the first conflict to be captured on camera in any detail. The best of these pictures were published

ALEX. GARDNER, Photographer,   Entered according to act of Congress, in the year 1865, by A. GARDNER, in the Clerk's Office of the District Court of the District of Columbia.   511 7th Street, V

Incidents of the War.

A SHARPSHOOTER'S LAST SLEEP.

Gettysburg, July, 1863.

Published by PHILP & SOLOMONS, Washington.

in the two-volume *Gardner's Photographic Sketch Book of the Civil War*.

Back in the East, John Thomson established a photographic studio in Singapore in 1862 and travelled widely in southeast Asia. He was the first person to photograph the temple of Angkor Wat, the images appearing in his book *The Antiquities of Cambodia*, published in 1867. Seven years later Thomson produced, in four volumes, *Illustrations of China and its People* – after which he turned his attention closer to home, with ground-breaking images of street life in London. In the early years of the twentieth century Sir Marc Aurel Stein, the explorer and archaeologist who acquired many of the items discovered at Dunhuang and other Silk Road sites (see Chapter 5), headed several expeditions to western China and took thousands of photographs.

The Middle East also proved a lure for photographic pioneers. As early as 1849 the French writer Maxime du Camp, a friend of Gustave Flaubert, produced a series of photographs of Egyptian temples: like Linnaeus Tripe, he made prints from paper negatives. In the 1850s Francis Frith, one of the best-known photographers of his generation, paid a long visit to the area, resulting in his two-volume *Egypt and Palestine Photographed and Described*, published in 1858 and 1859. In 1864 a party of Royal Engineers was sent to Jerusalem to improve its water supply. Among them was Sgt. James McDonald, who took several hundred

photographs, of which 87 were included in the official report. Far from being mere records of sanitary conditions in the city, many feature people as well as structures and the best have a moody quality. At the turn of the century D.S. George, based in Egypt, produced some lively images of the construction of the Aswan Dam, showing teams of labourers carrying stones to the site.

᪥ OPPOSITE

The American Civil War was the first conflict to be recorded extensively in photographs. The Scots-born Alexander Gardner (1821–82) toured the battlefields and in 1865 published *Gardner's Photographic Sketchbook of the War*. This image, which he named *A Sharpshooter's Last Sleep*, was photographed after the Battle of Gettysburg in 1863. Gardner is known to have staged some of his 'realistic' photographs and, although the main figure here was almost certainly dead, he might not have fallen in that precise position.

᪥ LEFT

Tower of Prea Sat Ling Poun, Bayon Temple, Angkor Thom, Cambodia, by John Thomson, 1867.

The construction of the Crystal
Palace in Sydenham, 1852.

Scenes of everyday life and work in Victorian Britain also proliferate in the Library's collections. There are photographs of the construction of London Underground tunnels and stations, and of the Crystal Palace in Sydenham, south London, where it was reconstructed in 1852 after housing the triumphant Great Exhibition in Hyde Park the previous year.

Portrait photography also flourished from the second half of the nineteenth century, and the Library holds an impressive collection of images of the leading figures of their age. The best-known photographer of that era is Julia Margaret Cameron: among her works is *Alfred, Lord Tennyson and his Friends*, a series of 25 portraits published in 1893. Other writers portrayed in photographs from around the turn of the century include Leo Tolstoy, W.B. Yeats and George Bernard Shaw – an enthusiast for the medium whose papers include an important collection of portraits by the leading society photographers of the early twentieth century.

The Library now actively collects modern photographs. A recent acquisition is the archive of the American photographer Michael Katakis and

⊱ LEFT
Alfred, Lord Tennyson, by Julia Margaret Cameron, 1893.

⊱ BELOW
A 'psychic photograph' from Fred Barlow's collection.

his wife Kris Hardin, an anthropologist. For nearly 30 years they have travelled the world together, recording personal and political triumphs and tragedies in moving words and photographs, some of which were exhibited in the Library in 2011 and are now freely available to researchers.

The most improbable item in the photographic collection is a two-volume set of 'psychic photographs' compiled by Fred Barlow, secretary of the Society for the Study of Supernormal Pictures. Formed in 1918, the Society's most eminent member was its vice-president, Sir Arthur Conan Doyle. In 1920 it issued a report ruling out fraud in any of the photographs it had studied; but it is apparent to the modern eye that the prints in these two volumes, showing ghostly apparitions haunting otherwise unremarkable compositions, have been doctored.

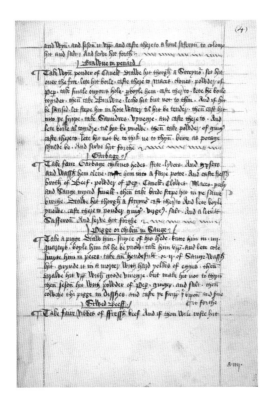

craftily and wholesomely', as well as dishes for special occasions – 'curious potages and meats and subtleties for all manner of states both high and low'. They include a range of dishes involving birds and animals that seldom grace our tables today – seals, cranes, curlews, herons and porpoises among them. Herbs and spices proliferate but the recipes, compared with today's, are imprecise, with no mention of quantities of ingredients or cooking times.

From the middle of the fifteenth century comes *A Boke of Kokery*, with 182 recipes. Students of etymology will be intrigued to observe how the words describing foods change their meaning over the centuries. For instance, a recipe for 'custard' is not for a creamy sauce, but for open pies containing marrow, dates, prunes and parsley, with a custard-like substance to bind them together. And 'garbage' is not what is put into refuse bins, but a dish made from animals' entrails – giblets, chickens' heads and feet, livers and gizzards. By the late sixteenth century, cookery writers had seen the need to specify quantities. *A Proper New Booke of Cookery*, published in 1575, has an updated recipe for custard – a quart of cream and five or six egg yolks, beaten well together. Calvesfoot jelly requires two calves' feet, a shoulder of veal, a gallon of water and a gallon of claret.

The Civil War of the 1640s and the ensuing Commonwealth period caused a temporary pause in the development of fine English dining. That, at least, was the view expressed by Robert May, a former chef to the aristocracy, in his book

Cookery books are among the oldest do-it-yourself manuals and the Library has a rich collection covering more than 600 years of gastronomy. Among the earliest is *The Forme of Cury* – not curry in the modern sense, but *cury* as the Middle English word for cookery. The manuscript contains 196 recipes and is thought to have been written in about 1390 by royal cooks working for Richard II. In the words of the authors, the recipes cover routine meals, 'common potages and common meats for the household, as they should be made,

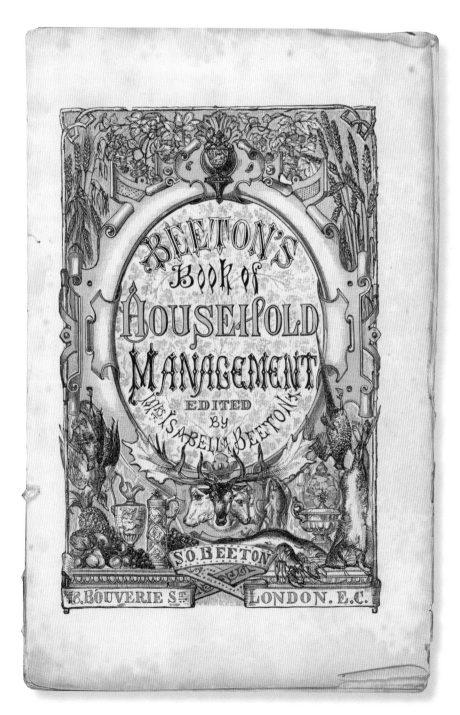

↪ RIGHT

The first edition of Mrs. Beeton's *Book of Household Management*, 1861.

The Accomplished Cook, published to mark the Restoration in 1660. He describes his recipes as being for dishes that were 'formerly the delights of the nobility, before good housekeeping had left England'. Some are tremendously elaborate, such as a swan pudding and a pastry stag filled with claret to simulate blood.

One of the first bestselling cookery manuals was Hannah Glasse's *The Art of Cookery*, published in 1747 and containing 972 recipes. Although directed at the servants of the wealthy, it proved popular with the general populace because of the author's accessible approach. 'If I have not written in the high polite style,' she explains, 'I hope I shall be forgiven; for my intention is to instruct the lower sort, and therefore must treat them in their own way. For example; when I bid them lard a fowl, if I should bid them lard with large lardoons, they would not know what I meant: but when I say they must lard with little pieces of bacon, they know what I mean. So in many other things in cookery, the great cooks have such a high way of expressing themselves that the poor girls are at a loss.' Unlike some of her more pretentious contemporaries, she preferred where possible to use inexpensive and readily available ingredients.

The nineteenth century saw the publication of two books with staying power: Isabella Beeton's *Book of Household Management* and Alexis Soyer's *Shilling Cookery for the People.* Mrs. Beeton's book bristles with homilies: 'A Christmas dinner with the middle classes of this empire would scarcely

⁜ LEFT

Alexis Soyer's *Shilling Cookery for the People*, 1855.

be a Christmas dinner without its turkey; and we can hardly imagine an object of greater envy than is presented by a respected portly pater-familias carving, at the season devoted to good cheer and genial charity, his own fat turkey, and carving it well.' Her didactic way of laying down the law on cooking (there are 2000 recipes) and other homemaking skills convinced people that she knew what she was talking about, even though she was only 25 when the first edition was published in 1861: 'I have always thought that there is no more fruitful source of family discontent than a housewife's badly-cooked dinners and untidy ways.' Yet it is hard to see how her advice on cooking vegetables (carrots, for instance, boiled for more than an hour) would have rescued many faltering marriages.

Alexis Soyer was for many years chef at the Reform Club in London. In 1851 he opened a restaurant opposite the Great Exhibition in Hyde Park, but it was not a success. He had, too, a social conscience, sailing out to the Crimea during the war there to cook nourishing meals for wounded soldiers. Soyer's *Shilling Cookery* of 1855 was aimed at a broader audience than Mrs. Beeton's work, and he avoided her tendency to talk down to readers by constructing his book as a series of letters to friends.

The introduction begins: 'Dear Eloise, More than a year has now elapsed since I wrote to you, with a promise that I would send you such receipts [recipes] as should be of use to the artisan, mechanic and cottager. … In the course of my peregrinations, I have made a point of visiting the cottages and abodes of the industrious classes generally, and have also closely examined the peculiarities and manners which distinguish each county, as well as the different kinds of labour; and I have viewed with pleasure the exertions made by philanthropic individuals to improve the morals of the labouring class, and render their dwellings more comfortable. But still I have found a great want of knowledge in that one object which produces almost as much comfort as all the rest put together, viz, the means of making the most of that food which the great Architect of the Heavens has so bountifully spread before us.'

Yet nine years later one author was still unimpressed by the number and quality of cookery books available, as well as by the standard of British cuisine. In *Host and Guest: a Book about Dinners, Wines, and Desserts,* Andrew Valentine Kirwan wrote: 'We have given birth to a Bacon, a Locke, a Shakespeare, a Milton, a Watt; but we are without a Vatel, a Bechamel, a Laguipierre, a Beauvilliers or a Carème. … We have given liberty to the slave, and preached the pure word of the gospel to the nations subjected to our dominion and sway; but we still eat butter badly melted with our roast veal, and we have not invented 364 ways to dress eggs.'

The hunger for instruction in the culinary arts is universal. Surely the oddest recipe book in the Library is the *Pidgin English Kuk Buk,* published

TAMATO SOS
Tomato Sauce — Grills, etc.

3 Tamato.
1 liklik sipun Anian (katim).
½ (hap) kap Wara.
Pepa na Sol.
Mint na Herbs.

Katim tamato liklik, putim long sosipan, putim anian, wara, pepa na sol wantaim.

Tekewei lip long mint, katim liklik, putim wantaim arapela long sosipan.

Sopos yu nogat mint, pasli, putim liklik herbs, tispela daraipela lip, oli ken baiem long stuwa, istap long galas.

Long taim tamato i kuk pinis, nau i no sitrong, kisim wantaim pleit na basin, igat planti liklik hul long im, putim antap long arapela sosipan, nau kapset tomato long im.

Tanim long sipun, long taim skin long tamato tasol istap.

Nau sos igo wantaim moa long stov, putim wanpela bikpela sipun plaua long im.

Tantanim long sipun gutpela, lukim i no gat sitrong-pela plaua long im, tanim gutpela.

Nau putim tamato na ologeta samting wantaim, tanim, tanim long taim em i boil.

c   33

in Papua New Guinea in 1964. To speakers of standard English some of the words are just about comprehensible, but the detailed instructions are hard to understand. The recipe for *tamato sas* includes an *anian, pepa* and *sol,* plus a *½ kap wara,* and it needs a *long taim em i boil.*

⅏ LEFT
'Tamato Sos' recipe from *Pidgin English Kuk Buk,* 1964.

Indian blue and pale red four-
anna stamps with the Queen's
head inverted, 1854-55.

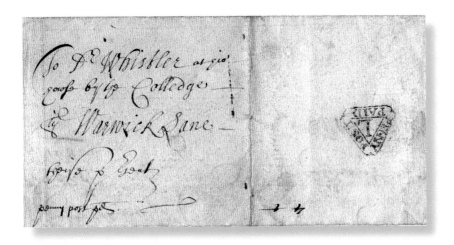

William Dockwra's London
penny post, 4th May 1682.

The Library's collection of stamps – estimated at about 50 million if you count each stamp individually – is the finest and most valuable in the world. It was begun in 1890 when Hubert Haes, a keen collector, donated two albums compiled by him and a friend to the British Museum to mark the fiftieth anniversary of the introduction of Rowland Hill's Penny Post and the first adhesive stamps. Haes declared that he had given the albums expressly to form the basis of a national stamp collection. The following year another dedicated philatelist, Thomas Tapling, a wealthy Member of Parliament, died of pleurisy, aged only 35. He bequeathed his much more substantial collection – described by the then Keeper of Printed Books as the most valuable gift to the Museum since the Grenville Library. During the twentieth century about 50 other collections were added through donations, bequests and transfers from Government departments.

The Tapling collection is held in a bank of retractable vertical display cases that keep the stamps in darkness when they are not being viewed – a form of exhibition developed by the British Museum in 1903 specifically for this collection and widely copied in postal museums. It fills 4,500 sheets, embracing stamps from 1840 to 1890, and includes nearly every basic issue from all over the world between those dates. A condition of the bequest was that it should be kept intact, and it is believed to be the only major nineteenth-century collection that has not been broken up. Like most collectors,

Tapling was fascinated by errors in production. He
has several examples of the phenomenon known
as *tête-bêche,* where adjoining stamps on a sheet
are printed different ways up. In 1855 some Indian
four-anna stamps were produced with the Queen's
head inverted: in the collection is a used envelope
sporting two of them, affixed upside-down by the
sender so that the head should appear the right way
up. And there is a Swedish issue where the value in
words does not match that of the numbers.

About half the items in the Library's philatelic
holdings are from Britain. Some of the rarest came in
1989 with the acquisition of the collection of Hugh
Greenwell Fletcher, who died in 1968. He had delved
into British postal history and unearthed such rare
items as a letter posted in 1682 bearing the stamp
of the first London-wide postal service, introduced
two years earlier by William Dockwra and Robert
Murray. For one penny, their couriers would deliver
mail to addresses within a ten-mile radius of the city
centre. Fletcher's collection also included many early
stamps from the reign of Queen Victoria.

The Library is rich in postal material from the
former British colonies and the Commonwealth.
In April 1890 the Secretary of State for the
Colonies instructed the authorities in territories
where Britain held sway to send examples of all
postage and revenue stamps and postal material.
The collection was held by the Foreign and
Commonwealth Office until 1992, when it was
transferred to the Library. Other material came

RIGHT

Examples from 1945 of
Third Reich stamps of Hitler
overstamped or corked.

BELOW RIGHT

Postcard carried by the
submarine 'C4' to blockaded
Menorca, 1938.

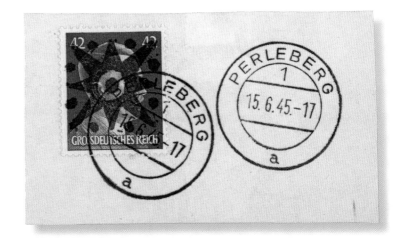

from the Crown Agents, who routinely received sets of mint stamps from the colonies and deposited them with the British Museum and later the Library. Their philatelic and security printing archive is also held – a comprehensive record of colonial and Commonwealth issues of the last 100 years, including the first printing of most issues, both postage and revenue. In 1966 the Board of Inland Revenue gave the Museum a collection of revenue stamps dating back to 1710. They include stamps printed in advance for taxes that, in the event, were not levied, such as a tax on matches proposed in 1871 and a 'luxury' tax that was considered during the First World War.

Outside Britain and the Commonwealth, a country strongly represented is Germany, whose complicated history can be traced through the stamps issued by the authorities that from time to time held sway over particular regions. This is best illustrated in the Model Collection, donated in 1956 by Dr Walther Model von Thunen, a Lutheran Pastor. A native of East Germany, he had been collecting stamps all his life but in May 1945 his house was looted by Russian soldiers and his collection lost. So he started again from scratch.

Ironically, the horror and dislocation of the war and its aftermath made it an exciting time for philatelists. With Germany divided into four occupied zones, the postal service was in chaos. Many post offices had been obliterated in the bombing and fighting, and in those that survived

the only stamps immediately available were those of the Third Reich, adorned with swastikas and portraits of Adolf Hitler. The authorities ordered these provocative images obliterated, a task achieved by overstamping them with crude cork stamps. In other cases the words '*Gebuhr bezahlt*' (fee paid) were stamped on the envelopes in a variety of styles. Before long the occupying forces began to issue their own stamps, and these have also provided rich material for collectors. In the same year that the Model Collection went to the Museum, the Foreign Office transferred its collection of the issues of the Allied Military Administration in Germany between 1945 and 1948.

A conflict that can be followed graphically through its stamps is the Spanish Civil War of 1936–39. In 2003 Ronald Shelley bequeathed his five-volume collection, mainly of covers used for communications to and from the International Brigades. Then in 2007 the Spanish Study Circle donated the 24-volume Bailey Collection, formed by Eric Bailey and covering a broader canvas than Shelley's. Bailey arranged his material topographically. In many cases, where control of a town switched from the Republicans to the Nationalists, stamps were overprinted with slogans of the victorious side.

Of special interest is a record of a unique submarine postal service, instituted by the Republicans in 1938 to carry mail from their Barcelona stronghold to the island of Menorca, passing beneath the naval blockade being enforced by the Nationalists. In the

event the submarine made only one voyage and the collection includes a postcard that was carried on it.

Finally, the philatelic collections boast possession of one of the largest objects in the Library: the Perkins D cylinder press, developed by Jacob Perkins in 1819. It was used to print the first adhesive postage stamps in 1840 and later produced many issues for Britain and its colonies. The press is on display near the stamp exhibition: its original patent is also held by the Library.

Prophecy is perilous. If you go to the Rare Books and Music Reading Room and ask to see item RB.23.b.1426, you will be handed a plain white A4 envelope containing a 16-page pamphlet, printed in 1681, entitled: 'GOOD AND JOYFUL NEWS FOR ENGLAND, or the prophecy of the renowned Michael Nostradamus that Charles II of Great Britain, France and Ireland, King, Defender of the Faith etc. shall have a son of his own body lawfully begotten, that shall succeed him in the imperial throne of Great Britain, and all other his Dominions; and reign long after his father, most fortunately and well beloved.'

Nostradamus's prophecies are notoriously ambiguous and often quite incomprehensible – although he did appear to be on the mark concerning Charles I's execution and an ensuing great plague. This pamphlet's author, J.B. Philaletes, pursues a tortuous argument to show, on flimsy evidence, that the seer predicted that Charles II's several unlawfully begotten sons would eventually be complemented by one conceived legitimately beneath the royal bedcover. History tells us that it did not happen.

Some argue that it is equally dangerous to predict the future of the British Library. Will the spread of digitisation mean that before long it will become simply a museum and storehouse for those archaic objects known as books and newspapers? Will its splendid Reading Rooms, so carefully designed by Colin St. John Wilson for maximum comfort and utility, be made redundant as we come to access more and more material on our home or office computers? And if any of that happens will the Government, which at present provides around three-quarters of the Library's funding, feel less obliged to give the Library the support it will always need?

It is a measure of the speed of modern technological developments that these questions have surfaced only in the last two decades. A glossy 64-page booklet published in 1989, *The British Library Past Present Future*, makes no mention of digitisation. The section headed 'The Future' contains just one paragraph, and that is partly about the past:

'The British Library, given its resources for an understanding of the past, the present and what we choose to make of the future, has no parallel in any country. It nourishes invention and curiosity; it provides for the needs of industry and commerce,

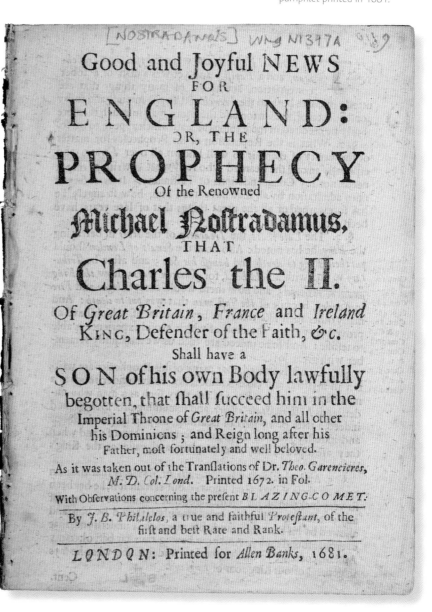

Good and Joyful NEWS
FOR
ENGLAND:
OR, THE
PROPHECY
Of the Renowned
Michael Nostradamus,
THAT
Charles the II.
Of *Great Britain*, *France* and *Ireland*
KING, Defender of the Faith, *&c.*
Shall have a
SON of his own Body lawfully
begotten, that shall succeed him in the
Imperial Throne of *Great Britain*, and all other
his Dominions ; and Reign long after his
Father, most fortunately and well beloved.
As it was taken out of the Translations of Dr. *Theo. Garencieres*,
M. D. Col. Lond.   Printed 1672. in Fol.
With Observations concerning the present *BLAZING-COMET*.

By *J. B. Philalelos*, a true and faithful *Protestant*, of the
first and best Rate and Rank.

LONDON: Printed for *Allen Banks*, 1681.

without which national prosperity withers; it sustains research, without which there can be no progress; it possesses the documentary sources for the evolution of thought in all countries at all times, without which we would be deprived of history. Before the invention of writing when history was an oral record, handed down from generation to generation, its custodians were honoured above all. Millennia later, libraries preserve that tradition. Among the many thousands of libraries throughout the world, the British Library is pre-eminent in its determination to serve those institutions and individuals for whom information is an imperative, to preserve the heritage of knowledge, and to demonstrate its belief in the unity of knowledge and the benefits which flow from such a belief.'

No hint there of systems that would enable readers to flip the pages of priceless manuscripts on screens in the Library or at home, or make available old newspapers with searchable texts. Yet only a year or two after that booklet was published, the Library's policy-makers, recognising that they had to start adjusting to the far-reaching changes that were now on the horizon, began developing plans to digitise large segments of the collections. Many of these schemes have now been rolled out, while digitisation targets have been progressively expanded. In 2008 the Library issued a paper setting out its strategy: 'We aim to help researchers advance knowledge by becoming a leading player in digitisation. We will produce a critical mass of digitised content,

reflecting the breadth and depth of our collection. We will provide a compelling user experience that facilitates innovative methods of research and meets twenty-first century requirements for interacting with content.'

The priority has been to complete the digitisation of the bulk of the newspaper collection, already well under way. At the same time ambitious programmes have been announced to digitise some out-of-copyright printed books in partnership with commercial concerns, making them readily searchable and available on computers and smart phones outside the Library. Another initiative allows readers with mobile devices to download entire ancient manuscripts, such as Leonardo da Vinci's *Codex Arundel*, for a small fee.

In 2010 the Library published a paper, *2020 Vision*, which set out its objectives for the next ten years. By 2020 an estimated 75 per cent of all titles worldwide will be published either in digital form only or in both digital and print. 'Our ambition is to preserve digital content for the long term in order to safeguard our intellectual heritage so that it can be used by future generations of researchers. … In the digital twenty-first century, where the flow of information is instantaneous and without boundaries, we must define the role of a national library in the global information network. … We will be a major hub in a truly global networked partnership for information.'

That does not mean that the books will be

allowed to crumble to dust on their basement shelves. The Library will adapt to changing conditions not by abandoning its former course and heading blithely in a new direction, but by embracing the future as a means of underpinning as well as expanding the core role envisaged by its founders. 'As digital formats become the norm, our rich resource of physical content will become more precious. It is thus vital that we continue to develop our world-class stewardship skills in conservation and preservation.'

Universal access remains a primary objective: 'At the heart of our vision is a passionate belief that everyone who wants to do research should have access to the rich resource of content held by the British Library. The digital environment provides an immense opportunity to democratise access to content through removing physical barriers. … We recognise that the learners of today are the researchers of tomorrow.'

A century and a half earlier Antonio Panizzi had expressed precisely the same sentiment: 'I want a poor student to have the same means of indulging his learned curiosity, of following his rational pursuits, of consulting the same authorities, of fathoming the most intricate inquiry, as the richest man in the kingdom, as far as books go, and I contend that Government is bound to give him the most liberal and unlimited assistance in this respect.' His successors in the Library today would not quarrel with one word of that.

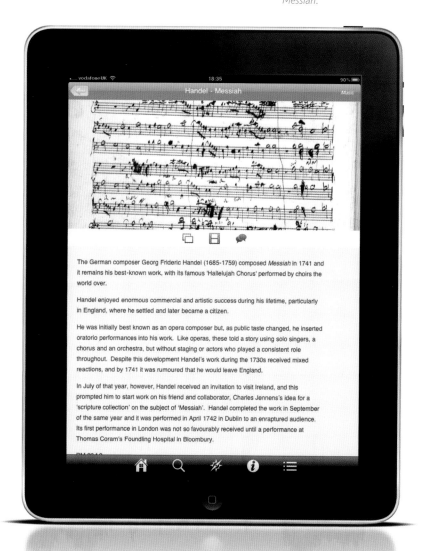

Index

Bibliography

Ackerman, Robert W. and Ackerman, Gretchen P., *Sir Frederic Madden, A Biographical Sketch and Bibliography*. Garland Publishing Inc, 1979.

Alston, R.C., *The British Library: Past, Present, Future*. British Library, 1989.

Barker, Nicolas, *Treasures of the British Library*. British Library, 2005.

Barwick, G.F., *The Reading Room of the British Museum*. Ernest Benn Ltd, 1929.

Birrell, T.A., *English Monarchs and Their Books: from Henry VII to Charles II*. British Library, 1987.

Birrell, T.A., *The Library of John Morris*. British Museum Publications, 1976.

The Book Collector, vol.45 (1), spring 1996, pp. 9–23.

British Library Journal, vol. 23 (2), autumn 1997 (special edition devoted to Antonio Panizzi).

Camille, Michael, *Mirror in Parchment: The Luttrell Psalter*. Reaktion Books, 1998.

Carley, James P., *The Books of King Henry VIII and his Wives*. British Library, 2004.

Day, Alan, *Inside the British Library*. Library Association Publishing, 1998.

Day, Alan, *The New British Library*. Library Association Publishing, 1994.

Fletcher, Chris, *1000 Years of English Literature: A Treasury of Literary Manuscripts*. British Library, 2003.

Fraser, Antonia, *Must You Go? My Life With Harold Pinter*. Weidenfeld & Nicolson, 2010.

Harland, Elizabeth, 'The Evanion Collection', *British Library Journal*, vol. 13 (1), spring 1987, pp. 64–70.

Harris, P.R., *A History of the British Museum Library, 1753–1973*. British Library, 1998.

Holroyd, Michael, *Bernard Shaw*. Vintage, 1998.

Howard, Philip: *The British Library: A Treasure House of Knowledge*. Scala, 2008.

Hudson, Graham: *The Design and Printing of Ephemera in Britain and America, 1720–1920*. British Library, 2008.

Jensen, Kristian (ed.), *Incunabula and their Readers*. British Library, 2003.

Jones, Peter Murray, *Medieval Medicine in Illuminated Manuscripts*. British Library, 1998.

Jones, Peter Murray: 'Witnesses to Medieval Medical Practice in the Harley Collection'. *Electronic British Library Journal*, article 8, 2008.

Kempe, Margery and Barry Wineatt (eds), *The Book of Margery Kempe*. Pearson, 2000.

Kenny, Sir Anthony, *The British Library and the St. Pancras Building*. British Library, 1994.

Larkin, Philip, *Required Writing: Miscellaneous Pieces 1955–1982*. Faber & Faber, 1983.

Lytle, G.F. and Orgel, S. (eds), *Patronage in the Renaissance*. Princeton University Press, 1981.

MacGregor, Arthur (ed.), *The Late King's Goods*. Oxford University Press 1989

McKendrick, Scot, Lowden, John and Doyle, Kathleen: *Royal Manuscripts: The Genius of Illumination*. British Library, 2011.

Mandelbrote, Giles and Taylor, Barry (eds), *Libraries Within the Library: The Origins of the British Library's Printed Collections*. British Library, 2009.

Meynell, Francis, *English Printed Books*. Collins, 1946.

Miller, Edward, *Prince of Librarians: The Life and Times of Antonio Panizzi of the British Museum*. Andre Deutsch, 1967.

Pallant House Gallery Magazine, no. 14, February–May 2008 (special edition devoted to Sir Colin St. John Wilson).

St. John Wilson, Sir Colin, *The Design and Construction of the British Library*. British Library, 1998.

Stonehouse, Roger and Stromberg, Gerard, *The Architecture of the British Library at St. Pancras*. Spoon Press, 2004.

Suarez, Michael F. and Woudhuysen, H.R. (eds), *The Oxford Companion to the Book*. Oxford University Press, 2010.

Summers, Anne, 'Sources on Twentieth-Century British Cultural History in the Department of Manuscripts of the British Library', *Contemporary Record*, vol. 9 (1), summer 1995.

Sutton, S.C., *A Guide to the India Office Library*. HMSO, 1967.

Picture credits

Unless otherwise stated all images are owned by the British Library.

10 Add. MS. 88931/1/3/18 f.25. Extract from Gormenghast by Mervyn Peake reprinted by permission of Peters Fraser & Dunlop (www.petersfraserdunlop.com) on behalf of the estate of Mervyn Peake; 12 Add. MS. 38182, f.1; 13 Add. MS. 41752, ff.22v–23; 14 Add. MS. 50582, f.28; 15 Add. MS.52619, f.34v. By kind permission of the Estate of Philip Larkin; 16 Add. MS.5 2430, f.44. © The Estate of W.H. Auden. Reprinted by permission of Curtis Brown Ltd; 18 Add. MS. 52903. By kind permission of the Estate of Philip Larkin; 19 Add. MS. 71956B, ff.6v–7r. © John Betjeman by permission of the Estate of John Betjeman; 21 J.G. Ballard Archive. © J.G. Ballard. All rights reserved; 22 Add. MS.5 1045, f.5; 23 LCP Corr 1964/4267 1; 24 Add. MS. 74415, f.220. By kind permission of the Terence Rattigan Charitable Trust; 26 Add. MS. 81539; 28 Cotton Nero MS. D.iv, f.27; 39 British Museum, London; 40 Cotton Vitelius MS. A.xv, f.132; 31 left British Museum, London; 31 right Cotton Otho MS. B.vi, f.26v; 32 Harley MS. 2788, f.109; 33 Harley MS. 4751, f.8; 34 649.c.26; 35 above British Museum, London; 35 below Sloane MS. 4016, ff.29v–30; 37 left Royal MS. 20.A.iv; 37 right Royal MS. 15 E.iv, vol.1 f.14; 38 Royal MS. 2.B.vii, f.1v; 39 Royal MS. 18.A.xiv, f.4r; 40 C.114.b.37; 42 British Museum, London; 44 747.f.3; 46 C.9.d.3; 47 British Museum, London; 48, 49 British Museum, London; 50–51 G.11586; 52 Add. MS. 33733, f.5; 54 British Museum, London; 55 Maps c.26.f.7; 57 BIP/The Kobal Collection; 59 Add. MS. 54579, f.1; 60 Add. MS. 54579, f.2; 72 By kind permission of the Estate of R.B. Kitaj/Marlborough Fine Arts; 80 Add. MS. 24098. f.29v; 81 Or. 7694; 82 Or. MS.14915; 83 Add. MS. 22406, ff.1v–2; 84 Or. MS. 2265, f.166; 85 Add. MS. 15297(1), f.138a; 86 Add. MS. 27210, f.12v; 87 Or. MS. 2627, f.136v; 88 Or. MS. 8212/84; 89 Add. MS. 43725, ff.89v–90; 90 Add. MS. 89000; 92 Cotton Claudius MS. B.iv, f.14; 94 Arundel MS. 60, f.13r; 95 left Add. MS. 18850, f.256; 95 right Add. MS. 42130, f.158; 97 Add. MS. 47682, f.15v; 98 Add. MS. 61823, f.1; 99 Add. MS. 39627, f.272v; 100–101 Add. MS. 88887, ff.4v–5; 102 left Add. MS. 80800; 102 right Or. MS. 481, f.110; 103 Add. MS. 11695, ff.147v–148; 104 G.12216; 105 Or. MS. 8210/P2; 106 C.50.a.15; 109 C.188.a.17; 110 C.132.h.46; 112 C.175.n.3; 113 G.11631; 114 C.30.f.6; 115 C.56.c.2; 116 680.k.12; 118 C.180.g.3; 119 left Ch.800/101. (3.); 119 right Add. MS. 46700, f.88; 120 HS.74/2143.

© DACS 2012; 121 C.43.c.16; 122 left Davis 660; 122 right C.68.i.1, C.68.i.2, C.68.i.10, C.68.i.4, C.68.i.11; 123 Davis 301; 124 Add. MS. 37000, f.1; 125 Add. MS. 47864, f.80; 126 Add. MS. 47497, ff.3v–4; 129 Egerton MS. 2711, f.66; 131 Add. MS. 36354, f.88; 132 Add. MS. 78342, f.58; 134 Add. MS. 4808, f.16; 135 Add. MS. 39839, f.35; 136 Egerton MS. 1610, f.60; 137 Add. MS. 39764, f.2; 138 Add. 59874, f.85; 139 Add. MS. 43474, f.1; 141 Add. MS. 57493; 144 Add. MS. 59840, f.35; 146 Add. MS. 51035, f.39; 147 Cotton Augustus MS. II.106; 148 Cotton Tiberius MS. B.i, f.26v; 147 Royal MS. 14.B.v; 148 Add. MS. 59678, f.35; 149 left Royal MS. 2.A.xvi, f.63v; 149 right C.18.c.9; 151 Add. MS. 22047; 152 Harley MS. 6986, f.23; 153 Add. 57555, f.23; 154 E.372. (19.); 155 Hs.74/1512.(6.); 156 Burney 121B; 158 P.P.5270; 160 Add. MS. 37953; 161 Add. MS. 56401, f.161; 162 Maps CC.5.a.546; 164 Maps G.35; 165 Cotton Tiberius MS. B.v, f.56r; 166 Royal MS. 14.C.vii, f.5; 167 Add. MS. 28681, f.9; 168 Maps *69810.(18.); 169 Add. MS. 5415A, ff.9v–10; 170 Cotton Augustus MS. I.i; 171 Maps C.29.c.13; 173 Royal MS. 18.D.iii, ff.33v–34; 174 Maps K.Top.CXXI, f.35; 175 Maps C.6.c.2; 177 Maps Crace 1.50; 179 left E.145; 179 right WD.2090; 180 Add. Or. MS. 2929; 181 left Photo 643(14); 181 right Or.78.a.11, 1; 182 MS. Pali 207; 183 above Add. MS. 15513, f.16; 183 below Add. MS. 27888, f.150; 184 8154.b.35; 185 G.12176; 186 T.271.(2.); 188 Harley MS. 978, f.11v; 189 Add. MS. 71148A; 190 Royal MS. 11.E.xi, f.2; 191 Mus.1591, f.105v; 192 RM 20.h.8, ff.55v–56; 193 above RM so.f.2, f.100r; 193 below Maps K.Top.41.27b; 194 K.10.b.12; 196 Zweig MS. 63, f.15v–16; 197 Zweig MS. 67, f.2; 198 Zweig MS. 81b; 199 Add. MS. 31766, f.2; 200 C.61.g.1; 201 1508/143; 203 Add. MS. 58004, f.38v; 208 Arundel MS. 263, f.73; 210 Sloane MS. 2839, f.1v; 211 Sloane MS. 1977, ff.49v–50r; 212 Harley MS. 5294, f.25; 213 Harley MS. 5311; 214 C.54.k.12; 215 34.l.12; 216 Add. MS. 5308C, ff.5v–6; 217 1651/829; 218 8755.cc.28; 220 2244.g.3; 221 Evanion 1172; 222 Evanion 411; 224 Evanion 6081, 225 Evanion 6072; 228 Talbot Photo 2.(49); 229 RH.9.x.268; 230 above Photo 922.(1.); 230 below Photo 35.(15); 231 Photo 353.(8); 232 1784.a.13; 233 Photo 983; 234 Tab.442.A.5; 235 left 1757.b.14; 235 right Cup.407.a.1.(23); 236 Harley MS. 4016, f.4; 237 C.133.c.5; 238 RB.23.a.21664; 239 YL.1987.a.940; 240 above Philatelic Collections/The Tapling Collection; 240 below Philatelic Collections/The Fletcher Collection; 241 Philatelic Collections/The Foreign and Commonwealth Office Collection; 242 above Philatelic Collections/The Model Collection; 242 below Philatelic Collections/The Bailey Collection; 245 RB.23.b.1426.

DATE DUE

Demco